CW00959916

Cathal O'Byrne and the
in Ireland, 189

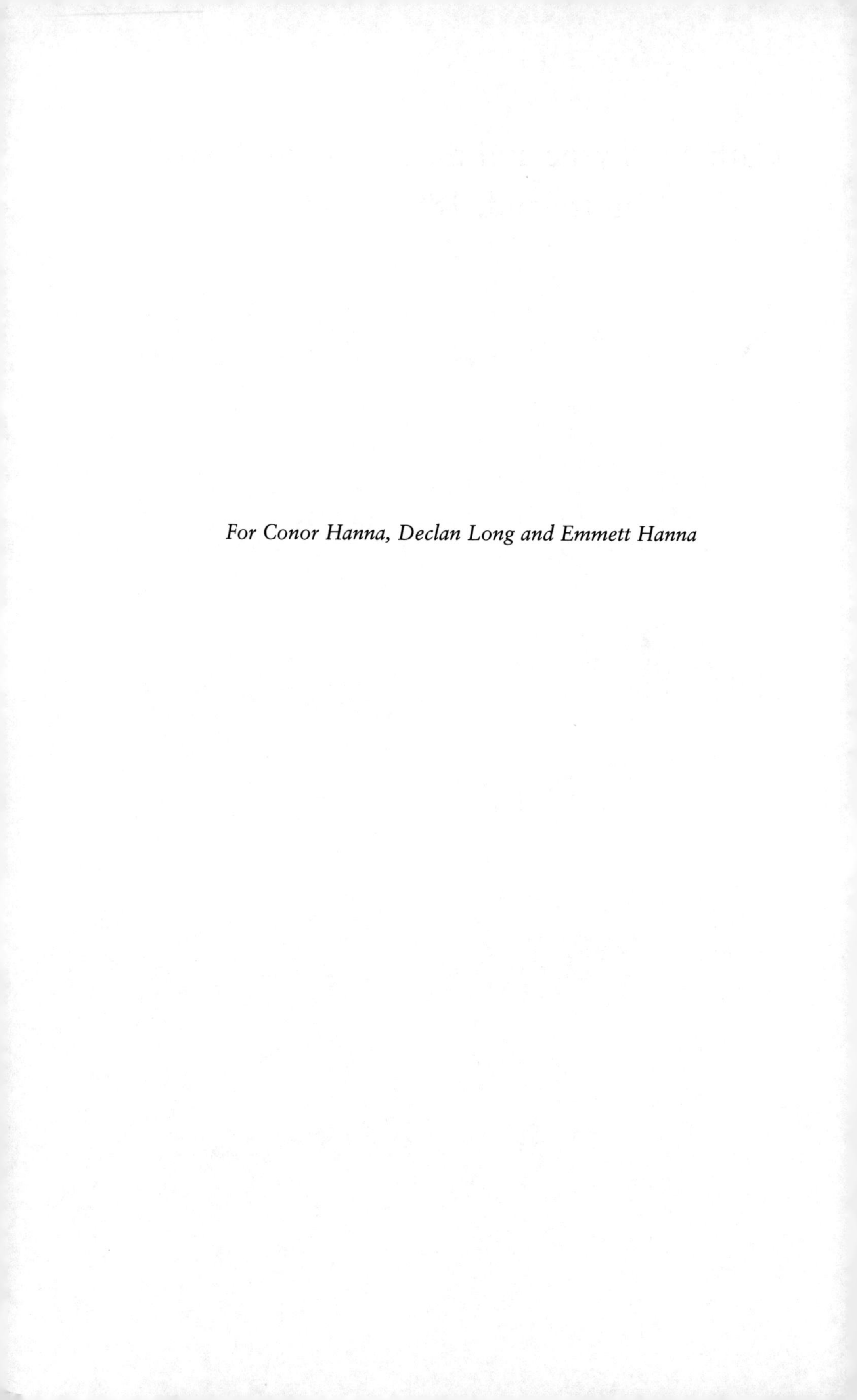

For Conor Hanna, Declan Long and Emmett Hanna

Cathal O'Byrne and the Northern Revival in Ireland, 1890–1960

Richard Kirkland

LIVERPOOL UNIVERSITY PRESS

First published 2006 by
Liverpool University Press
4 Cambridge Street
Liverpool L69 7ZU

Copyright © 2006 Richard Kirkland

The right of Richard Kirkland to be identified as the author of this work has been asserted by him in accordance with the Copyright, Design and Patents Act 1988.

All rights reserved. No part of this book may be reproduced, stored in a retrieval system, or transmitted, in any form or by any means, electronic, mechanical, photocopying, recording, or otherwise, without the prior written permission of the publisher.

British Library Cataloguing-in-Publication data
A British Library CIP record is available

ISBN 1-84631-023-7 cased
ISBN 1-84631-045-8 limp

ISBN-13 978-1-84631-023-2 cased
ISBN-13 978-1-84631-045-4 limp

Typseset in Sabon by R. J. Footring Ltd, Derby

Printed in the European Union by Bell and Bain Ltd, Glasgow

Contents

Contents

Preface and acknowledgements

I FIRST encountered the work of Cathal O'Byrne when I was a postgraduate student at the Queen's University of Belfast in the early 1990s. Searching the library in a slightly desultory way for books that might tell the story of the city I had made my home and about which I was meant to be writing, I came across the 1982 edition of *As I Roved Out*, with its maroon dust-jacket, cover image of the long since demolished Smithfield Market, and John Hewitt's affectionate, if slightly bemused, Foreword. Few considered O'Byrne's work worthy of much study at that time. The dense, interlocking series of stories, myths and memories of old Belfast that make the book unique was out of step with a city attempting to regenerate its public spaces and retail centres – a spirit embodied perfectly by the hulking architectural banality of the recently opened CastleCourt shopping centre on Royal Avenue. Alongside this neglect, any Belfast writer who did dare to cite O'Byrne's work in reference appeared to do so only with the sternest warnings of its many historical and factual errors and the seductions of its nostalgic nationalism. Luckily, at this stage of my studies I was too ignorant to have encountered these strict entreaties and I found myself immediately engrossed by the hypnotic weave of O'Byrne's technique. I left the library five hours later having read the entire book without pause.

My interest in O'Byrne might have ended there – little more than a paragraph in the eccentric narrative of Northern Irish writing that at that time I doubtfully thought of as my thesis – had it not become gradually clear to me that O'Byrne's style, rather than being a relic of a historical moment that had long since passed, was in fact reappearing in a new generation of Irish writers, most obviously in the startling experiments in poetics found in Ciaran Carson's 1989 collection *Belfast Confetti*.

Clearly, nothing disappears without a trace. Far from being culturally residual, the possibility arose that some of the ideas and preoccupations in O'Byrne's work might be re-emerging. Other forces were also at work. Interest in the tragic life and legacy of O'Byrne's friend and confidant Roger Casement gained a remarkable momentum during the course of the 1990s, while a number of academics and postgraduate students – often working without knowledge of each other – were turning their attentions to the previously neglected cultural life of the North in the early years of the century. There were a number of reasons for this new-found emphasis. Most pressingly, the increasingly exhausted rituals of a thirty-year period of political violence in Northern Ireland seemed to demand a renewed attempt to understand some of the cultural forces that had led to that violence's inception. Certainly, too much of the tumultuous period in the North between 1900 and 1920 remained either obscured or – perhaps more dangerously – was seen as self-evident in its subsequent effects. Alongside this were other, more enabling possibilities. A developing academic interest in the long-suppressed histories of dissident sexualities in Ireland, the emergence of new voices in Irish cultural studies and exciting new analyses of the Irish literary revival provided the inspiration for further research.

By this stage, O'Byrne was causing me other moments of aggravation. Beyond my ongoing fascination with *As I Roved Out*, I had come across snippets of information about his life: vague and often contradictory rumours about his friendships, travels and activities. At one level O'Byrne remained entirely mysterious – few could assert with confidence any single verifiable fact about his early years – and yet myths and stories clung to his legacy with a stubborn irreducibility. Clearly, something had to be done. I cleared my desk of other projects and decided to focus entirely on his life and writing. This book is the result. That it is impossible to tell the story of Cathal without also speaking of Francis Joseph Bigger, Roger Casement, Joseph Devlin, Alice Milligan, the *Irish News*, the Ulster Literary Theatre, and the heady, if brief, excitement of the Northern Revival is something that I have accepted as a happy inevitability.

Cathal O'Byrne and the Northern Revival in Ireland, 1890–1960 is, then, the result of fifteen years' discontinuous study. Over such a prolonged period one's debts to others mount up in a daunting manner, but I would like to record my particular thanks (in no particular order) to Emily Jones, Michael Allen, Edna Longley, Eamonn Hughes, Jeff Dudgeon, Nora McGreavey, Brian Kirkland, David Alderson, Joe Graham, J. J. Tohill, Catherine Morris, John Cronin, Colin Graham, Shaun Richards, Edward Larrissy, Richard Madden, Raymond Piper, the families of Denis McCullough and Joseph Connolly, Robbie Meredith, Sandra Dodson, Ralph Footring, Learning Design, the library and archive staff of the *Irish News*, and the British Arts and Humanities Research Board. During the period of this book's composition I have held lectureships at the universities of Keele and Manchester and at King's College London, and I am grateful to these institutions for the support they have given to my research. Finally, this work has benefited immensely over the years from the perceptive insights and critical wisdom of three Northerners: Conor Hanna, Declan Long and Emmett Hanna. I dedicate this book to them with my thanks and love.

Prologue

Strange portents were abroad in the city of shipyards, factories, foundries and stubborn negations. A wind of idealism was blowing over the arid wastes of political controversy, and tiny flowers, full of hope and promise, began to unfold in the most unexpected places. Not for nothing had Ethna Carbery and Alice Milligan toiled to remind the North of the deep, enduring realities that underlay all the slogans and catch-cries. Just as, on a spring morning, one hears a lone songster in a copse, and then realises that one after another has joined him, so it was in Belfast in those golden days. Every week one heard the name of a new poet, a new playwright, a new painter, a new story-teller. Joseph Campbell had published his first volumes of verse, and was contesting Colum's claim to be regarded as the most racial of our singers. Richard Rowley, Cathal O'Byrne, Padraic Gregory, John Stevenson and Florence Wilson were writing ballads and lyrics shaped in the national mould. W. B. Reynolds, a brilliant journalist-musician, was editing a quarterly called *Uladh* which supported the newly-founded Ulster Literary Theatre and the cultural movement generally. John McBirney's long supremacy was being challenged by younger artists like Frank McKelvey, the Morrow brothers, Charley Lamb, William Connor, and John Campbell, whose emigration to America deprived Ireland of a superb black-and-white artist. The Ulster Theatre had produced Davy Parkhill's 'The Reformer' and 'The Enthusiast', Rutherford Mayne's 'The Turn of the Road' and 'The Drone', and Harry Morrow's 'Suzanne and the Sovereigns' and 'Thompson in Tirnanogue'. Carl Hardebeck, a Belfast man by adoption, Herbert Hughes and Hamilton Harty were finding inspiration in the folk-music that had survived the withering centuries. 'Bliss was it in that dawn to be alive, but to be young was very heaven.'

Hugh A. MacCartan, 'Belfast: some backward glances', in *Capuchin Annual* (Dublin: Capuchin Franciscan Fathers, 1943), pp. 176–7

CHAPTER ONE

Cathal O'Byrne and the Northern Revival

> Cathal O'Byrne is a poet. He is a gaelic poet, as authentic as the bards who sang the epics of the giant-men before St Patrick, as the minstrels who wove a fairy magic over the lives of the saints, as the martial poets of vision who kept the faith in Erin during the black days of persecution. He is a storyteller of that ancient breed which traces back through all the generations of Ireland, the weaver of words who would seat himself before the peat fire and relate his wondrous tales through fastly slipping hours to bulging eyes and gaping mouths. Cathal O'Byrne comes of a long tradition, and he would be recognised by his forebears as one of themselves.
>
> *America Magazine*[1]

> Familiar though his name may be to us, the storyteller in his living immediacy is by no means a present force. He has already become something remote from us and something that is getting ever more distant.... The art of storytelling is coming to an end.
>
> Walter Benjamin[2]

IN September 1957 a young family prepared to take possession of their new home, 43 Cavendish Street, a small terraced house just off the Falls Road in Belfast. After gaining the keys but still awaiting the delivery of their furniture, they were alarmed to discover chaotic piles of papers, books, maps, letters and manuscripts in nearly every room. Time was pressing and, with the arrival of their possessions imminent, it was to the family's good fortune that a passing tradesman with a horse and cart agreed to take the unwanted archive to the local tip for a small fee. They gave the matter little more thought. The previous resident of the property and hoarder of this material had been Cathal (or Cahal) O'Byrne, a writer, singer, storyteller, actor and historian. Cavendish Street had been his home for thirty years until illness had obliged him to take refuge in the care of the sisters at Nazareth House on the Ormeau Road from 1954. Although by the time of his death many had forgotten his achievements, with his passing Belfast lost one of the last major figures of the Northern Revival, that brave, eccentric and neglected movement that in the early years of the twentieth century had done so much to brighten the habitually crepuscular landscape of the city's art and culture. Certainly, the story of the Northern Revival cannot be told without telling the story of O'Byrne, and yet this is an act that the too hasty clearance of 43 Cavendish Street rendered – if not quite impossible – extremely difficult.

Even at the point of beginning, then, it is clear that a narration of O'Byrne's life will be shadowed by gaps, ellipses and omissions. At different times a figure of both periphery and centre, his thread emerges and disappears in the fabric of Irish history from the fall of Charles Stewart Parnell in 1890 through to the austere years following World War Two. There are, however, more profound reasons why his creative legacy has fallen into neglect, beyond the lack of substantive biographical papers. Described perceptively by the Belfast poet John Hewitt as 'someone from the Northern margin of the Celtic Twilight',[3] too often the pervasive nationalism expressed in O'Byrne's work is peculiarly univocal and seemingly incapable of self-realisation to hold a sustained interest for modern readers. As a result its tone can appear unremitting. What we find in his often near obsessive litanies of dispossession and injustice are the politics of despair: the voice of Irish nationalism in the North during the post-partition period, when the sense of abandonment was most acute and the possibility of popular mobilisation to the cause of a united Ireland in Ulster most distant. It is in this way that O'Byrne's shifting allegiances and preoccupations speak of larger tendencies and cultural movements. As O'Byrne surveys the dissociation taking place between North and South and (perhaps for him more importantly) the different visions of the Irish nation developing on either side of the border, so his work turns from the attempted imaginative encapsulation of the entire island in his early poetry to the increasingly microscopic dwelling on the particular found in his major work, *As I Roved Out*, from 1946, an extraordinary elegy for Catholic nationalism in the North of Ireland. Many readers have lacked the patience for such a project. When Patricia Craig, in her anthology of autobiographical prose from Ulster, *The Rattle of the North*,[4] is forced to explain the absence of *As I Roved Out* from the contents, her prose assumes the slightly weary, slightly superior tone that much of his work seems to instil in modern critics: O'Byrne's writing, she comments, though full of 'interesting information', is at the same time 'unacceptably banal'.

As Craig's dismissal indicates, the appeal of O'Byrne's writing belongs to a different epoch and one that can lie quite beyond the sensibility of a modern reader. Indeed, if, as I have already indicated, his aesthetic and historical sense was refined through the activities of the Northern Revival, so this movement, in turn, has occupied an uncertain and often uncomfortable place in twentieth-century Irish cultural history. When compared with the monumental cultural achievements of the movement in the South, the Revival in the North was fragile in its existence and uncertain in its aims. If the Irish Revival proper takes its place as part of an independence narrative, its role having been to provide canonical texts upon which assertions of national cultural autonomy could be guaranteed, the Northern Revival, in contrast, found itself hopelessly compromised by the very different narrative of partition in 1920, an event which ran counter to all the activity of the Revival and one to which it seemingly had no answer. Such considerations suggest the reasons why the Northern Revival has rarely been understood as an integral part of the Revival movement as a whole, while they also indicate that even the term 'Northern Revival' itself is a problematic label: a term that appears to speak of the very partitionist instinct that the movement fundamentally opposed. Perhaps it is for this reason that, when we look for coherency in its objectives, we find fragmentation and discord; when we search for its cultural achievements, we find sporadic and often inconclusive activity that ultimately collapses into a post-partition despair. All this means, of course, that to reconstitute the Northern Revival is by no means a straightforward task, for if it is viewed in the light of subsequent events, its fleeting coherency, its sense of itself as a movement, dissolves. We have lost what Benjamin (quoted above) terms the 'living immediacy' of the Northern Revival in its historical moment, but the present study takes its momentum from the belief that something of its vibrancy remains relevant to an Ireland that is still in many ways experiencing the fallout of the Parnell crisis of 1890.

Significantly, then, the Northern Revival had a quite different character to the Revival in the South and this is identifiable not just in the cultural forms through which the two movements made themselves manifest, but also in the narratives of their progress. The classic Revival narrative cites as a beginning the fall of Parnell in 1890 and a subsequent disenchantment, both in Ireland and elsewhere, with hegemonic nationalist political activity, what W. B. Yeats described in his famous 1923 Nobel lecture to the Royal Academy of Sweden as 'a disillusioned and embittered Ireland turn[ing] from parliamentary politics'.[5] This disappointment was seen to lead to an increasing concentration on cultural activity and the political invigoration of interest in Celtic antiquarian study, which had been steadily gaining momentum through the course of the nineteenth century. The major events and texts from this point on are well known – a narrative summarised at its most mechanical by the literary historian Ernest Boyd in 1916 as a 'new spirit' that 'culminated in the rising of 1916'[6] – but it is usually assumed that the Northern Revival finally petered out around 1922 with the end of the Anglo-Irish war the previous year and the bitterly satirical portraits of Revival figures found in James Joyce's *Ulysses* of that year. At this point – so the story runs – Protestants vacated the cultural stage and were replaced by the resurgent, often triumphalist, Catholic bourgeoisie.

It is in this latter transition that events in Yeats's least-favourite province were most obviously different. While post-Parnellite disillusion can, without doubt, be identified in the North – even if it was often disillusion with Parnell himself rather than with those forces that brought him down – the Northern Revival was much more profoundly Catholic and clerical in its allegiances than most Anglo-Irish narratives of the Revival in its entirety can accommodate. Similarly if, as I have suggested, a continuity (no matter how fraught) can be traced between the activities of the Revival in the South and the subsequent manifestation of the independent state, it is less easy to recognise the work of the predominantly Belfast-based Northern Revival in the cultural and political life of Northern Ireland. In fact, the dissolution of the movement in the North was so sudden and overwhelming that its aspirations can often only be recognised in subsequent Northern Irish culture as a fleeting, and often embittered, presence. In these terms the energy of the Northern Revival was typically potential rather than kinetic.

That said, nothing disappears entirely without trace. Consider, for instance, the following descriptions of street life in Belfast. The first is from *As I Roved Out*, the second from Ciaran Carson's prose poem 'Question time', published in his collection *Belfast Confetti*, from 1989:

> Cutlers, dyers, grocers, publicans, bakers, cabinet-makers, tailors, butchers, builders, bookbinders, were all represented within the confines of the narrow thoroughfare, and where we passed between the busy shops and the cosy dwelling-houses, an air of brisk prosperity and comfort and contentment seemed to lie over all the old world place and make it glad.[7]

> I get on my bike, and turn, and go down the Falls, past vanished public houses – The Clock Bar, The Celtic, Daly's, The Gladstone, The Arkle, The Old House – past drapers, bakers, fishmongers, boot shops, chemists, pawnshops, picture houses, confectioners and churches, all swallowed in the maw of time and trouble, clearances.[8]

Although separated by a gap of forty-three years, the cultural residues that resonate through the comparison suggest stylistic and formal continuities. Looking beyond the obvious biographical similarities shared by the two writers (to put it bluntly, they are both male, Catholic and writing out of the geography of the Falls Road) there is in both pieces a preoccupation with the effective forces of litany, memory and nostalgia. In Carson's poem, the protagonist has cycled from the Shankill Road to the Falls and, so suspicious are his movements, he finds himself apprehended and interrogated by paramilitaries. It is only his intimate knowledge of the local area – his precise recollection of who lived in which house thirty years ago – that convinces his captors to release him. As the poem observes, 'I am this map which they examine, checking it for error, hesitation, uncertainty'. He cycles on, and the world that was briefly recreated through the interrogation dissolves away, back into the modern. In O'Byrne's piece, the author has placed himself under the guidance of 'an old, old man', and they walk together through the Belfast of the 1940s, seeing the city as it had existed in the previous century. The vision that is described is fleeting and ephemeral, a glimpse of an organic community. As with the Carson poem, the new is quite helpless to prevent the fantastical reappearance of that which has long since vanished; it is written over by the past. It is for this reason that O'Byrne observes in the opening to the piece – and to *As I Roved Out* as a whole:

> Places have a soul, and men make it for them by living in them. And even after the men pass away, and the place with the soul has become depopulated and deserted, something, if it be only a memory, remains.[9]

The important continuity here is that in both pieces nostalgia is deployed as a mode of survival. In 'Question time' this is relatively obvious: it is only memory that prevents something dreadful – something material – happening to the protagonist. For O'Byrne, the deployment is more embedded, but resides in his conviction that only nostalgia can compete with what he saw as the appalling reality of a partitioned Ireland and the existence of the Northern Irish state. This describes the larger project of O'Byrne's volume. *As I Roved Out* is best described by its subtitle, 'being a series of historical sketches of Ulster and Old Belfast', but these sketches merely repeat the same narrative of betrayal in various forms – the narrative that takes Ulster from Henry Joy McCracken and the United Irishmen to partition. Indeed, so preoccupied is *As I Roved Out* with this story that at times it can appear to do little more than gaze with horror on the modern symptoms of the decline it articulates. This disgust heightens the work's prelapsarian tone and gives intensity to the secular hymns to social harmony and civility that dominate the book. However, these visions are rarely allowed to endure, and the typical progression of a story in the collection is one that moves from the present, via a moment of epiphany gained by a revelation of the past, to the recognition of irretrievable loss. As Thomas MacGreevy noted in a perceptive review, for O'Byrne 'the individual note in the music of humanity tends always to be muted'.[10] It is for these reasons that *As I Roved Out* can be read as the obituary of the Northern Revival, the very movement that created the preconditions for its existence in the first instance. The book revisits the cultural possibilities of the Revival as they existed before 1916 but only with the awareness that such possibilities were soon to appear hopeless anachronisms. The nostalgia that this gave rise to was, however, something other than retrograde, in that it articulated a mode of survival for Northern Catholic nationalism that was, for O'Byrne at least, appropriate to the new circumstances of the Northern Irish state. In place of constitutional political agitation, O'Byrne offers instead the forces of memory, cunning and abstention; and these are the strategies that Carson's 'Question time' inherits and deploys.

In asserting this comparison, then, it is possible to glimpse the continuity of a tradition insofar as the mode of nostalgia that O'Byrne perfects through *As I Roved Out* can be interpreted as the signature discourse of Belfast Catholic nationalism in the latter half of the last century. To speak broadly, while a case can be made that Northern Protestant writing in this period finds itself preoccupied with questions of territory and space,[11] the Catholic imagination is, instead, increasingly dominated by the temporal: the possibility of inhabiting many historical locations beyond the fallen present. Protestant writing urges revision, redefinition and assertion of presence, while Catholic writing is, instead, often circular – it returns repeatedly to the moment of the fall, it dwells on loss and it frequently finds the beginning of a new narrative to be a fraught and laboured procedure. In terms of representations of Belfast, Protestant writing returns obsessively to the mud and the swamps from which the modern city was claimed,[12] an act of heroic communal endeavour, while Catholic writing emphasises instead the accumulated layers of oppression built into the fabric of the city itself. In the necessary revisions and circlings that this technique involves we can glimpse the revitalisation of a storytelling/*shanachie* tradition and, indeed, O'Byrne is perhaps best understood as an urban *shanachie*: a writer deploying repetition, folklore, Ulster English, comparative and non-linear forms of storytelling to create an effect which can be near-hypnotic. In this way, O'Byrne was the protector of a popular tradition of storytelling and history in Belfast at a time when it was threatened with eradication – in Hewitt's words, he provides a way of making 'sense of the streets we traverse, and their street names which encapsulate so much of their tangled history'.[13] Moreover, O'Byrne's ability to reinvigorate the *shanachie* tradition to encompass the urban space and the modernity it embodies galvanises folk memory as a force hostile not only to institutional historiography but also to the collective amnesia implicit – as he sees it – in the expansive energies of capitalist industrialisation. Carson has been explicit about the nature of his debt to O'Byrne's work,[14] and his work since *The Irish for No*, from 1987,[15] has frequently appeared heavily influenced by these formal explorations. In a subsequent collection of Belfast stories and histories, *The Star Factory*, from 1997,[16] Carson 'acknowledge[s] O'Byrne's ghostly presence at my shoulder' in a manner reminiscent of Yeats's evocation of Lady Gregory and J. M. Synge in 'The bounty of Sweden'.[17] Ultimately, *The Star Factory* takes the imaginative principles of *As I Roved Out* further than O'Byrne was able, but in both there is a desire to preserve the memory of that which has gone – an instinct in this case closer to reclamation than nostalgia. Carson is not alone in recalling O'Byrne through his creativity. A similar influence can also be identified in the creative writing of Gerry Adams (especially his collection of essays and stories *Falls Memories*[18]) and in modern forms of popular culture in the North – the vernacular sentimentality of the Falls Road-based community magazine *Rushlight* being perhaps the best example. In O'Byrne's sometimes fevered imagination were forged the stories that Catholicism in the North of Ireland has told itself, the destinies to which it clings.

These patterns can be traced in the life as well as the work of O'Byrne. Born as Charles Burn in 1876[19] in County Down but of Wicklow parents, he spent his childhood in Balmoral in the relative comfort of the lower middle class. Although autobiographical references in his work are surprisingly rare for such a prolific writer, in *As I Roved Out* he records boyhood excursions to Malone, Stranmillis and the Botanic Gardens and describes a world of slightly fragile bourgeois Catholic respectability. He was educated at St Malachy's College on the Antrim Road in Belfast and his first job was as a manager of a spirit grocery on the Beersbridge Road in Ballymacarret with his sister and lifelong companion, Teresa. This was not coincidental. Because of the highly segregated and sectarian nature of employment opportunity in Belfast, the liquor trade was one of the few areas in which Catholics could gain not just employment but a career. Indeed, as Michael Farrell has observed,[20] by 1911 some 80 per cent of publicans and wine and spirit merchants in Belfast were Catholic – a preponderance that, to some extent, still pertains. O'Byrne would give up this job in 1902 as demand for his singing and journalism increased. As a youth he counted the great Northern nationalist politician Joe Devlin as a friend and was a member of the Sexton Debating Society – a society that sought to protect and advance 'Irish Ireland' culture in Belfast and which had Devlin as president. At this time Devlin was manager of the spirit grocer Kelly's Stores on Bank Street, and O'Byrne divided his time between there and the Linen Hall Library, where he obsessively studied books, maps and newspaper articles on Belfast and its history. Such scholarly interests led naturally enough to a more general preoccupation with the political possibilities of the rapidly growing Revival movement. O'Byrne became a leading member of the Gaelic League in Belfast and was prominent in the cultural politics of nation building, alongside the Protestant solicitor and Northern Revivalist par excellence Francis Joseph Bigger. His friendship with Bigger was the most important of his life and one that endured until Bigger's death in 1926, an event that for many symbolised the passing of an era.

The story of O'Byrne's adult life subsequent to this adolescent activity is one that this book will relate in more detail, but something of the curious joy of what he was to become was well captured by a vivid pen-portrait of O'Byrne (anonymous although probably written by the Protestant republican writer and memoirist Denis Ireland) published in the *Irish Times*[21] towards the end of his life:

> The creator of this *comédie humaine* was a handsome young man with a luxuriant head of hair and a moustache so magnificent that it might have been invented by Ouida. You saw him at concerts of Irish music, a striking figure in his Irish kilt: a singer of Gaelic songs, a musician, a poet, a dramatist, an essayist – above all, a superb raconteur. He was a friend of Ethna Carberry and Alice Milligan in the days when they were reviving the *Shan Van Vocht*, the days of the '98 centenary. He was a friend of Francis Joseph Bigger, and at Bigger's house, Ard Righ, on the Antrim road overlooking Belfast Lough, met Roger Casement, Patrick and Willie Pearce [*sic*], Sean McDermott, the Countess Markievicz, Maud Gonne MacBride – indeed looking back, it seems as if he met the whole cavalcade of nationalist and revolutionary Ireland.

As this memoir indicates, the significance of O'Byrne lies in part in the fact that he was connected to nearly all the major figures of Irish nationalism in the first half of the century. Constantly engaged in a shifting series of coteries and intimacies, he moves from a commitment to Home Rule, through a period of Hibernianism and on to a more resolute republicanism in a manner that was typical of the progression of many nationalist activists during this time. Moreover, in his roles as singer, actor, poet and journalist he was, in many ways, the archetypal figure of the Northern Revival itself. In his later years, following the partition of the island and a residency in the United States, he reinvented himself as a folklorist, storyteller and Catholic mystic. Indeed, stated in such simple terms, the symmetry of O'Byrne's career – pre-partition optimism set against post-partition nostalgia – suggests itself as the template for a more extensive understanding of the fate of the Northern Revival in its entirety. Before partition, the movement can be identified as a self-confident and quite assertive force mobilising itself around a number of interlinked organisations, journals and coteries, such as the Gaelic League, the Ulster Literary Theatre (ULT), the Irish Folksong Society, the Henry Joy McCracken Literary Society (another project funded by Bigger) and the group of intimates gathered at Bigger's house, Ardrigh, in north Belfast. Such organisations were partly based on Revival movements operating elsewhere in Ireland but were also, in their concerns and structure, often unique to the North. Following partition and the 'loss' of the North, these movements either collapsed or radically reshaped themselves. From being a confident and fundamentally optimistic discourse, the language of Northern cultural nationalism after 1921 became insular, melancholic and preoccupied with images of memory and loss. As this suggests, the speed and extent of the Northern Revival's growth were matched only by the suddenness of its collapse. Central to this, of course, was partition and the feelings of abandonment and shock that it generated among Northern nationalists, but it is also important to recognise the seismic shift of the Easter Rising in 1916 – an event from which the North was curiously removed.[22] In the cultural sphere, the Northern Revival could find little adequate response to the transformed post-1916 political landscape. Certainly, in writing of the movement it is impossible not to be struck by the qualitatively different nature of experience in this period, when events moved at an often bewildering speed. Individuals, organisations and political ideas could pass from an emergent to an obsolescent state within a matter of months and the imperative to respond to the latest developments in Irish politics was to become a typical feature of the Northern Revival's frequently ephemeral preoccupations.[23]

Understood as such, the Northern Revival was a distinct movement, one that was nationalist in orientation, connected to Revival organisations elsewhere and yet still unique in its methods and temperament. However, this distinctiveness is so marked that for some cultural historians the movement in the North disappears from the Revival radar altogether. As John Wilson Foster argues:

> It is not surprising that fictional realism during the years of the Irish Renaissance can be found in the North of Ireland where commerce and industry, and an associated middle class, as well as an urban working class, flourished. The novels of [Shan] Bullock, [Forrest] Reid, and St. John Ervine cannot be accounted part of a literary revival that preferred romanticism to realism. Nor could the reality of the North of Ireland be accommodated by a cultural nationalism directed from Dublin.... Ulster writers, such as Bullock, went to England (or if they stayed at home, like Reid, wrote for English readers) or, like Ethna Carbery (née Anna Isobel Johnston), Alice Milligan, Seosamh MacCathmaoil (né Joseph Campbell), AE (né George Russell), and Moira O'Neill (née Nesta Higginson), they joined the romantic nationalist movement, in the process Gaelicizing or otherwise altering their identities. This they had to do, for the Protestant North, with its incorrigible nonconformism, industrialism, and political unionism, was not to be part of the cultural revival.[24]

Foster's reading has an internal cogency, although recent research qualifies the terms of his analysis in important ways. Most obviously, the existence of a seemingly inevitable tension between an urban and commercial middle class and romantic cultural nationalism is increasingly hard to identify with any confidence. More properly, one might argue that the development of the latter is in many ways beholden to the vibrancy of the former. In these terms the Revival, even in its most fantastical peat-smoked reveries, is clearly a function of the modernity it appears ostensibly to despise. As Joyce's satires on the Revival in *Dubliners* portray in withering detail, such tendencies (and the humour that they provoked) were readily identifiable in Dublin, but Revival instincts in Belfast also emerged from the city's commercial centres and were frequently driven by the energies of its Ulster Protestant industrial ascendancy. As such, one persuasive way of reading the Revival movement in all its different manifestations is as a means of relating changing economic and material conditions to national identity. Issues of religious identity can be read in similar terms. What Foster calls the Protestant North's 'incorrigible nonconformism' was, for figures such as Bigger and Alice Milligan, precisely that which they claimed led them to reject the sentimental attachment to faith, class and unionism in Ulster. As a result, the Presbyterian spirit of the North was read as a radical strand embedded deep in a Northerner's political instinct and this was an element seen to be sadly lacking in their co-religionists in the South. As this suggests, Foster is surely correct when he observes that 'the reality of the North of Ireland' could not 'be accommodated by a cultural nationalism directed from Dublin', but this in turn did not prevent the North developing its own movement directed instead from industrial Belfast.

The fact that the Revival in the North operated in these distinct ways illustrates that the Irish Revival movement as a whole was never homogeneous. Indeed, even in its earliest period – before the kind of fragmentation one might expect to find in such an ambitious cultural project had set in – the movement tended towards the incorrigibly diverse. As W. P. Ryan noted in 1894, in one of the earliest accounts of the Revival as a recognisable entity:

> literary Ireland consists of many fragments, very far apart and very strange to one another. Even our leading literary societies, working for the same purposes, are not yet like the wings or sections of the same organisation. Literary Ireland in fact does not know itself.[25]

Ryan's sense of 'literary Ireland' is important for it emphasises that such an entity – Ireland as a textual phenomenon – was at no point entirely concomitant with Ireland as a physical space. Instead, 'literary Ireland' was a moment of cultural perception and, as the Revival was to prove, was therefore as likely to flourish in London as it was in Dublin. Or indeed Belfast. As Ryan's account of the scattered locations from which the Revival grew observes:

> for ten years the Belfast Young Ireland Society has been a virile Celtic centre in the northern capital. It has had an essentially missionary career, and is justly looked back to as a national Alma Mater by many.[26]

There is little exaggeration in his description. The Young Ireland Society met weekly through the 1890s in St Mary's Hall on Bank Street under the leadership of William McGrath and it was directly responsible for educating and galvanising a generation of nationalist politicians, writers and editors. Indeed, the fact that by 1894 the eventual leader of Belfast nationalism, Joe Devlin, had succeeded McGrath as its president further indicates the extent to which the organisation was a template for the future structure of Northern nationalist political culture. Aside from its regular lectures and readings, the Society was enthused by practical acts of commemoration and, most notably, erected a cross over the grave of 'the Belfast Man' Francis Davis, the nineteenth-century weaver, poet, journalist and, ultimately, assistant librarian of Queen's College. The significance of this ceremony derived from the Society's assertion that the legacies of figures such as Davis had been forgotten in a city driven primarily by an unceasing self-delight in the achievements of its industrial progress. The cultural and historical amnesia often said to typify Belfast and its citizens might well be the price that this forward gaze demands.

As this example indicates, the Northern Revival in its earliest manifestations was not a phenomenon of high or indeed print culture, but rather was typified by an emphasis on ceremony, commemoration and performance. Moreover, and I think crucially, much of the Northern Revival was informed by popular culture – most obviously the traditions of music hall and vaudeville that captivated huge swathes of the city's working population most nights of the week. In this way, many of the events that typify the Northern Revival (in Belfast at least) can be understood as a sometimes unlikely series of negotiations between middle-class Catholic nationalism and the working-class (or lower-middle-class) genre of music hall. To put this more elegantly, it can be suggested that the Revival took from the latter in order to energise the former. One can identify this cross-pollination in the seemingly endless series of so-called 'Irish nights', recitals, variety evenings, 'smoking concerts' and pageants organised by groups and institutions as diverse as the Ancient Order of Hibernians (AOH), the Gaelic League, the Irish Folksong Society and the Belfast National Literary Society. Indeed, from 1898 – a year of celebrations for the centenary of the United Irishmen and a crucial moment in the Revival's sense of its own project – to the outbreak of World War One in 1914, the ideal of a Northern Revival gained its definition and coherency through the extraordinary range and vitality of its public events. On reflection this is unsurprising. The formation of a confident sense of Irish national identity in an atmosphere as unpromising as late-Victorian Belfast demanded constant rehearsal and repetition. It also demanded a certain self-consciousness. The Northern Revival was never shy of recognising itself as a coherent and self-contained movement, although sometimes the logic of all this disparate activity was so submerged that only Northern Revival propagandists writing for the *Irish News* or the *Northern Whig* could trace its contours. However else we imagine this period, it is clear that revivals are not spontaneous; rather, they are willed into existence.

Inevitably, however, the Ireland that was constructed through this feverish activity was quite distinct from the Irelands simultaneously being created in Dublin and London. Although the movement emphasised the quality of 'Ulsterness' as the means through which a non-sectarian Irish identity might gain a foothold in the North (and thus imagined that its native genius derived from what it saw as the bluff common sense and satiric instinct that was indigenous to the area), in reality the Ulster it constructed was a projection, or often a fantasy, of a peculiarly Belfast mindset. In these terms the Northern Revival was largely a Belfast phenomenon, the product of an industrialised modernity that did not so much reject the signs of capitalist imperial expansion that surrounded it as engage dialectically with it. As for the actual Ulster that lay beyond Belfast, its complexity and unevenness remained largely unexplored by a cultural movement that was usually prepared to encounter the rest of the province only through idealised assumptions of a Northern Gaelic essence. For example, despite his status as a prominent amateur historian and archaeologist, Bigger was happy to imagine a fifteenth-century colonial merchant's castle in Ardglass to be the fortress of a Gaelic chieftain, while other members of the Ardrigh coterie repeatedly read the Glens of Antrim as nothing less than the home of an unpolluted Celtic spiritualism. As Lynn Doyle joked in his *An Ulster Childhood* of 1921, 'the Gaelic Revival has repopulated the other three provinces, and the glens and mountains of Ulster, with fairies and leprechauns, whose airy tongues syllable a new language that is also old'.[27] Indeed, much of the Northern Revival's efficacy depended on a carefully policed distinction between the country and the city. As Milligan insisted in the *Northern Patriot* in December 1895: 'Belfast is not Ulster, nor even representative of that province. There is a Native North, as thoroughly Celtic as any part of our island.'[28]

Milligan's mistrust of Belfast was shared by other important figures in the Revival movement. As Roger Casement asserted in 1898: 'Belfast is really I think a very stupid ill-bred town and although I have not (fortunately) been in it for 7 years until this visit I hope it may be fourteen before I come to it again'.[29] Meanwhile, for O'Byrne, Belfast, 'with its interminable miles of mean streets was one of the ugliest cities in the world'.[30] For O'Byrne the unsightliness of the city's industrial architecture was a direct result of the uncompromisingly austere unionism of the city fathers and, indeed, for many in the movement Belfast remained little more than 'Bigotsborough', the pseudonym it assumes in James Douglas's interesting although neglected 1907 novel *The Unpardonable Sin*. Developing this, St John Ervine, during his period of enthusiasm for the Home Rule cause in 1913, described Belfast as an 'upstart city; it is without breeding and tradition; its people are assertive and full of contempt for those who have not made money. Each man suspects his neighbour of evil designs.'[31] Meanwhile, when the painter Paul Henry was finally able to flee Belfast, the city of his childhood, and escape to London, he wrote simply of himself: 'I was the caged bird which had been set free'.[32] However, as much as Northern Revival writing about Belfast disdains the city, it also demonstrates a helpless fascination with the dynamism of the place. O'Byrne's *As I Roved Out* would prove to be the ultimate expression of this complex relationship but a similar preoccupation can be found in the work of Bigger, Milligan and the poet Joseph Campbell. Resistant though they usually are, at various times these writers all succumb to the allure of what H. A. MacCartan in 1921 called the 'glamour of Belfast'.[33] Certainly the energy of the city could be infectious. In 1891 Belfast overtook Dublin as the biggest city in Ireland and by 1900 it was the fastest growing city in the British Isles, a place that was rapidly becoming one of the major cities of Western Europe. More than simply an industrial and commercial hub, Belfast was also the centre of scientific and technological research in Ireland during this period, a remarkable modern experiment in capitalism rendered all the more startling by its close proximity to deeply traditional rural economies of labour.

Central to much of this activity was the Belfast Natural History and Philosophical Society, a vibrant organisation that sheltered a considerable number of smaller organisations, such as the Belfast Naturalists' Field Club (BNFC), in its headquarters on College Square North. From its foundation in 1821 the Society structured much of the intellectual life of the city for the next century at least, shaping its distinct concerns and disseminating what it deemed to be good scientific practice. Inevitably the Society was drawn predominantly from the city's Protestant middle class and, although politics and religion were the two subjects forbidden for discussion,[34] a distinct streak of liberalism is visible in its preoccupations. This is important because of the degree to which the concerns of the Society appeared to move quite naturally from science and technology to areas that would eventually prime the Revival, such as archaeology, Irish antiquity and the study of the Irish language. It is no coincidence that the foundation of the Belfast branch of the Gaelic League developed as a result of the success of the Irish-language classes organised by the BNFC. Partly because of the restless energies of Bigger, by the 1890s the Society's areas of enquiry had widened dramatically and could incorporate subjects as arcane as 'Irish fairy lore', the title of a lecture W. B. Yeats delivered to the BNFC in November 1893,[35] or indeed 'Local Gaelic place names', Bigger's own contribution to the lecture series in April 1894. As John Wilson Foster has pointed out,[36] one of the important aspects of this transition is that it reminds us that Protestant industrial or mercantile culture was not, in itself, antipathetic to later Revivalist activity, and indeed it was only the subsequent rewriting of the history of the movement by Revivalists themselves that created the opposition. The extent to which this division has ultimately shaped the cultural memories and self-perceptions of the two parts of the partitioned island remains hard to judge, but certainly it can be argued that a figure such as Bigger appears anomalous as a Revivalist in this period only because of his seemingly comfortable occupation of both camps.

Bigger, of course, was exceptional in many ways, but the cultural position he maintained was not restricted to the realms of the dedicatedly eccentric. In the years before the Ulster crisis of 1914 there was in fact an enduring and often energetic interest in Irish Ireland among Belfast's Protestant middle class. In 1905 the Belfast Industrial Development Association organised an 'Irish exhibition' on Queen Street, which was remarkable not least because of the manner in which it presented Belfast industries alongside Irish traditional crafts from the four provinces, and invited the visitor to see the continuum. We know of this detail thanks to the images of Alexander Hogg, the event's official photographer.[37] Born into a Presbyterian family in 1870, Hogg was a pioneer of photography in Ireland and, more importantly for this argument, was perhaps the key chronicler of Belfast in all its forms during the early years of the century. The variety of his portfolio remains striking: from the technology of the shipyards and the mills, to the music halls and theatres, to the pathetic lives of those lost in poverty and exclusion, Hogg recorded all that he encountered. He was also a member of the BNFC and, naturally enough for the time, was deeply immersed in interests that we would now consider to be classically Revivalist – interests indicated clearly by his floridly Celtic business cards and advertisements. There is no real evidence to suggest that Hogg was anything other than a unionist, albeit one with strong liberal sympathies, and yet he was happy enough to join with Bigger on a number of Revival projects, including taking a series of striking photographs of Bigger's restoration of Shane's Castle in Ardglass, the history of which I will relate in Chapter 4. If the range of Hogg's images – from the *Titanic* to recreations of Tír na nÓg – suggests a contradiction, it was a contradiction that could be creatively (and perhaps even politically) enabling.

A similarly productive tension could be found in the activities of the Ulster Arts Club, a society that is still in existence. Although the Club would eventually become part of Belfast's middle-class unionist social culture, at the time of its inauguration in 1902 it bore all the hallmarks of Revivalist cultural politics. As Patrick Shea noted in his official history of the Club:

> illustrations on some of the early concert programmes were executed in Celtic designs. Club dinners were held on St Patrick's night; and it was usual to have a short poem about Ireland specially composed and printed on the menu card.[38]

These tendencies were doubtless the work of the Club's founding inspiration, Harry Morrow, an artist who, as I will discuss in Chapter 3, would later find success as a playwright with the ULT under the pseudonym Gerald MacNamara. Alongside Morrow, the fact that both Bigger and O'Byrne were longstanding members of the Club indicates something of the welcome it was prepared to offer to committed Irish nationalists. Indeed, it was at the Arts Club's premises on Fisherwick Place that such disparate figures as O'Byrne, the novelist Forrest Reid and Alex Hogg could socialise – an opportunity that could never be taken for granted in Belfast's habitually suspicious and partitioned social realm. Despite the Club's interest in Irish Ireland, however, it was never a nationalist organisation. One of its first acts was to decorate the Club's headquarters in celebration of the royal visit of King Edward VII and Queen Alexandra in 1903. As a newspaper reported at the time:

> The Ulster Arts Club had a large banner suspended in front of their premises with the motto 'Caed Míle Failte' interwoven with shamrocks, a flag of Erin and a Union Jack suspended on either side. On the footpath, students dressed in white monks' robes performed a mime and with their quips and pranks kept the crowd in the vicinity fully amused.[39]

That said, there were clearly other Belfasts in existence beyond Fisherwick Place and College Square North, with their formal lectures and mannered debates. Although still principally a Protestant city, the influx of rural Catholics hired to work in the burgeoning linen mills gradually began to change not only the demography of Belfast but also its social practices and habits. This transition was culturally energising for a city that had become increasingly monolingual in the stories it told about itself, but it was also dangerous for those who existed in the liminal spaces of the city's now secure sectarian geography. Serious rioting between the two communities was a regular feature of Belfast life during the Revival period, but the social and political causes of this violence were rarely acknowledged by a Belfast middle class who preferred instead to view such events through the prism of late-nineteenth-century theories of racial difference.[40] Although the Northern Revival ultimately created only a limited dialogue between Catholic and Protestant, given this context the existence of any kind of dialogue at all was by no means a small achievement. Similarly, although the Revival movement was surely class ridden in its hierarchies, the fact that a figure such as O'Byrne could move with apparent ease between the near poverty-stricken working-class Catholic communities clustered along the Falls and the upper-middle-class Protestant world of Bigger, Casement and Milligan suggests that some internal mobility was possible.

The Belfast of this period, then, was one of constant surprises. It was an urban space that defied easy categorisation and one that often energetically contested the clichés of those who sought to disparage it. In the cataclysmic years of the Parnell tragedy and its aftermath, through the period of Home Rule agitation and on to the Ulster crisis, Belfast presents both tolerance where one might expect to find bigotry, and intolerance in places we might assume to be liberal. It was also a city in permanent and sometimes bewildering flux. Even as recently as the early 1880s the dominant characteristics of Belfast were that of a semi-rural town, a city described by Forrest Reid as 'somehow likeable, and surrounded by as beautiful a country as one could desire'. Indeed, for Reid, even the anti-Irishness of the Protestant middle class was 'not so apparent while the whole town was more homely, more unpretentious'.[41] Few writers yield as easily to the idealisations of nostalgia as Reid, but even taking this tendency into account it is significant that his Protestant suburban memory chimes with O'Byrne's Catholic lower-middle-class perception of the city during the same period as a predominantly rural market town.[42]

Such a condition was not to endure. Granted city status in 1888, by the turn of the century Belfast had grown rapidly and become a city that both alienated Reid and occasionally frightened him. This change was not merely a matter of its rapid industrialisation – spectacular though this was – but was also manifest in the transformation of its social structures, the city's sense of *civitas*. This more intangible shift was most vividly embodied by the building of Belfast's City Hall on the site of the old White Linen Hall between 1903 and 1906. With its ornate wedding-cake design and extensive use of Portland stone and marble it was described in the lavish advertising brochure *Fashionable Thoroughfares of Great Britain and Ireland* as 'unmatched for beauty of design and nobility of structure by any similar edifice in the United Kingdom'.[43] It was also, of course, a powerful symbol of unionist industrial ascendancy and as such has been cordially loathed by the city's nationalist population ever since, a building of 'formal pomposity' as Brian Moore described it in his 1955 novel *The Lonely Passion of Judith Hearne*.[44] As this suggests, the rapid industrialisation of Belfast came with a concomitant hardening of political and social attitudes and it would not be long until something close to a Protestant unionist hegemony pertained. The economic and industrial dynamism of the city in the early years of the century was underwritten by a profound cultural and social surveillance and, as such, Belfast as a physical space became an increasingly regulated and policed entity. The ideological apparatuses of the society – whether imagined in terms of religion, class, geography or family – wove themselves tightly around all forms of cultural practice and invariably circumscribed the early activities of the Northern Revival. Certainly, while the cultural nationalism of a Protestant and Freemason such as Bigger was merely an eccentricity in 1895, an activity to be indulged or patronised, by 1911 it was nothing short of an absurdity, and a dangerous one at that.

This was a condition that appeared most tangible (and, indeed, most stifling) during Belfast's seemingly endless Sundays, the day of the week when the clamour of the city's industries gave way to a concomitant, and no less striking, silence. Joseph Connolly, a member of Bigger's Ardrigh coterie and a close friend of O'Byrne, describes the unsettling atmosphere of those days in arresting terms:

> Belfast was and maybe still is a Sabbatarian city. The Belfast Sunday of my youth was a day of gloomy depression. The brightest Sunday in summer was made melancholy by the almost sullen silence of the streets and the black-garbed stream of solemn church-goers.... As a young boy I could not and did not attempt to analyse it but, even now, I feel an involuntary shudder when I recall the effect of it. I can only describe it as a sense of loneliness or homesickness, a depression that was atmospheric, and it can only have been caused by the solemnity and the appearance of severity which the church-goers presented.[45]

The powerful sense of *unheimlich* that Connolly describes here constitutes a form of monad – the moment when ideology reveals itself through material practice. Indeed, so total was this observance – and so dispiriting for those who craved stimulation on their day of rest – that, as O'Byrne joked in *As I Roved Out*, it sometimes seemed that even Ulster's crows were strict Sabbatarians.[46]

As this suggests, the few traces of Protestant radicalism that had lingered in Belfast up to this time were, on the whole, helpless to prevent the growing polarisation of the two communities as the Ulster crisis worsened. Indeed, by 1913, the London *Times* could report that 'Ulster Liberalism is very like the Cheshire cat in *Alice in Wonderland*. It has vanished until only its grin lingers furtively in a corner of Co. Antrim.'[47] That corner was Ballymoney in North Antrim, where traces of an old anti-landlord radicalism remained among Protestant farmers. These beliefs were articulated most consistently in the early years of the century by the Presbyterian minister and advocate of Home Rule James B. Armour. It was Armour who organised the famous 'anti-Covenant' meeting of 24 October 1913 in Ballymoney Town Hall that attracted a crowd of 500 Protestants to hear speeches by the radical nationalist historian Alice Stopford Green, as well as by Captain Jack White and, making his debut in political oratory, Sir Roger Casement.[48] As the presence of these participants indicates, this event was probably the closest the Revival movement came to one of its greatest desires – the reinvigoration of the radical Presbyterian tradition in Ulster – but even Armour's meeting was, in truth, something of a chimera and no significant political movement ensued. Despite this, it is easy to understand the appeal of this tradition for both Revivalists and subsequent historians of this period, for not only did it distort the 'two nations' theory of Ulster that could so relentlessly trample on the complexities of the North's social and political micro-landscape, but it also spoke of an older continuity: the final links with an eighteenth-century Protestant republicanism that it was usually assumed evaporated after the fall of the United Irishmen. Unfortunately, like the bones of McCracken, so assiduously protected and then ceremonially reburied by Bigger in one of the Northern Revival's more peculiar episodes, the few remains of the tradition that could still be identified were probably erroneous and certainly historically misleading.

If the internal structures of unionism in this period were becoming increasingly ossified, the same could not be said of Northern nationalism, which remained in a potentially volatile state. As the next chapter will discuss, the tensions within the nationalist movement in Belfast, which had been starkly revealed by the Parnell crisis, did not fade away but subsequently re-emerged in the struggles between Devlinite and anti-Devlinite factions, constitutionalism against republicanism, the clash of ideologies between Sinn Féin and the Irish Parliamentary Party (IPP), and even arguments about specific events such as the Spanish Civil War – a conflict which generated inter-Catholic violence on the streets of West Belfast.[49] Inevitably, these divisions had at their epicentre the constantly shifting fault-lines that lay between the Catholic Church and the aims of Irish nationalism – a tension still readily identifiable in Northern nationalist political culture today. Indeed, then as now, the major way in which this breach was healed, or at least temporarily overlooked, was through the assertion of a communal unity demanded by the continued hostility of Orangeism and the political structures that buttressed it. For this reason, it can be argued that one of the more remarkable characteristics of Ulster Catholicism was not the frequency with which it divided against itself, but rather the often remarkable unity of voice and aspiration it managed to display. Allied to this was a determined capacity for self-reliance, both before and after partition, which distinguished the community from its co-religionists elsewhere on the island. In many ways this was an instinct fostered by necessity and can be seen as an inevitable aspect of life for the minority community in the North, but, even taking this account, some of its achievements were extraordinary. Devlin's boast in 1914 that

Belfast Catholics had built seventy schools for their children at a cost of £180,000 indicates the scale of the projects undertaken.[50]

Inevitably, this self-reliance was not just economic but cultural. During this period the Catholic Church in Belfast became the main focus of social as well as spiritual life for its communicants and was usually a reliable supporter and sponsor of many Revival events and initiatives. This dominance would become all the more marked in the years following partition, when it would be no great exaggeration to suggest that the Church became a form of internal government for a community that felt itself disenfranchised within Northern Ireland and abandoned by the South. This, in part, accounts for what can be identified as a distinctive attitude towards the Church that one encounters repeatedly among Northern Catholics: a frustration with – or even resentment of – the often socially suffocating and conservative structures though which the Church organised its community, alongside a recognition of the central role that the Church played in maintaining social cohesion and, therefore, a reluctance to reject its ultimate authority. The other major aspect of this self-reliance was a tendency towards insularity. The inward gaze of Northern Catholicism was increased not only by constant emigration but also by a distinct hostility to external ideas and influences that might be said to be a logical result of living within a state of imaginative siege.[51] Indeed, the fossilisation of the Catholic North's intellectual life was not the least of partition's effects, and it is only in this context that the startling artistic renaissance of the late 1960s and 1970s can be properly appraised. Certainly, as historians such as Marianne Elliott, Fionnuala O'Connor, Oliver Rafferty and Eamon Phoenix have demonstrated,[52] the story of the Catholics of Ulster during the twentieth century is nothing short of remarkable.

Although recognising the uniqueness of unionist and nationalist identities in Ulster during the period of the Northern Revival is, of course, a necessary process, it is also one of the aims of this book to suggest something of the limits of this two-community model of Ulster society when assessing the constant fluidity of cultural performance, both in its production and in its reception. Indeed, ultimately it is the cultural dynamics of 'Northernness' itself that needs to be appraised, for the extent to which this concept could be mobilised within Irish nationalism (or indeed mobilised as a means of contesting that aspiration) remained a point of both cultural and semantic instability. In fact, one of the constant risks attendant on the Northern Revival was the danger that this 'Northernness' would become culturally self-sufficient: a radical, even disquieting, proposition that was, I think, quite distinct from the regionalist movement that gained brief momentum in Northern Ireland later in the century. Partition made the future trajectory of this possibility impossible to judge but certainly it can be argued that while there are now valuable academic studies of such key Northern Revival organisations as the ULT, the Gaelic League in the North and the numerous periodicals and magazines that emerged in this period, 'Northernness' itself will only emerge if these movements are understood in the totality of their effects as a series of interconnecting forces. This demands a critical practice that is able to read the few remaining fragments of what was once a complex pattern and, with this, to take a guess at those aspects of the Northern Revival that have yet to be inherited. There is much in the legacy of the movement that constitutes unfinished business.

One important element to this reconstruction involves having to recognise connections and inheritances that might more comfortably be overlooked. In many literary historical accounts of the possibilities and limitations of the Northern Revival movement there is a clear, if usually barely acknowledged, division between 'good' Revival movements, which contain some element of secular nationalism and so are worthy of further study (for instance, the ULT), and 'bad' Revival movements, which promote a unified version of national and Catholic identity and so must be marginalised (for instance, the AOH).[53] In terms of the revisionist and post-revisionist discourses of Irish history and cultural studies, the reasons why this distinction has occurred are understandable, but it is not a division that appears to have been recognised at the time with anything like the same sensitivity. These moments of interpenetration should not, then, be suppressed, not least because they allow us to glimpse something of a wider truth about the efficacy of Revivalism as a means of instilling and disseminating national feeling. When recognising the extent to which much of the Northern Revival insisted on a strict alignment of nation, faith and culture, it is inevitable that we notice also the considerable number of times when these factionalised cultural identity politics simply failed to achieve anything close to their intended purpose. Indeed, we can argue that such failure is almost the inevitable result of the initial aspiration. To emphasise this point is not to fetishise the liminal, the marginal or the hybrid as the centre of cultural performance but rather to recognise a simple (and perhaps energising) truth: we are never entirely concomitant with our identity and in the gap that exists reside emergent meanings, misreadings, over-compensations and suppressions.

This is possibly why the Revival as a whole was so reliant on discourses of self-satire. As Terence Brown has argued, the cultural nationalism that underwrote much of the Revival's basic beliefs was nothing less than the 'conviction whereby the essential, spiritual life of a people is assumed to subsist in its culture, bequeathed to it from antiquity and pre-history'.[54] It was in this way that Revivalism could enter into a dialectical relationship with political or even revolutionary movements towards independence. To this end, the necessary and concomitant recognition of the essential impossibility of cultural nationalism as so defined was as important to its achievement as the monotonous singularity of the primary discourse itself. The fact that the Northern Revival appeared to grasp this realisation before the revivals of Irish sensibility that were occurring in Dublin, London and New York at the same time is, I would argue, one of its most profound achievements. Perhaps it is for this reason that a willingness to risk ridicule – to recognise the impossibility of the task undertaken – typifies many of the Northern Revival's major events and individuals. As the example of Cathal O'Byrne vividly demonstrates, it was at such moments that the Northern Revival was not only at its most compelling, but also its most dangerous.

NOTES

1 Quoted in anonymous, 'Bookman's gossip', *Irish Bookman*, 1.2 (September 1946), p. 73.
2 Walter Benjamin, 'The storyteller: reflections on the works of Nikolai Leskov', in *Illuminations*, ed. Hannah Arendt, trans. Harry Zohn (London: Fontana, 1973), p. 83.
3 John Hewitt, Foreword, in Cathal O'Byrne, *As I Roved Out* (Belfast: Blackstaff, 1982). All subsequent page references are to this volume.
4 Patricia Craig, *The Rattle of the North* (Belfast: Blackstaff Press, 1992), p. 10.
5 W. B. Yeats, *Autobiographies* (London: Macmillan, 1992, first published 1955), p. 559. There is, of course, much to question in this model. Indeed, perhaps because most of the key work on the Revival has been undertaken by literary and cultural critics, the assumption that political disenchantment led automatically to cultural revitalisation has been accepted too easily. In fact, as Roy Foster has pointed out, nationalist politics – both constitutional and revolutionary – continued to function with some vitality after Parnell's fall. For a more detailed analysis of this pervasive belief, see Foster's essay 'Thinking from hand to mouth: Anglo-Irish literature, Gaelic nationalism and Irish politics in the 1890s', in *Paddy and Mr Punch: Connections in Irish and English History* (London: Penguin, 1993), pp. 262–80.
6 Ernest Boyd, *Ireland's Literary Renaissance* (London: Grant Richards, 1923, first published 1916), p. 5.
7 Cathal O'Byrne, *As I Roved Out*, p. 3.
8 Ciaran Carson, 'Question time', in *Belfast Confetti* (Dublin: Gallery Press, 1989), p. 63.
9 O'Byrne, *As I Roved Out*, p. 1.

10 Thomas MacGreevy, 'Cathal O'Byrne, Dublinman', *Father Mathew Record* (May 1948), p. 11.
11 We might note, for instance, that it is this preoccupation that connects such different writers as the mid-century 'planter poet' John Hewitt to the modern Belfast novelist Glenn Patterson.
12 Again, the poetry of Hewitt and Patterson's novel *Fat Lad* (London: Chatto and Windus, 1992) serve as good examples of this tendency.
13 Hewitt, Foreword.
14 I expand on this influence in the essay '"The shanachie of Belfast and its red-brick Gaeltacht": Cathal O'Byrne', *Bullán: An Irish Studies Journal*, 4.2 (winter 1999/spring 2000), pp. 67–82.
15 Ciaran Carson, *The Irish for No* (Dublin: Gallery Press, 1987).
16 Ciaran Carson, *The Star Factor* (London: Granta, 1997), p. 191.
17 'But certainly I have said enough to make you understand why, when I received from the hands of your King the great honour your Academy has conferred upon me, I felt that a young man's ghost should have stood upon one side of me and at the other a living woman sinking into the infirmity of age.' Yeats, *Autobiographies*, p. 571.
18 Gerry Adams, *Falls Memories* (Dingle: Brandon Books, 1983).
19 This is according to his death certificate. Hewitt's Foreword to *As I Roved Out* proposes 1883 while Padric Gregory's *Modern Anglo-Irish Verse* (London: David Nutt, 1914) suggests 1877. Meanwhile the *Northern Whig* suggested 1874 ('Prince of storytellers is dead', 3 August 1957, p. 1). On the matter of O'Byrne's origins it is interesting that 'Burn' and 'Burns' were very common names in County Down and had become so due to the nineteenth-century Anglicisation of the local Irish name McBrin. O'Byrne's own Gaelicisation of his previously Anglicised surname then indicates something of the perpetual threat of etymological amnesia attendant on the process of renaming and translating.
20 M. Farrell, *Northern Ireland: The Orange State* (London: Pluto Press, 1976), p. 367.
21 *Irish Times*, 23 July 1955, p. 12.
22 Witness, for instance, Bulmer Hobson's opposition to the entire enterprise and Roger Casement's seeming misunderstanding of the Rising's aims and intentions.
23 Bulmer Hobson, co-founder of the Ulster Literary Theatre, provides an interesting example of this phenomenon. At one time regarded by British Intelligence as 'the most dangerous man in Ireland', after 1916, because of his opposition to the Easter Rising, he had been almost entirely marginalised and largely forgotten.
24 John Wilson Foster, *Fictions of the Irish Literary Revival: A Changeling Art* (Syracuse: Gill and Macmillan, 1987), p. 176.
25 W. P. Ryan, *The Irish Literary Revival: Its History, Pioneers and Possibilities* (London: privately published, 1894), p. v.
26 Ryan, *The Irish Literary Revival*, p. 154.
27 Lynn Doyle, *An Ulster Childhood* (Dublin: Maunsel, 1921), p. 21.
28 Alice Milligan, 'The boys who are true to Erin oh!', *Northern Patriot*, 3 (1895), p. 33.

29 Jeffrey Dudgeon, *Roger Casement: The Black Diaries* (Belfast: Belfast Press, 2002), p. 176.
30 O'Byrne, *As I Roved Out*, p. 116.
31 St John Ervine, 'The return to Belfast', *New Age*, 14.4 (27 November 1913), pp. 102–4, p. 103.
32 Paul Henry, *An Irish Portrait* (London: Batsford, 1988, first published 1951), p. 8.
33 H. A. MacCartan, *The Glamour of Belfast* (Dublin: Talbot Press, 1921).
34 According to Seán Lysaght's *Robert Lloyd Praeger: The Life of a Naturalist* (Dublin: Four Courts Press, 1998), p. 27, the BNFC 'functioned as a kind of freemasonry where religious discourse had no place'.
35 Letter to F. J. Bigger, week of 13 November 1893, in *The Collected Letters of W. B. Yeats. Vol. 1: 1865–1895*, ed. John Kelly (Oxford: Clarendon Press, 1986), p. 367. According to the letter, Bigger offered to 'dedicate' the day after the lecture to Yeats's 'whims'. They spent the day touring County Antrim. During this visit to the North Yeats also called upon Alice Milligan, thus beginning a long, if not always comfortable, acquaintanceship. A humorous account of Yeats's expedition can be found in Denis Ireland's *From the Jungle of Belfast: Footnotes to History 1904–1972* (Belfast: Blackstaff Press, 1973), pp. 17–19.
36 John Wilson Foster, 'Natural history, science and Irish culture', in *The Poet's Place: Ulster Literature and Society. Essays in Honour of John Hewitt, 1907–1987*, eds Gerald Dawe and John Wilson Foster (Belfast: Institute of Irish Studies, 1991), pp. 119–29.
37 For more on Hogg see W. A. Maguire's *Caught in Time: The Photographs of Alexander Hogg of Belfast, 1870–1939* (Belfast: Friar's Bush, 1986).
38 Patrick Shea, *A History of the Ulster Arts Club* (Belfast: Mayne, Boyd, 1971), p. 6.
39 Shea, *A History of the Ulster Arts Club*, p. 4.
40 See Jonathan Bardon's *A History of Ulster* (Belfast: Blackstaff Press, 1992), p. 400.
41 Forrest Reid, *Apostate* (London: Constable, 1926), p. 51.
42 See for instance the numerous childhood reminiscences of Belfast collected in O'Byrne, *As I Roved Out*.
43 Anonymous, *Fashionable Thoroughfares of Great Britain and Ireland* (London: Advertising Concessions Company, 1911).
44 Brian Moore, *The Lonely Passion of Judith Hearne* (London: Penguin, 1959, first published 1955), p. 42.
45 J. Anthony Gaughan, ed., *Memoirs of Senator Joseph Connolly (1885–1961): A Founder of Modern Ireland* (Dublin: Irish Academic Press, 1996), p. 50.
46 O'Byrne, *As I Roved Out*, p. 429.
47 25 October 1913. See also J. R. B. McMinn's *Against the Tide: A Calendar of the Papers of Rev. J. B. Armour, Irish Presbyterian Minister and Home Ruler 1869–1914* (Belfast: Public Record Office of Northern Ireland, 1985), p. lviii.
48 See McMinn, *Against the Tide*, for a full description of this event and also J. R. B. McMinn, 'Liberalism in North Antrim 1900–14', *Irish Historical Studies*, 23.89 (May 1982), pp. 17–29.

49 It is interesting to note that, according to Maguire's *Caught in Time* (p. 155), one of the major strongholds of support for fascism in Belfast was within the city's small but vibrant Italian community, centred on Little Patrick Street.

50 See Oliver P. Rafferty's *Catholicism in Ulster 1603–1983* (London: Hurst, 1994), p. 173.

51 One of the most vivid embodiments of this condition in literature is again Moore's *The Lonely Passion of Judith Hearne*, the major part of which takes place in a Catholic boarding house on Camden Street in South Belfast. For Moore, the writer in exile, the ignorance, conservatism and petty-minded bigotry of the various residents encapsulated a wider truth about the insular state of Catholic life in Northern Ireland during this depressing period.

52 Respectively: Marianne Elliott, *The Catholics of Ulster: A History* (London: Penguin, 2000); Fionnuala O'Connor, *In Search of a State: Catholics in Northern Ireland* (Belfast: Blackstaff Press, 1993); Rafferty, *Catholicism in Ulster 1603–1983*; Eamon Phoenix, *Northern Nationalism: Nationalist Politics, Partition and the Catholic Minority in Northern Ireland 1890–1940* (Belfast: Ulster Historical Foundation, 1994).

53 For an example of such marginalisation, see what is also one of the most detailed and stimulating accounts of the Northern Revival, Flann Campbell's *The Dissenting Voice: Protestant Democracy in Ulster from Plantation to Partition* (Belfast: Blackstaff, 1991).

54 Terence Brown, 'Cultural nationalism, 1880–1930', in *The Field Day Anthology of Irish Writing, Vol. 2*, eds Seamus Deane *et al.* (Derry: Field Day, 1991), p. 516.

CHAPTER TWO

The political and cultural origins of the Northern Revival

Question 13. – 'Has not Ulster Bigotry much to do with the Irish opposition to Home Rule?'

Answer: – 'Ulster Bigotry' is a term of reproach invented by Irish Roman Catholic Nationalists to explain the well-reasoned opposition to Home Rule which has always existed, and always will exist, in the northern province. The people of Ulster are largely Protestant. They believe – and who are capable of judging better? – that a Home-ruled Ireland would be an Ireland mainly dominated by the ideas of the Irish Roman Catholic hierarchy and clergy, who claim authority as much in temporal or secular affairs as they do in matters religious or spiritual. In reality, 'Ulster Bigotry' is only 'Ulster Self-Defence'.

The Irish Unionist Pocket-Book for the Use of Unionist Workers in Great Britain[1]

HOME RULE MEANS ROME RULE

The Heckled Unionist: Hints to Irish Unionists on English Platforms[2]

PERHAPS the dominant way in which cultural historians have sought to understand the phenomenon of the Irish literary Revival is to read it as a movement emerging from the activities of a small and quite tightly organised coterie of intellectuals and artists from the South, and especially Dublin. As such, many of the Revival's preoccupations illustrate the negotiations between the classes and factions of that city, and the corresponding manner in which a new form of national and personal identity was created. Most prominently, this required a transformation of Anglo-Irish identity that may have been, to return to John Wilson Foster, 'unrealistic',[3] but which remained revolutionary in its implications, in that it validated the potential emergence of a secular Irish national identity. It is on this claim that the Revival's historical significance is based and this perception was, if anything, intensified by the fact that subsequent events in post-partition Ireland showed just how fragile such an identity was. It was also precisely for this reason that Ulster's role in the Revival has remained uncertain. If many Revivalists in the South were prepared to contemplate (at least) the uncoupling of religion and nationalism in the search for a more inclusive shared identity, a comparable gesture was always unlikely in a province where religion remained the most crucial determinant of selfhood. Rather than an attempt to short-circuit the current of sectarianism by offering a more attractive alternative, much of the Northern Revival's cultural output can be perceived instead as simply old antipathies reconfigured in the light of new cultural possibilities.

This is not to suggest that the Northern Revival lacked ambition, but rather to recognise the extraordinarily difficult environment in which it attempted to grow. While the possibility of tentative cultural exchange across religions was one of the preconditions for the development of the Revival in the South, in the North no such space existed. Instead, in the crucial years between 1900 and 1920, it is more usual to find a hardening of attitudes and a concomitant reliance on a peculiarly Ulster mode of dogmatic assertion. For instance, when faced with what it termed 'radical questions' about the Home Rule issue, *The Irish Unionist Pocket-Book for the Use of Unionist Workers in Great Britain*, from 1911, proposed that the individual unionist need do no more than repeat the model answers it proposed. As it suggested:

> If these answers are carefully read, and their salient points memorised, Unionist workers will be able to reply off-hand, with brevity, and effectively, to most of the queries that proceed from those in Great Britain whose support of Home Rule is largely due to misunderstanding.[4]

If, to a large extent, the energies of the Revival in the South derived from a startlingly new sense of how one could be an individual in society, in the North such individualism was viewed with a sceptical eye. In this context, the Northern Revival's tendency to operate from within established political and religious institutions becomes explicable.

Whatever else it was, then, the Northern Revival struggled to be a forum for cross-community dialogue. As I have discussed in the previous chapter, although the Protestant dissenting tradition in the North was still identifiable in areas such as North Antrim and in organisations such as the Independent Orange Order, its influence among the general Protestant population remained tiny. This is an important caveat for, despite the work of the cultural historian Flann Campbell in his pioneering book *The Dissenting Voice*,[5] it is hard to dispute J. R. B. McMinn's assertion that, ultimately, radical Protestantism 'was a structure built upon the sand of political illusion, rather than on the rock of political reality'.[6] Instead, Protestant politics remained transfixed by the spectacle of the mass movement, and deliberately sought to suppress its internal antagonisms of region or class in the interests of asserting a unified voice. This was both Orangeism's greatest strength and its secret weakness, but it was also no small achievement on an island that remained dogged by an ever-increasing factionalism. Certainly, it was a capability that would earn the despairing respect of, among others, James Connolly.

But what of Ulster's Catholic community? In comparison with the highly visible formations of Protestant politics, typified most obviously by the Orange parading tradition, the province's minority religious grouping had remained largely invisible as a political force, both within Ulster itself and when seen as part of Catholic Ireland as a whole. The cause of this was not political apathy but rather the lack of a tradition of mobilisation and the particularly intimate relationship that Ulster Catholics (especially those in Belfast and Derry) had with their political antagonists – a situation not found elsewhere in Ireland. As a result, and as George Boyce has argued, 'nineteenth-century Irish nationalism bore no imprint of Ulster Catholics'.[7] The implications of this for nationalist Ireland were both serious and unsettling. The Ulster minority was not a defeated community and yet its response to an intensely unjust political structure had been closer to quiescence than rebellion. Clearly, if Irish nationalism as a whole was to advance its claims, then the galvanisation of the Ulster Catholics was an urgent requirement. It is in this context that the events described in this chapter should be viewed. The creation of a political and revolutionary class in Ulster in the years leading up to partition was remarkable, not just because of the speed with which it was achieved, but also because it had such unpromising origins.

The Northern Revival was to play a large part in this transformation. As I will discuss in the next chapter, while the origins of the movement in both the North and the South can be seen in the antiquarian interests and political commitment of wealthy Protestants, in the North at least its transformation into a mass movement was dependent on its adoption by the Catholic community. It is for this reason that the Revival in the North was much more profoundly Catholic and clerical in its allegiances than most narratives of the Revival in its entirety can allow. Although Protestants such as Bulmer Hobson, Roger Casement, Francis Joseph Bigger and Alice Milligan played major roles in its development, they were exotic figures in the often sectarian atmosphere of Northern nationalism while remaining, as Jonathan Bardon has observed, 'utterly unrepresentative of the mass of Ulster Protestants who were repelled by these new interpretations of cultural identity'.[8] Even Casement, himself something of a rare flower in the atmosphere of early-twentieth-century Ulster, realised that people thought of Bigger as 'a crank – a banner and pipe maniac'.[9] Indeed, rather than the continual uneasiness with the hierarchy and ritual of the Catholic Church that we find in many of the writings of Protestant Southern Revival figures, the more usual strategy of Northern Protestant Revivalists was a submersion into Catholicism, in both its theological and its social forms. For instance, although Milligan often made great play of the fact that she was a Protestant nationalist, she was also quite capable of subordinating her Methodism to a sympathetic understanding of, and identification with, the Catholic Church,[10] while it is revealing that Bigger, perhaps the most eccentric Northern Revival figure in what is, by any measure, an extraordinary cast of characters, was persistently described in the words of his friend, the novelist Shane Leslie (himself a convert to Catholicism), as 'a Protestant with Franciscan leanings'.[11] Even Casement, another close friend of Bigger, converted to Catholicism immediately before his execution (although he had, in fact, been secretly baptised into the faith as a child, rather like Oscar Wilde). Cathal O'Byrne considered the significance of this act in some detail in an article from 1937, 'Roger Casement's last will',[12] which describes Casement as carrying a rosary as part of his personal possessions and once stating that 'no one could love the Irish people without loving the religion that made them what they were'. The devout O'Byrne was always alert to the possibility of converting his Protestant friends and, as such, Casement's conversion represented a considerable trophy.

If inter-faith tensions, then, were curiously lacking from the Northern Revival (even though they were more obvious in other areas of Ulster society), the movement can be better understood as a competition for hegemony within Catholic Ulster as a whole. Such competing forces included the usual suspects: pro- and anti-Parnellite opinion (the anti-Parnellites having considerable strength in Ulster), the fault-lines between republicanism and nationalism (to be most clearly exposed in the violence surrounding the 1918 election in the Falls Division when Devlin triumphed over de Valera), and clerically based organisations mobilising against nascent labour movements. It is precisely because of these tensions that the figure of Joseph Devlin, who was Home Rule MP for West Belfast from 1906 to 1918 and ideologue behind the revitalisation of the exclusively Catholic Ancient Order of Hibernians (AOH), dominates the political landscape of the period. Devlin was born in 1871 in a working-class area of the Falls in Belfast and was particularly finely attuned to the sensitivities of the Ulster Catholic micro-climate. More specifically, his genius lay in his ability to encompass the different aspects of Catholic identity in its various forms across the North, and to maintain the contradictions thereby generated in a mode of creative tension. While, as Michael Farrell has recognised, Devlin's primary loyalty was to 'the interests of the Northern Catholic business class and the Church',[13] he can also be found in this period supporting socialist and neo-socialist movements (as in his support for Jim Larkin's strike call in 1907), backing John Redmond's call for nationalist enlistment in World War One, and playing on purely sectarian fears and aspirations though the AOH. Understood in these terms, Devlin can be seen as the archetypal Northern politician of this period – and would be an inconceivable figure in any other part of Ireland. If Northern Catholic politics, like the Northern Revival, can be understood as a strictly internal row – or a family feud – it was at times only the cult of Devlin that prevented complete fragmentation.[14]

As this suggests, Devlin's ascent to political power corresponded very closely with the development of the Revival itself and some consideration of his adolescent activity indicates the extent to which the two phenomena were interwoven. O'Byrne's *As I Roved Out* is again the key text here:

> With us, in our memory, 'Kelly's Store' will be forever associated with the name of Joe Devlin, for it was while he was manager of the place that we first got to know him. At that time, in our young youth, we were a member of a literary circle – the Sexton Debating Society – of which Joe was the President. He could not have been more than nineteen years old at the time, if so much. There were not many opportunities for the acquiring of our native Irish culture in the Belfast of that day. There was no Gaelic League, no Irish Language or Dancing Classes, no Gaelic Football or Hurling Clubs, and so, those of us who made up the roster of our Society had to do the best we could. From time to time, and by distinguished people, we had lectures on subjects of Irish interest. We read and studied Irish History, and held debates on phases of it – that we certainly did – and took ourselves very seriously, too. We had a fairly comprehensive library of Irish literature. We organised concerts and sang Irish songs, and all of these things we did with the lad named Joe Devlin as our Chairman.[15]

This description is undoubtedly touched by the desire to assert a myth of first beginning (a tendency found in many personal accounts of Revival history) and yet it still reveals a number of important features of the movement's early activity. O'Byrne's estimate of Devlin's age dates this memory to the years 1890–91 (O'Byrne himself would have been fifteen) – the time, of course, of the Parnell crisis, and the point at which it is assumed that activism in the cultural sphere begins to replace constitutional Home Rule politics.

This, then, was the Revival's year zero, or, as Seumas MacManus put it with a great deal more dramatic effect when chronicling the beginning of the nationalist journal the *Shan Van Vocht*, the time when 'Ireland had slipped into the Slough of Despond – when the nation's hopes seemed shattered – and all patriotic work for Ireland was completely arrested'.[16] It is, of course, necessary to question the reality of such a clean distinction but it is not easy to doubt the effective significance of the date in Revival mythology. Perhaps, however, the most significant aspect of O'Byrne's account is that it reminds us that the Revival sprang from diverse sources. Although the movement would soon be apprehended as a singular entity – a perception wrought for the most part by the movement's own zealous propagandists – it developed from a number of more or less semi-autonomous coteries and creative intimacies across Ireland and, indeed, the United States and Britain. This heterogeneity has often been overlooked and yet without its recognition it is difficult to decode many of the later tensions implicit in the movement and, of course, the manner in which it would eventually collapse. Certainly, the group described by O'Byrne – a Northern Catholic urban coterie determined upon a course of self-education – is as good an example as any of the Revival's heterogeneous origins and an early indication of its varied aims.

Devlin had formed the Sexton Debating Society in 1885 and Thomas Sexton himself – West Belfast MP from 1886 to 1892 – was its patron. Sexton was an early role model for Devlin, and his emphasis on the importance of learning debating skills can be understood as a direct attempt to create a nationalist political class. Certainly for Catholic Ireland, this was a pressing need – and would prove to be a precondition for the events leading up to and beyond 1916. At no time, however, was this political class unified and even in O'Byrne's account of Devlin's early activities we can identify incipient traces of what would become bitter divisions. This can be seen in O'Byrne's further recollections of the period:

> Once, on a day, we had to call at 'Kelly's Store' to consult with Joe about some of our Society's projected activities, and going in we found him in his office – Joe was manager of the place – he did not serve at the bar – declaiming to the four walls, a black cat, some chairs and the office furniture generally, a 'piece of elocution' he was preparing for a competition, and there and then he pressed us into service (an audience of one) and made us sit in judgement on his efforts. The name of the piece – and how well we remember it – was 'Shiel's Reply to Lord Lyndhurst,' a turgid bit of old style oratory of the kind that was popular with all the Belfast teachers of elocution of that day – and they were not few.[17]

It is easy to overlook the significance of the incidental detail that O'Byrne includes here. The account asserts a moment of political possibility and yet so fragile is this that even in its asides and sub-clauses the passage reveals implicit tensions and subsequent factionalism. For instance, in O'Byrne's insistence that Devlin 'did not serve at the bar' is a passing reference to the idea of Devlin as 'the Wee Bottlewasher', the sarcastic name his political opponents would use when they wished to draw attention to his class origins and his bourgeois aspirations. O'Byrne's correction insists on the more respectable status of Devlin's position, and in so doing reveals something of the extent to which Northern Catholic nationalism was fissured by class politics. More tellingly, James Connolly would revisit this accusation in 1915 in his fury at Devlin's energetic support for enlistment. As he noted then:

> The sarcasm is pointless. A bottlewasher was an honest occupation, but a recruiting sergeant luring to their death the men who trusted him and voted him into power is – ah well, let us remember the Defence of the Realm Act.[18]

Even the subject of Devlin's exercise contains a nostalgia born of subsequent political division. 'Shiel's [*sic*] Reply to Lord Lyndhurst' was an oration praising the skills of Irish soldiers delivered by Richard Lalor Sheil in response to Lord Lyndhurst's accusation that the Irish were 'aliens in blood, in language, and in religion'. In this oration, Devlin's later constitutional nationalism and role within the Irish Parliamentary Party (IPP) is made explicit and the irony of this position's subsequent impossibility is not lost on O'Byrne. As Connolly wryly observed in his *Labour in Irish History*, 'Shiel considered the above phrase of Lord Lyndhurst an insult; modern Irish Nationalists triumphantly assert the idea, embodied in that phrase, as the real basis of Irish nationalism'.[19]

As these details indicate, the political beliefs of O'Byrne and Devlin would eventually diverge, and in this cooling intimacy can be seen in microcosm something of the wider dissociation that would take place within nationalism as a whole as militant activists gradually lost patience with Redmondite constitutional politics. In these terms, the violent disagreements over enlistment that would take place during World War One were only the most obvious symptoms of a more protracted argument. As O'Byrne notes: 'Later in life Joe and ourselves parted company with regard to many Irish issues, major and minor, but the firm friendship of our boyhood days, we are glad to say, remained unbroken to the end'.[20]

If Devlin was to provide the inspiration for the resurgence of Catholic Irish nationalism in Ulster, the *Irish News* was to shape the specific contours of its political and cultural identity. The Northern Revival itself was crucial to this identity in that the movement provided a coherent rationale for the idea of indigenous artistic production and, with this, an assertion of cultural autonomy. The *Irish News* was not slow to recognise the potential of this and it provided the movement with unfailing publicity and support, effectively becoming its house organ. For this reason, it is not possible to understand the Revival's popular appeal without recognising the unique place the paper occupies in modern Ulster history.[21] In a similar manner to the Revival itself, the *Irish News* had emerged from the disastrous split in nationalist opinion caused by the revelations surrounding Parnell's private life. In December 1889 Captain William O'Shea had cited Parnell as co-respondent in a divorce petition and the subsequent outrage that this generated in both Ireland and Britain prompted Gladstone, the prime minister, to state that the Liberal–nationalist alliance – the vehicle for the delivery of Home Rule – could not continue if Parnell remained leader of the IPP. In effect, Irish nationalist opinion was forced to make a stark choice between the promise of Home Rule or the continued support of its once assured leader. The old joke about the English finding an answer to the Irish question only for the Irish to change the question was now reversed and the result was both swift and devastating. Nationalist Ireland divided into two bitterly opposed camps – the majority against Parnell – and the tide of Home Rule receded once again.

While Dublin was to remain one of Parnell's strongholds, nationalist opinion in the other great conurbation on the island, Belfast, was more dangerously divided. The major Northern nationalist (or, at least, not pro-unionist) newspaper, the *Belfast Morning News*, had initially vacillated in the face of the crisis, moving from an anti-Parnellite to a pro-Parnellite position. This dramatic shift incurred the displeasure of the Northern Catholic hierarchy and drew attention to the fact that the North lacked a newspaper willing to provide a consistent platform for the views and teachings of the Church. The most energetic proponent of this position was Dr Patrick McAlister, the Bishop of Down and Connor, who identified 'the great necessity which exists at the present time for a really Catholic and nationalist daily journal in Ulster'.[22] Parnellism, it seems, was no longer compatible with Catholicism and it was with this belief that the *Irish News* was created. With the key support of the Church, Catholic business and the fledgling Northern Catholic bourgeoisie, the momentum for the new paper gathered pace and the first issue appeared on 15 August 1891. Its success was immediate. The *Belfast Morning News*, despite abandoning its own pro-Parnell position, could provide no adequate response and, after a year of competition, it was subsumed into the younger paper. Driven by its sense of mission and (more importantly) healthy sales figures, the *Irish News* maintained its pursuit of Parnell until his death, as a broken and ill figure, in October 1891. It was an inglorious, if strategically necessary, beginning.

The success of the *Irish News*, then, provides evidence of the strength of anti-Parnellite feeling among Northern Catholics as well as of the manner in which subsequent Revival activity could happily coexist alongside a quite narrowly defined sense of Catholic national identity – the intersection which O'Byrne's work would later occupy and illustrate. However, despite the seemingly stark terms of the schism created by the Parnell crisis, the two opposing positions were never as monolithic as they may now appear. As Roy Foster has observed,[23] some priests remained with the Parnellite cause, while anti-Parnellism was, in the North especially, often a troubled and contradictory position. It was, perversely perhaps, these doubts that saved the *Irish News* from becoming merely the mouthpiece for stifling and conservative clerical opinion. Despite its unpromising beginnings, after Parnell's death the paper realised the necessity of appealing to a wider spectrum of nationalism and it became a lively and often stimulating journal driven by talents such as the young Devlin and T. J. Campbell, the paper's editor from 1895 to 1908. Devlin was to have a fraught relationship with the paper until, after a bitter power struggle, he was elected to its board in 1905 (he became managing director in 1923). During the turbulent years of 1900–16, the paper was to play a crucial role in Devlin's attempts to build a Home Rule consensus within Northern nationalism.

It can be argued, then, that the most distinctive element of the *Irish News* in this period, and perhaps the major reason for its initial success, was not a slavish devotion to clerical principle, but rather its ability to maintain a highly protean editorial position – a quicksilver tendency it shared with Devlin himself. The paper in general represented the interests of the urban Catholic business class, espoused the politics and aspirations of Home Rule, and yet was quite capable of startling shifts in perspective and argument, according to the strategic demands of everyday political life. There is, perhaps, nothing surprising in this. As I have already suggested, the Northern Catholic constituency that the paper represented was, in many ways, also searching for a coherent political position, in relation not only to nationalist aspirations across Ireland but also to the threat posed by the increasingly militant assertions of loyalist politics closer to home. Moreover, the paper understood and constructed its readership as anything but a beaten community. Rather than the repetition of grievance and dispossession, the *Irish News* urged its readers to embrace the possibilities of economic and educational advancement and to mimic the structures of the organised Protestant business community. This accorded with the similar role that Devlin envisaged for the AOH, in that both organisations provided him with a means of mobilising the electorate at such times as was necessary, while tying the disparate aims and activities of Northern Catholic business to an overall political objective. Certainly, in the years up to 1916 it is difficult to see the AOH movement and the *Irish News* as anything other than a political whole. The final important factor in the constitution of the *Irish News*' editorial line was the ever-present threat that the disastrous schism in Catholic opinion caused by the fall of Parnell could easily reassert itself in a different form. Despite the passing of time, the Northern Catholic community remained intractably divided on this issue and the polarised terms of the debate suggested that no resolution was possible. In the face of this, the *Irish News*' eventual policy of tactical silence on the subject was understandable – even though it is hard to avoid the suspicion that the ghost of Parnell hovered over many of its subsequent editorials.

Despite its success, the *Irish News* could not, of course, encompass all shades of nationalist opinion and it is in the often bitter criticism it received that it is possible to gain a fuller picture of its distinctive features and readership. The most vocal of its early critics was undoubtedly Connolly. As the *Irish News* had been created in order to provide Catholic moral leadership and was, by 1905, firmly committed to the achievement of Home Rule, this was scarcely surprising, but Connolly's disdain was to initiate a century of consistent republican hostility to the paper.[24] Connolly had returned to Ireland in 1910 after a period of political activity in the United States, and had become Ulster organiser of the Irish Transport and General Workers' Union. Based in Belfast, he was well placed to witness the success of the paper, even if it was, for him, often a depressing and slightly mystifying phenomenon. As he wrote in 1913 in the article 'Press poisoners in Ireland':[25]

> We have in Belfast a Home Rule journal, the *Irish News*, a careful study of whose columns would be an enlightenment to those Socialist comrades in Great Britain who imagine in their innocence that an enthusiasm for Labour is the inevitable accompaniment of the advocacy of a measure of political freedom for Ireland.
>
> They would find that that journal is one of the most deadly enemies of the Labour movement that this country possesses, and that it never lets slip any opportunity to wound that movement even whilst softly purring its sympathy for Labour on all possible occasions. In all Ireland there is no journal more ready to proclaim from the housetops its readiness, and

> the readiness of the party whose mouthpiece it is, to do something for the working class, and in all Ireland there is no journal more ready with the poniard to stab to the heart every person or party that dares to organise the workers to do anything for themselves.

Connolly's attack, voiced from the self-consciously internationalist perspective his writing always occupied, identifies the newspaper's habit of strategically shifting loyalties and sees in this tactic nothing less than a conspiracy to subvert the cause of workers' unity he had devoted his life to achieving. It is with this belief that he interprets the paper as 'more thoroughly modern than its rivals in the Tory press', in that its strategy of propaganda is based not on editorials (which usually contain 'a sloppy sentiment sloppily expressed in favour of Labour') but a more insidious policy of giving 'undue prominence' to any news story 'that tells against Labour'. As he develops his argument:

> It never moves against Labour by direct attack. It suppresses here, exaggerates there, distorts this bit of news, omits this qualifying sentence from some speech, drops casually a favourable paragraph from the report of some strike or Labour meeting, and is ever alert to seize every opportunity to spread the slime of poisonous suggestion over the most apparently innocuous report of the activities of Labour.

Connolly's accusations are perceptive insofar as they go on to identify one of the key fault-lines within Northern Catholic nationalism: that which lay between the authority of the Church and the demands of organised labour. As with the Parnell split, however, this was by no means a clear distinction. Individual priests, especially in Belfast, were often highly supportive of the labour movement, while the powers of trade and industrial combination were often mobilised for factional or sectarian ends. It could hardly have been otherwise. In the increasingly polarised atmosphere of early-twentieth-century Ulster it was certainly not easy for an individual worker to determine where sectarian oppression ended and class oppression began. Moreover, as Boyce has recognised, for many Ulster Catholics a dislike of England and its politics was secondary to a 'hatred of Protestants, and especially Orangemen'.[26] The role of the *Irish News* in this was, however, neither as simple nor as intriguing as Connolly suggests. In truth, the paper's uneasy relationship to organised labour was less due to a fully realised policy of anti-socialist propaganda as a more haphazard recognition that the Home Rule coalition needed to encompass as many different elements of nationalism as possible. Certainly, the paper well understood that the Home Rule argument could be fought on the factory floor as well as from the pulpit and it was in this manner that it made its appeal.

Connolly himself was well aware of the significance of this issue for the Home Rule argument. While the Northern Catholic bourgeoisie – the constituency who had supported the foundation of the *Irish News* and who had, for the most part, turned against Parnell – were the natural supporters of Home Rule in the North, the unskilled Catholic workers of Belfast were less compliant. As Connolly recognised, they constituted a class 'whose instincts are all rebellious and revolutionary, and who are therefore drawn towards the Labour movement'.[27] As his 'Press poisoners in Ireland' argues, the support of this class was crucial to Devlin if he was to retain control of his West Belfast parliamentary seat, for if he alienated even a small percentage of that grouping then the seat would pass into unionist hands. It was Devlin's ability to maintain this control that both infuriated Connolly and earned his grudging admiration. By mobilising the *Irish News* and the AOH (an organisation which, according to 'Press poisoners in Ireland', was involved in attempting to break the tram workers' strike in Dublin during this same period) Devlin created a stronghold for Home Rule in Belfast that was to endure long after the argument had ceased to be an attractive proposition elsewhere in Ireland.

This is not to suggest, however, that Devlin's record in labour politics in Belfast was merely cynical. In fact, he was committed to the cause of improving conditions for the working class in Belfast for both communities throughout his political life and even historians such as Farrell, who might be expected to be hostile to Devlin and his politics, recognise the sincerity of his welfare work.[28] Indeed, it can be argued that, despite Connolly's suspicions, threats to Devlin's power base were more likely to develop from the clerical and middle classes than from the often adoring workers of West Belfast, who, according to Paddy Devlin, 'idolised Devlin because of his efforts to win them better conditions'.[29] As an anonymous piece of doggerel published in the *Irish News* in 1905 put it:

> Sprung from the common people, he loves the commonweal.
> In factory, mill and workshop, his worth is known and prized
> By old and young, by weak and strong, in actions realised.[30]

The politics of Home Rule, perhaps because the term itself was open to a number of interpretations, always involved a loose coalition of interests and often seemingly contradictory impulses. Connolly himself, with his record of defending the Catholic faith and the institution of marriage against those socialists who claimed such things were inimical to Marxism,[31] may well have recognised something of his own political philosophy in Devlin's ideological pirouettes.

The popular appeal of the *Irish News* can be comprehended only if it is placed in the context of two other Devlinite organisations in this period: the AOH and the United Irish League (UIL). All three organisations were to serve the cause of the IPP during the early years of the century and, in each instance, this influence had been gained through a process of infiltration and committee manipulation. This was one of Devlin's particular areas of expertise and a key factor in his success as a politician. By 1905 he had gained control of the *Irish News*, become national president of the AOH and general secretary of the UIL. No other nationalist leader had a local power base of such strength and, indeed, it can be argued that because of his political energies there was now a template for the exercise of coherent Catholic nationalist belief in Ulster, which was unprecedented. Reading the *Irish News*, joining the AOH and subscribing to the precepts of the UIL provided individual Catholics with a set of ideological principles that enabled them to reconcile the different elements of family, faith, work and politics. Moreover, the Northern Revival would soon provide both a cultural context and a range of leisure activities appropriate to that belief system. When compared with the fragmented state of Northern nationalism after the fall of Parnell, this was an extraordinary feat achieved in a very short period. It was, however, also a coalition of interests utterly dependent on the presence of Devlin himself. The talismanic promise of Home Rule had remained the primary objective, but even when that agenda crumbled under the twin assault of World War One and Easter 1916, Devlin's own popularity remained.

A closer examination of the AOH movement in this period further illustrates these talents. The organisation was originally founded in 1836 as an Irish American benevolent society in New York, a city in which the Order's often baleful influence has remained.[32] Heavily influenced in both its constitution and its ritual by secret societies from both the nationalist and unionist traditions, the AOH sought to protect its members' interests and to promote and defend the status of the Catholic Church. While popular in America, it remained a minority movement in Ireland itself until the beginning of the twentieth century, when its powerful call for religious solidarity across classes found a natural home in Ulster's increasingly sectarian atmosphere. Unlike the UIL, the Hibernians made their popular appeal on the basis of religion rather than land and, as such, their views were particularly well suited to the province's unique religious micro-climate, a location where political grievance was readily communicated in the discourse of faith and sacrifice. As a result, it soon became, in Bardon's words, 'a Catholic mirror image of the Orange Order',[33] giving the iconography and parading tradition of the Protestant organisation a vivid green makeover. If it differed from the Orange Order, this was only because, as Farrell has observed, it 'never had the power over the Catholic population the Orange Order had over the Protestants since it had no patronage to distribute or privileged position to defend'.[34] Despite this, and as Devlin recognised, the AOH was both a threat to his power and, potentially, an important ally. The Order's supreme governing body, the Board of Erin, constituted the movement's elite, and it was this that Devlin established and controlled, a process that culminated in July 1905, at the Order's convention in Dublin, with the movement's new constitution endorsing the IPP's Home Rule policy. As Patrick Pearse, among others, recognised,[35] this created a situation where Protestant nationalists, no matter how dedicated to the cause of Irish freedom they might be, were unable to join one of the leading and most active nationalist organisations in Ireland. The AOH itself was uncompromising on the issue. As 'Mr. A. Newman' reported to Division Forty-Five of the Order in St Mary's Hall, Belfast, in March 1913:

> The Ancient Order of Hibernians is the secular arm of the Church and it remains for the few who do not recognise that fact to recognise it as soon as possible. It has come to this – a man cannot become a Hibernian unless he is a practical Catholic: and if he is a Hibernian, one may be morally certain that he is a practical Catholic.[36]

Devlin remained national president of the AOH until 1934 and, while it was another one of the organisations whose relevance would be swept away by the events of 1916, in the years leading up to the Rising it was an influential and powerful movement, with over 120,000 members, a constituency that proved particularly useful in mobilising the nationalist vote. Moreover, the Catholic character of the Order enabled Devlin to exert some control over the more religious elements of nationalist opinion in the North, thus preventing further schisms of the type revealed so disastrously by the Parnell crisis. As Connolly recognised, one purpose of the AOH for Devlin was 'as a weapon against clerical dictation in politics'.[37] Finally, but significantly, it also enabled the links between Irish nationalism and Irish America to be further reinforced. This, in itself, was one of the vital preconditions for the growth in militant agitation (of a type far beyond what the Order would have sanctioned) and, ultimately, the Rising itself. As is so common in this period of Irish history, the relationship between aims and outcomes was by no means predictable.

Another aspect of the Hibernians movement that it shared with the *Irish News* was the degree of venom that the organisation attracted from both republicans and unionists. This was mainly due to the conservative form of nationalism the Order espoused, but its shadowy influence on local political and economic affairs as well as the almost Masonic tone of some of its rituals and initiations were also heavily criticised. According to *The Irish Unionist Pocket-Book for the Use of Unionist Workers in Great Britain*, the AOH was 'the most powerful of all sectarian Irish associations',[38] while, from an opposing perspective, Connolly declared that the Board of Erin was 'the foulest brood that ever came into Ireland'.[39] Connolly was well aware of the peculiarly symbiotic relationship the AOH had with the Orange Order and argued that:

> were it not for the existence of the Board of Erin, the Orange Society would long since have ceased to exist. To Brother DEVLIN (Grand Master A.O.H.), and not Brother Carson is mainly due the progress of the Covenanting Movement in Ulster.[40]

Republican attacks on the AOH tended to rely on the symmetry of this parallel, and it was an accusation that the Hibernians found difficult to refute. Indeed, for the Protestant nationalist T. A. Jackson, the only real difference between the two organisations lay in the fact that the Hibernians were, if anything, even more corrupt than their Orange fellow Ulstermen. As he notes in his history and memoir, *Ireland Her Own*,[41] the Board of Erin:

> [despite being established] ostensibly to protect Catholic traders and work-people from the Orange racket ... [soon] degenerated into a Catholic 'racket', which reproduced, and outdid, the worst sectarianism of the Orange racket. The falling away of mass support from the Party created an opening for the racketeers to gain complete control of the Party machine.

If this accusation is unfair, then it is only because the Orange Order was itself falling into new depths of sectarianism during the same period.

It is, then, important to recognise that the three organisations Devlin controlled – the *Irish News*, the AOH and the UIL – played a complex if vital role in Ulster politics during this time. It is, however, their connections to the Northern Revival that are of primary significance to this study. For the *Irish News* especially, the Revival became a potent force, as the paper was the first in the North to recognise that through its activities the movement could enact a wholesale cultural revitalisation of nationalist aspirations. To illustrate the extent of this commitment it is interesting to consider the development of the paper between the years 1902 and 1904. While in 1902 the *Irish News* was certainly aware of what cultural nationalist activity there was taking place across the North (and was willing to publicise it), within two years the newspaper had been quite transformed and was dominated by lengthy reports from such groups as the AOH, the fledgling Ulster Literary Theatre (ULT), the Gaelic League, the Irish Folksong Society and the Belfast National Literary Society (another organisation presided over by the ubiquitous Devlin). These groups, in turn, frequently cross-pollinated with organisations that had less obvious cultural interests, such as the UIL and the Irish National Foresters, and, at times, no clear distinction in their activities or membership can be drawn. Moreover, the *Irish News* was quite happy to group together all of this disparate activity under the general term of the 'Revival movement', and in this promoted the cause of the Revival as a spur to economic regeneration and spiritual awakening. Significantly, this was as much a regionalist as a national cause, and in the newspaper's editorialising there was a constant desire to stress the distinctive social conditions pertaining in the North and the consequent importance of the Revival's achievements. If Ulster was still regarded as an inherently philistine province by many both inside and outside its borders, then the achievements of the Northern Revival were all the more laudable. Certainly, it is legitimate to wonder what the Abbey Theatre made of an assertion in a 1909 *Irish News* editorial that 'The Ulster Literary Theatre has always been the most virile organization of its kind in Ireland'.[42]

As this example indicates, the *Irish News* was prepared to stretch (although not, perhaps, quite break) the limits of credulity in its desire to encourage the Revival's activities and prestige. Similarly, it is important to recognise that for the paper the concept of 'Revival' encompassed a range of cultural activity and that it refused to acknowledge any clear distinction between high art and popular entertainment. In this, the intent of a Revival text or event was seen as less important than its effect and, as such, any Revival event that promoted popular sympathy for the aims of Irish nationhood was to be applauded. Consider, for instance, the *Irish News*' report of a 'Smoking Concert' organised by the West Belfast branch of the UIL in May 1904.[43] The event ('which was packed to suffocation') began with 'a selection of Irish airs on the gramophone, skillfully manipulated by Mr. Cormac Kelly', and then featured a number of amateur and professional singers, including Cathal O'Byrne (who performed the popular songs 'An Irish reel' and 'Little Mary Cassidy'). If such an event can be understood as Revivalist in tone and aspiration, it is that version of the Revival which aspires to Catholic bourgeois respectability, a phenomenon mercilessly satirised in Dublin by James Joyce in his short story 'A mother', of 1905. In the same manner, the perceived exclusivity of the UIL was recognised as an important attraction. As the *Irish News*' report of the Smoking Concert went on to observe, many had been unable to join the branch because they had failed to prove themselves to be 'sound, genuine nationalists'.

If this was one of the places from which the Northern Revival would grow, it is important to acknowledge that many of the groups and organisations that typified it would disorientate a scholar of the Revival familiar only with its manifestation in the South of Ireland. This is not merely because the Revival in the North obviously disrupts that reading of the movement which Robbie Meredith has recently defined as 'Revival as a duplicitous Ascendancy project'[44] (although that is the case), but also because it was so often extraordinarily dependent on the good will and political support of the local Catholic Church. As such, clericism became one of the project's defining characteristics. This notice of a typical Northern Revival event from the *Irish News* of 20 December 1912 well illustrates this reliance:

> A planned 'Irish Night' will take place at the Boys' Brigade Hall, Falls Road on Sunday night next. The Christian Brothers, with their traditional readiness to assist the Gaels, are sending their special choir, which made so notable a success at the Ulster Hall lately. Cahal O'Byrne has also placed his splendid professional services at the disposal of the committee, and everyone knows that Cahal is a host in himself, by personality, vocal ability, and more so, perhaps, by the fact that he was among the first to discover and interpret in prose and verse the blend of humour and pathos in the temperament of the Irishmen of the Counties which the Lagan keeps apart. Cahal may not give 'The Battle of Scarva' or 'Comber Fair,' but he has others as racy quite.

The various components of this bill indicate in microcosm the constituent parts of the Northern Revival in its entirety. Alongside the strong clerical support for the event, there is a determined assertion of regional distinctiveness and a pronounced element of music hall – an aspect of much Revival activity now often overlooked. Similar events took place almost every night in Belfast and the diversity of the entertainment offered was remarkable. For instance, alongside O'Byrne on the bill for the Irish night, there was also a performance by his mentor, the blind musicologist Carl Hardebeck,[45] while it was anticipated that 'Miss R. Irwin's six midgets will dance a Highland Reel to pipe music'.

There were clear benefits for the *Irish News* in promoting the Revival and asserting itself as the movement's major supporter. Most obviously, the paper could bask in the reflected light of the movement's early dynamism, and find in that excitement a cause that the paper could adopt. It was, perhaps, for this reason that the *Irish News* described the Revival as a much more coherent movement than it was in actuality. By committing so much of its newsprint to Revival activities, the paper not only began to look markedly different to other Northern papers, but also became a good deal more varied in its appeal. This was no small advantage for a newspaper still regarded by many as narrowly clerical and residually anti-Parnellite. In these terms, the Revival story, understood as an entirely positive development, was a happy opportunity.

This was, perhaps, less obviously the case for the movement itself. By insisting on the homogeneity of the Revival cause, the *Irish News*' coverage implicitly unified a phenomenon that had drawn its initial strength from the sheer variety of its activities. That these activities were then perceived as operating within the IPP's Home Rule agenda was an inevitable outcome of the paper's patronage. As a result of this, the work of Revival figures such as Bulmer Hobson, the radical republican co-founder of the ULT, was frequently misunderstood. It can be argued that only in the pages of the *Irish News* and the more extreme sectors of the Orange press could the activity of the AOH be allied to the development of revolutionary Marxist republicanism and understood as constituent parts of a singular entity. As this suggests, while the *Irish News* enabled the Revival to become, at least in Belfast, a mass participation movement, this was at the price of making it appear a much more fundamentally Catholic enterprise – a dangerous development in a province where interaction between the two communities was always tentative at best. As I have already argued, the first stirrings of the Revival in Ulster came from the work of Protestants such as Hobson, Bigger and Milligan. While their work was to continue through the early years of the new century, its distinctively Protestant characteristics were more easily elided.

The individual most obviously responsible for the *Irish News*' Revival enthusiasm was T. J. Campbell, the editor of the paper from 1895 to 1908. Campbell was a thoughtful political strategist and after, leaving the paper, went on to become an MP for the Nationalist Party and a county court judge. His real talents were, however, as a newspaper man and it was in this role that he steered the *Irish News* through its early turbulent years and forged its distinctive editorial line. Campbell's book *Fifty Years of Ulster: 1890–1940*,[46] published in 1941, contains vivid accounts of this time and reveals the extent to which the Revival project was considered to be an integral part of the nationalist movement in the post-Parnell years. As he observed:

> The revival was a genuinely literary Irish revival in prose, poetry and drama, and was productive of remarkable books and plays and a notable school of acting. It was original, independent in thought and action,

> racy of the soil, and brimful with the Irish aspiration for nationhood. It betrayed a critical tone and temper, made the Irishman laugh at himself, and even made merry at the expense of certain aspects of Irish revolutionary feeling.[47]

Campbell's recollection of the homogeneity of the Revival in this account accords with the manner in which his paper understood the movement at the time. Indeed, it could appear so coherent only in subsequent years because of the work of individuals such as Campbell in forging its collective identity. In this manner, difference, or the satiric impulse of much Revival work, is understood as a form of sameness or, to put this another way, those aspects of the Revival which criticised nationalist pieties were assimilated into the overall 'aspiration for nationhood' as a necessary release valve. That this underplays the extent to which much work now seen as part of the Revival had serious reservations about the nationalist project to which it was allied is undeniable, but it was, perhaps, also a distinctively Northern way of understanding the movement. Certainly, individual writers like the novelist Forrest Reid felt unable to commit themselves to the Revival movement because, as John Boyd observed some time later, 'the leaders of the "Ulster" school had come to the curious conclusion that the "Ulster genius" was satiric'.[48] Curious or not, the extent to which satire was the dominant mode of address for much of the literary and dramatic work of the Ulster Revival is notable, the comedies of the ULT being only the most famous examples.[49]

Although the *Irish News* was probably genuine in its belief that the Revival had 'renew[ed] Belfast's almost forgotten reputation as a "Modern Athens"',[50] its support for local cultural activity proved to be conditional. Following partition, the paper was less willing to advocate the cause of Northern artists and writers, if only because such a stance might reinforce what it saw as the artificial division of the national territory. Indeed, the radically changed circumstances created by the Government of Ireland Act of 1920 signalled the death not just of the Revival but also of those institutions and social forces that had enabled its growth. Such conditions led inevitably to political marginalisation, and there was to be no Northern Catholic representation at the subsequent Anglo-Irish Treaty negotiations of 1921. Alongside this, many of Ulster's radical republican leaders, such as Hobson, had been sidelined by the sheer speed of events and were unable to respond effectively to phenomena such as the dramatic rise of Sinn Féin in the South. Although some form of expedient partition of the island had increasingly appeared inevitable, this awareness did nothing to ease the sense of betrayal felt by Northern Catholics at the manner in which their cause had been undermined. Partition was to set Northern nationalists an entirely new set of questions; the answers, however, proved elusive.

Following the establishment of the Northern Irish state, Devlin, whose personal popularity remained strong, led the Nationalist Party through a period of largely ineffective opposition. Conservative by nature and instinct, the Party proved itself obsessed by the border question and little interested in social issues. As John Darby has observed, 'its organisation, strategy and policies all reveal an acceptance of a permanent minority position, and either unwillingness or inability to do anything about it'.[51] With the possibility of Home Rule a distant memory, the Party saw no profit in attempting to sell its message to non-Catholics and settled instead into a semi-quiescent state, rousing itself only occasionally, when called on to attack the abuses of the Stormont regime. In the absence of an imaginative or coherent policy statement, and faced with the impossibility of holding significant power and the fact that nationalists in the South were preoccupied with building their own state, the Party placed its faith in Catholic birth-rate statistics, hoping to achieve through biology what it could not attain through politics. This depressing aspiration was always likely to prove illusory. Catholic emigration remained high and skilful gerrymandering by the unionist regime prevented any significant shift in the balance of power. Despite his political tenacity, in truth Devlin belonged to the era of Redmond and Gladstone, and that era had long since passed. He died in January 1934, and had been, as the *Irish News*' headline proclaimed, the 'last of the great leaders of the Home Rule movement'.[52]

Such was the unhappy state of Northern nationalist politics that it was inevitable that Devlin's death would leave a power vacuum. The degree of authority that he had wielded had been immense, and because of the personality-driven nature of nationalist political culture in the North his party was ill equipped to compensate for his loss. Certainly, Devlin's successor, T. J. Campbell, proved himself to be an inadequate replacement, his talents as a newspaper editor notwithstanding. Perhaps, however, Campbell's failure was inevitable. Despite Devlin's often-stated desire to reach out to the Protestant community, the Party that he left behind remained overwhelmingly Catholic in its composition, and his failure to create any form of secular nationalist consensus was to disable after his death the cause he had served for decades. In this sense, partition brought to full circle the events that had begun with the fall of Parnell. In 1891 Northern nationalism had been weak, divided and bewildered; thirty years later it was in a similar position. As Shane Leslie observed in 1938:

> Today Ireland is a rather forgotten island beyond the Isle of Man, from which proceed depressions in the weather, horses and jockeys and sweepstake tickets. Irish politics seem something between an ancestral dream and a distant muddle. That they can ever upset British statesmen and British governments again seems impossible.[53]

Considering the date, it is difficult to overlook the rashness of this prophecy, but what is of more interest is Leslie's utter certainty that partition had imposed a kind of final settlement on Ireland, a state of permanence that lay beyond the process of history. As he further commented:

> an entire generation of Unionists and Nationalists has passed away. All that they fought for or against was obliterated after the rising of 1916. They died bewildered and saddened on both sides of the fence.[54]

As it had been for Devlin, so it was for the organisations he left behind. Although the Rising had effectively destroyed the relevance of the AOH and the UIL, their activities did not cease immediately but instead gradually faded into the background of daily life. The *Irish News* had similar difficulties in adapting to the changed circumstances. Its circulation had been badly hit by the partition of its natural hinterland and by the 1920s it was suffering serious financial difficulties. In place of the often feverish reports of political and cultural activity that had typified the paper at its most energetic, it became increasingly Catholic in its emphasis and usually restricted its intervention in local political issues to ineffectual attacks on the inbuilt biases of the Stormont regime. Its coverage of local culture was much reduced, while its interest in heritage, genealogy and tradition increased. A long-running (and usually dull) series on the history of popular Ulster surnames typified this change of emphasis. Indeed, it can be argued that the paper was not to regain its momentum until its coverage of the Papal Eucharistic Congress in June 1932, an event it was happy to describe as the 'greatest day in Ireland's history'.[55] Considering the series of depressing events it had witnessed in its relatively short history and the degree to which its readers' aspirations had been frustrated, the hyperbole was, perhaps, forgivable.

NOTES

1 Anonymous, *The Irish Unionist Pocket-Book for the Use of Unionist Workers in Great Britain* (Dublin: Unionist Associations of Ireland, 1911), p. 64.
2 Anonymous, *The Heckled Unionist: Hints to Irish Unionists on English Platforms* (Dublin: E. Ponsonby, 1906), p. 15.
3 John Wilson Foster, *Fictions of the Irish Literary Revival: A Changeling Art* (Syracuse: Gill and Macmillan, 1987), p. xvii.

4 Anonymous, *The Irish Unionist Pocket-Book*, p. 5.
5 Flann Campbell, *The Dissenting Voice: Protestant Democracy in Ulster from Plantation to Partition* (Belfast: Blackstaff, 1991).
6 J. R. B. McMinn, 'Liberalism in North Antrim 1900–14', *Irish Historical Studies*, 23.89 (May 1982), p. 29.
7 George Boyce, *Nationalism in Ireland* (London: Routledge, 1991), p. 275.
8 Jonathan Bardon, *A History of Ulster* (Belfast: Blackstaff Press, 1992), p. 422.
9 Letter to Alice Stopford Green, 21 September 1913. See J. R. B. McMinn, *Against the Tide: A Calendar of the Papers of Rev. J. B. Armour, Irish Presbyterian Minister and Home Ruler 1869–1914* (Belfast: Public Record Office of Northern Ireland, 1985), p. lv.
10 See Brighid Mhic Sheáin, *Glimpses of Erin. Alice Milligan: Poet, Protestant, Patriot* (Belfast: Fortnight Educational Trust Supplement, undated), pp. 4–5.
11 See, for instance, Shane Leslie's novel *Doomsland* (London: Chatto and Windus, 1923, p. 171), which features the character Francis Joseph MacNeill, a thinly disguised representation of Bigger.
12 Cathal O'Byrne, 'Roger Casement's last will', *Irish Monthly*, 65 (October 1937), pp. 668–9.
13 Michael Farrell, *Northern Ireland: The Orange State* (London: Pluto Press, 1976), p. 367.
14 Something of Devlin's charisma can be felt in the following memoir by H. A. MacCartan, 'Belfast: some backward glances', in *Capuchin Annual* (Dublin: Capuchin Franciscan Fathers, 1943), p. 176:

> He was probably the smallest man in the crowd, but all eyes were centred on him in admiration or hostility. He had the square chin and pugnacious nose of the born fighter, but there were kindly ripples about the large, mobile lips, and the wistful grey eyes were full of dreams too great, perhaps too vague, ever to come true. It was one of those faces which, once seen at close quarters, are never forgotten.

15 Cathal O'Byrne, *As I Roved Out* (Belfast: Blackstaff Press, 1982, first published 1946), p. 15.
16 Seumas MacManus, 'A memoir of Ethna Carbery', in *The Four Winds of Eirinn: Poems by Ethna Carbery* (Dublin: M. H. Gill, 1918). See http://digital.library.upenn.edu/women/carbery/carbery.html.
17 O'Byrne, *As I Roved Out*, pp. 15–16.
18 James Connolly, 'Wee Joe Devlin', *Workers' Republic*, 28 August 1915, p. 2.
19 James Connolly, *Labour in Irish History* (Dublin: New Books, 1973, first published 1910), p. 144.
20 O'Byrne, *As I Roved Out*, p. 16.
21 Any analysis of the historical significance of the *Irish News* has to acknowledge the pioneering work of Eamon Phoenix. Much of what follows is indebted to his *Northern Nationalism: Nationalist Politics, Partition and the Catholic Minority in Northern Ireland 1890–1940* (Belfast: Ulster Historical Foundation, 1994) and the collection of essays he edited, *A Century of*

Northern Life: The Irish News and 100 Years of Ulster History 1890s–1990s (Belfast: Ulster Historical Foundation, 1995).

22 Eamon Phoenix, 'The history of a newspaper: the *Irish News* 1855–1995', in *A Century of Northern Life*, p. 13.

23 Roy Foster, *Modern Ireland: 1600–1972* (London: Penguin, 1989), p. 424.

24 See, for instance, Gerry Adams' attack on the paper's anti-republican bias in his collection of stories and recollections *Falls Memories* (Dingle: Brandon Books, 1983), p. 54:

> In 1918, Éamon de Valera was nominated for the Falls Division and was soundly thrashed by Devlin, from whom he seems to have had no chance of winning the seat. The *Irish News* coverage of the election makes interesting reading, for that paper appears to have acted as an election periodical for the Irish Parliamentary Party. Nowhere in its coverage of the election for the Falls Division was one Republican statement, speech or election manifesto reported and reporting of Republican election activity was minimal. Exposure of Joe Devlin went to the other extreme, and pages were filled with details of his sponsors, expansive reports of his meetings, parades, election addresses and statements.

Interestingly, the other direction from which the *Irish News* has been attacked has been from those, whether Republican or otherwise, who have perceived it as a symbol of all that it is most intolerant, stifling and conservative about Catholic Northern life. The novels of Brian Moore are particularly attuned to this aspect of the paper's identity. See, for instance, his novel *The Emperor of Ice-Cream* (London: Paladin, 1987, first published 1965), p. 36, which contains an account of the paper's typical stories in the 1930s, including:

> a Jewish name discovered in an account of a financial transaction, a Franco victory over the Godless Reds, a hint of British perfidy in international affairs, an Irish triumph on the sports field, an evidence of Protestant bigotry, a discovery of Ulster governmental corruption.

25 James Connolly, 'Press poisoners in Ireland', *Forward*, 30 August 1913. From the collection *Ireland Upon the Dissecting Table* (Cork: Cork Workers' Club, 1975), from the Marxists' Internet Archive at http://www.marxists.org/archive/connolly/1913/08/press.htm.

26 Boyce, *Nationalism in Ireland*, p. 277.

27 Connolly, 'Press poisoners in Ireland'.

28 See Farrell, *Northern Ireland*, p. 367:

> [Devlin] identified closely with his constituents and did a lot of social welfare work, such as organising excursions for mill-girls. Though he represented the interests of the Northern Catholic business class and the Church, he retained strong working class support through his welfare work and through taking a fairly radical line on social and economic issues.

29 Paddy Devlin, *Straight Left: An Autobiography* (Belfast: Blackstaff, 1993), p. 12.
30 K. McPhillips, *The Falls: A History* (Belfast: private publication, undated), p. 25.
31 Boyce, *Nationalism in Ireland*, p. 301.
32 Most obviously in the fact that the Order retains responsibility for the organisation of New York's annual St Patrick's Day parade. Since 1990 it has vigorously resisted attempts by the Irish Lesbian and Gay Organization to take part in the celebrations. For a detailed discussion of this ongoing controversy see Kathryn Conrad's 'Queer treasons: homosexuality and Irish national identity', *Cultural Studies*, 15.1 (January 2001), pp. 124–37.
33 Bardon, *A History of Ulster*, p. 423.
34 Farrell, *Northern Ireland*, p. 370.
35 Ó Buachalla, S., ed., *The Letters of P. H. Pearse* (Gerrards Cross: Colin Smythe, 1980), p. 276.
36 'Ireland's future: the great work which lies before the Ancient Order of Hibernians', *Irish News*, 1 April 1913, p. 7.
37 Connolly, 'Press poisoners in Ireland'.
38 Anonymous, *The Irish Unionist Pocket-Book*, p. 64.
39 T. A. Jackson, *Ireland Her Own: An Outline History of the Irish Struggle for National Freedom and Independence* (London: Cobbett Press, 1946), p. 351.
40 Jackson, *Ireland Her Own*, p. 362.
41 Jackson, *Ireland Her Own*, p. 351.
42 *Irish News*, 22 May 1909, p. 4.
43 'Report on the West Belfast United Irish League', *Irish News*, 4 May 1904, p. 8.
44 Robbie Meredith, 'The *Shan Van Vocht*: notes from the North', in *Critical Ireland: New Essays in Literature and Culture*, eds Aaron Kelly and Alan A. Gillis (Dublin: Four Courts Press, 2001), p. 179.
45 Carl Gilbert Hardebeck (1869–1945) was one of the most important figures in traditional Irish music during this period. Born in London to a wealthy German father and Welsh mother, he came to Belfast in 1895 to open a music shop. When this venture failed he remained in the city and spent increasing amounts of time in composition, teaching and, most crucially, the transcription of traditional songs (using an innovative Braille technique). The resulting volume, *Gems of Melody* (Dublin: Pohlmann, 1908), is a key Revivalist work. From 1918 he became master of the Cork Municipal School of Music, but returned to Belfast in 1923. His final years were spent in reclusive semi-poverty in Dublin. The relationship between Hardebeck and O'Byrne was mutually beneficial. O'Byrne owed his extensive knowledge of Irish music to Hardebeck's teaching, while O'Byrne was an extremely gifted performer of Hardebeck's arrangements.
46 T. J. Campbell, *Fifty Years of Ulster: 1890–1940* (Belfast: Irish News Ltd, 1941).
47 Campbell, *Fifty Years of Ulster*, p. 192.
48 John Boyd, 'Ulster prose', in *The Arts in Ulster: A Symposium*, eds Sam Hanna Bell, Nesca A. Robb and John Hewitt (London: George G. Harrap, 1951), p. 116.

49 For instance Gerald MacNamara's plays *Suzanne and the Sovereigns*, co-written with Lewis Purcell, 1907, and reprinted in Kathleen Danaher, 'The plays of Gerald MacNamara', *Journal of Irish Literature*, 18.2–3 (1988), pp. 24–55, *The Mist that Does Be on the Bog* (1909, unpublished) and *Thompson in Tír-na-nÓg* (Dublin: Talbot Press, 1912).
50 *Irish News*, 22 May 1909, p. 4.
51 John Darby, *Conflict in Northern Ireland* (Dublin: Gill and Macmillan, 1976), p. 95.
52 *Irish News*, 19 January 1934, p. 9.
53 Shane Leslie, *The Film of Memory* (London: Michael Joseph, 1938), p. 368.
54 Leslie, *The Film of Memory*, p. 391.
55 *Irish News*, 27 June 1932, p. 4.

CHAPTER THREE

The genres of the Northern Revival

– Wife well, I suppose? M'Coy's changed voice said.
– O yes, Mr Bloom said. Tiptop, thanks.
He unrolled the newspaper baton idly and read idly:
What is home without
Plumtree's Potted Meat?
Incomplete.
With it an abode of bliss.
– My missus has just got an engagement. At least it's not settled yet.
Valise tack again. By the way no harm. I'm off that, thanks.
Mr Bloom turned his largelidded eyes with unhasty friendliness.
– My wife too, he said. She's going to sing at a swagger affair in the Ulster hall, Belfast, on the twentyfifth.
– That so? M'Coy said. Glad to hear that, old man. Who's getting it up?

James Joyce, *Ulysses*[1]

THURSDAY 16 June 1904, the day on which Joyce set *Ulysses* and consequently the most famous day in Irish literary history, was almost as uneventful in Belfast as it was in Dublin. At the Palace Theatre there was a performance of Michael Balfe's opera *The Bohemian Girl* (the music of which echoes through Joyce's novel) while the Ulster Hall played host to Mary Anderson, considered, by the *Irish News* at least, to be 'the world's greatest actress'.[2] The event was part of her farewell tour and included, among other highlights (and despite the fact that she was in her late forties), a performance of the balcony scene from *Romeo and Juliet*. Although in the 'Hades' episode of *Ulysses* Martin Cunningham makes a direct comparison between Molly Bloom and Mary Anderson,[3] it is doubtful that Molly's intended concert at the same venue on the twenty-fifth of the month would have attracted the same level of eager anticipation – not least because by that date the paper's attention was firmly fixed upon the upcoming Feis organised by Francis Joseph Bigger in Glenariff. Despite its potentially appalling consequences, the *Irish News* appeared sanguine about an outbreak of smallpox in the city, although the possibility of Molly contracting the disease during her visit troubles Leopold Bloom and leads him to consider whether she would tolerate being vaccinated against it.[4] Elsewhere in the paper there is a report of a 'determined suicide' in Dromara, while the racing section is preoccupied – in the same way as many of the characters of *Ulysses* – with that day's Royal Ascot Gold Cup. Red Hand, the paper's tipster, sees little hope for Throwaway, the eventual winner and the horse associated throughout the novel with Bloom's own progress, and predicts, instead, a victory for Sceptre, the horse symbolically linked with Bloom's love rival, the phallic Blazes Boylan. In this context, the admiration expressed by the *Irish News*' unionist rival, the *Belfast News-Letter*, for the 'staying attributes of Throwaway'[5] seems entirely fitting.

Ulysses, then, is fleetingly aware of the cultural, political and economic connections that existed between the two great cities of Ireland, and such moments serve to contextualise the general parochialism that Bloom encounters during his wanderings. It is, however, impossible to read Belfast through the lens of Joyce's novel without becoming aware of one overwhelming, if obvious, cultural discrepancy: the fact that not only is there no Belfast *Ulysses*, but there is no significant Belfast novel from this period whatsoever. Of course, the reasons for this have, in part, to take cognisance of Joyce's unique imaginative power (in that sense the revolution he initiated was no less than a European phenomenon) and yet the perception of early-twentieth-century Belfast as an unwritten city indicates other absences and discontinuities. Despite his geographic and temporal distance, the microscopic gaze that Joyce fixes on the Dublin of June 1904 suggests a belief in the recuperative properties of the city's quotidian history. This remained the case in spite of the shattering events of the intervening period: the literal destruction of much of Dublin's physical fabric that took place as a result of the Rising, and the violence and repression of the Anglo-Irish War. To this, we can also add the burning of many of the city's newspaper holdings in 1922 during the Civil War – an event contemporaneous with the publication of *Ulysses* and one freighted with intense symbolism. It is in response to these acts that *Ulysses* offers its mode of remembrance. The book recognises that the mundane life event is the most fragile of memories, the one most easily rendered alien by the emergence of a new order, and it is because of this that it deploys its mythic structure. For if myth deals with types, so it provides a template on which memory can be shaped, a process that culminates, in the novel, in the ultimate ordering of experience as unity. In this way, while *Ulysses* takes its mythic structure from Homer, it, in turn, offers its own mythic template as an aide-mémoire for the dispossessed of the actual city.

Could such a project ever have been attempted in Belfast? While the city's experiences in this period were as traumatic as those endured in Dublin – for the horrors of the Civil War one may substitute the Belfast pogroms of 1920–22 – such acts took place in the context of a sectarian fragmentation that was inimical to any sense of an underlying unity of experience. Despite the painful loneliness of many of its characters, ultimately *Ulysses* acknowledges a shared community, or at least imagines a city in which the intimacy of disdain allows for the realisation of a communal vision. Bloom and Boylan, for instance, may reject and dislike the values that the other represents, but at the same time they are obliged to recognise the roles they play in each other's lives and the extent to which their histories are intertwined. It is upon this supposition that the book's mythic method is reliant. By comparison, the incorrigibly plural communities of Belfast in this period appear to have been lost in parallel universes. We can gain some indication of this simply by placing editions of the *Irish News* and the *Belfast News-Letter* for any given day alongside each other. The Belfasts that the two papers imagine and construct are not only markedly different (in politics, sport, entertainment and commerce) but also subliminally opposed. For this reason Belfast itself can sometimes appear sporadic, discontinuous and forgetful. As a bewildered Joseph Tomelty remarked in 1947: 'The Dublin of Joyce is still the Dublin of O'Casey, but the Belfast of Forrest Reid is so different to the Belfast of St. John Ervine and Michael McLaverty, that it almost ceases to be Belfast at all'.[6] This indicates something of the underlying difference between the two cities: if the *Ulysses* myth provided Joyce with a suitable template for the reconstitution of Dublin, Belfast's literature has always been more indebted to the *Illiad*.[7]

The art of the Northern Revival, then, was an art that had to express itself in the face of irreconcilable histories. It is for this reason, above all others, that it gained its particular characteristics. Molly's 'swagger affair' at the Ulster Hall would have taken its place in these negotiations.[8] As Bloom tells M'Coy, like many such events, her tour was funded by a committee on a 'part shares and part profits'[9] basis, and the fact that her and Boylan were intending to perform 'Love's old sweet song' indicates something of the sentimental Irish flavour of the planned evening. Certainly, in Belfast at this time there was a large audience for such events. The year 1904 was one of the most vibrant of the Northern

Revival and the notices section of the *Irish News* was invariably full of advertisements for concerts similar to Molly's. This, in itself, indicates the extent to which the Northern Revival was a phenomenon of popular, rather than elite, culture: its theatre companies relied upon a staple diet of trusted comedies, its poets produced popular inspirational verse, and its writers were humorists and storytellers. To express this differently, the aesthetic of the Northern Revival was one which Molly would have appreciated and one from which Stephen Dedalus would have recoiled in horror.

Another way of recognising this distinctive texture is to consider those who felt unable to declare themselves for the movement. For instance, had the Protestant Belfast novelist Forrest Reid been born in Dublin rather than Mount Charles he may, perhaps, have found himself at home among the sceptical Protestant Revivalists of that city: individuals who were prepared to explore the possibilities of attaining an Irish identity but who remained aware of the cost of that transformation. As it was, and as I noted in the previous chapter, the Revival's more robust Northern manifestation alienated him, and he felt little able to contribute to a movement that he believed was too reliant on a belief in the transformative powers of satire. Reid's account of his encounter in 1904 with W. B. Reynolds, editor of the Ulster Literary Theatre's short-lived journal *Uladh*, music critic for the *Belfast Evening Telegraph* and key propagandist for the concept of a Northern Revival, well illustrates this reticence:

> Although Irish, I had never been interested in politics, had never distinguished in my mind north from south, and the Ulster propaganda did not particularly appeal to me. It was not what to-day would be called Ulster propaganda, since it was definitely nationalist, and merely insisted that Ulster should play its part in the Irish Revival. I had no objection to that naturally, but I could not see why there should be two camps, nor why what Reynolds called 'the Ulster genius' should necessarily be, as he said it was, satiric. If it came to that, it was the first time I had heard of 'the Ulster genius', and I had certainly seen no sign of it. Therefore I listened to Reynolds without conviction. I didn't know what 'Ulad' meant; I didn't know why Joseph Campbell should call himself Seosamh MacCathmhaóil. It seemed to me to be a most difficult name to pronounce, and since Reynolds got over it by pronouncing it Joe, the difficulty still remains. I asked him what he would like me to write, and received a sudden clue as to the real bent of his interests when he replied without a moment's hesitation, 'an essay on *The Future of Irish Opera*'.[10]

Although entirely bewildered by the meeting and convinced that Reynolds held his theories 'firmly embedded in his soul',[11] Reid did contribute an essay on the Lane collection of pictures and a short story, but his conviction that what Reynolds called the 'Ulster renaissance' was in all ways inimical to the artistic life of the individual remained with him. For John Boyd, it was in this instinct that Reid most clearly revealed his origins, for 'rooted to Ulster in body and in mind, Reid had too much independence of character to belong to a school of writers'.[12] The judgement is surely misplaced. In fact, Reid's reluctance more obviously derived from his adherence to the classic form of English late liberal humanism as articulated by his friend and mentor E. M. Forster, an ideology typified by a pessimistic mistrust of all forms of combination, whether they be manifest in art, nationalism or politics. Despite his long residence in Belfast, it was for this reason that, as John Wilson Foster has recognised, Reid remained 'culturally orientated towards England'.[13] As Reid himself observed of his meeting with Reynolds, 'I didn't believe in either the past, present, or future of Irish opera. It was not that I couldn't imagine it; it was rather because I could – in all its dreadfulness.'[14]

The significance of this is that it demonstrates that, as a middle-class Ulster Protestant, Reid was aware that he had a choice of allegiance more complex than a simple declaration for a sectarian faction. This explains, in part, why relatively few of his class aligned themselves with the Revivalist cause. If the factionalism of Revival aesthetics was deemed repellent, then the alternative was an artistic individualism which was absent in Ireland, but which, in Reid's case at least, could be discovered at Cambridge. Understood as such, it is no coincidence that one of the constant themes of Reid's fiction is the necessity of escape: the desire to flee from the fallen (and usually Ulster Protestant) present and to inhabit, instead, the realms of childhood and reverie. For Reid this was nothing less than a declaration of imaginative independence, and one that Forster strongly endorsed when he wrote after Reid's death:

> He was the most important man in Belfast, and, though it would be too much to say that Belfast knew him not, I have sometimes smiled to think how little that great city, engaged in its own ponderous purposes, dreamed of him, or indeed of anything. He who dreamed and was partly a dream.[15]

Such was the martyrdom of Forrest Reid, an artist destined to remain unrecognised amid the calcified emotions of modern urban life. Indeed, for Forster, Reid's fate was all the worse for the fact that, in this case, the modern urban was specifically a modern Belfast urban. Forster, however, was correct in suggesting that his work was little regarded by the people of the city. Perhaps one result of Reid's ideological migration was that his art remained out of step with contemporary taste in both England and

Ireland, and he remained puzzled as to why, in Boyd's words, 'the reading public apparently took no interest in his novels'.[16] Since his death, however, Reid's reputation has grown. The emergence of the publishing genre of gay fiction and the rise of queer studies in universities has given his work a new constituency and provided fresh contexts for his preoccupations. Reid might not have been of the Northern Revival but his legacy now takes its place as part of a quite different cultural tradition.

Not all Ulster Protestants shared Reid's alienation. Indeed, an event often recognised as one of the crucial precursors for the Revival movement in both the North and the South took place in October 1895, when the Methodist Alice Milligan collaborated with the Catholic Anna Johnston (who used the pseudonym Ethna Carbery) to edit the Henry Joy McCracken Literary Society's paper, the *Northern Patriot*. Seumas MacManus, who was later to be Johnston's husband, describes this moment with typical hyperbole and yet his account indicates something of its subsequent emblematic status:

> When, after the debacle of the Nineties the Irish cause was at its lowest ebb, the morale of even brave men broken, and boldest fighters in retreat, two Belfast girls – poets – Alice Milligan who had smashed off her the shackles of alienism whereunto she was born, and Ethna Carbery, daughter of the North's Fenian leader, stepped in the gap and in noble numbers sounded an electrifying rallying call. By their brave chants in dismal hour was their country's chilling heart cheered, her sinking soul lifted and steeled again.[17]

Whatever else might be said about MacManus's casually sectarian reference to 'alienism', it is clear that, in actuality, Milligan's background was anything but an inheritance that had to be disowned. Coming from a reasonably wealthy and liberal family meant that Milligan had both independent means and access to education (at the Methodist College in Belfast and later to study English literature at King's College London), a combination that enabled her to live a life of extraordinary political activism. Moreover, her father, Seaton Forrest Milligan, was not only a successful businessman but also an Irish antiquarian and a member of both the Royal Irish Academy and the Belfast Natural History and Philosophical Society. Placed in the context of the time, he was of his century and yet also a model for later Protestant nationalist antiquarians, such as Bigger (who would follow him into the pages of the *Ulster Journal of Archaeology*). Certainly, Seaton Milligan encouraged his daughter's interest in Irish culture, and she would contribute to his antiquarian study *Glimpses of Erin* in 1890. Alice's commitment to Irish nationalism, however, was to a degree far in excess of her father's essentially cultural and historical preoccupations, and yet she did not feel that her background was an impediment to her political convictions. Like many of the small minority to which she belonged, she had converted to the nationalist cause after the fall of Parnell, and in this context she viewed her inherited Methodism as a dissenting tradition naturally opposed to the abuses of an unjust political system. In 1893 Milligan's family moved to the Antrim Road in Belfast and thus came within the force field of ideas and political energy emanating from Bigger's nearby home, Ardrigh. As with Bigger, her dissenting background led inevitably to a fixation with the United Irishmen and a concomitant belief that the qualities of 'Ulsterness' had to be an integral part of an inclusive Irish national identity. The maintenance of this position involved a complex series of avowals and denials, an implicit hostility to that version of Ulster typified by industrial achievement and Orangeism, and a concomitant insistence on the continuity of a tradition of Ulster nationalist resistance that reached back to the example of Cuchulain. Predictably, perhaps, such arguments were not for the benefit of Protestant Northern unionists – who would have viewed them with bemusement at best – but instead took place solely within the discourse of Irish nationalism; this was a noisy and usually ineffective debate with those, such as W. B. Yeats, who doubted whether north-east Ulster was properly part of Ireland at all.

Sympathies such as Milligan's were fully displayed in the pages of the fiercely regional *Northern Patriot*. Alongside features such as 'This month's martyrs', Milligan and Johnston constantly reminded their readership of the need to recognise the distinctive contribution of Northern nationalists to the cause of Irish freedom, and with this attacked the educational system of the time for its perceived failure to teach Ulster children of their dissenting heritage. One can assume that such sentiments would have come naturally to Johnston, the daughter of Robert Johnston, a Fenian leader and council member of the Irish Republican Brotherhood (IRB), and cousin to Joseph Campbell, but, in truth, Milligan was the more politically committed of the partnership and sought for the paper a role that went some way beyond an interest merely in the historical literature of nationalist Ulster. For instance, it gave strong support to Maud Gonne's calls for an amnesty for the Irish prisoners convicted of involvement in the English dynamite campaigns of the 1880s, while Milligan made little effort to conceal her pro-Parnellite opinions. Clearly, this was too much for the literary society whose views and news the *Northern Patriot* was intended to represent, and Milligan and Johnston were removed from their posts at the beginning of 1896, after only three issues. Far from being a setback, however, it is clear that the *Northern Patriot* had already outlived its usefulness for the two editors and, with the help of Johnston's father, they immediately established their own paper, the *Shan Van Vocht*, with Milligan as editor and Johnston as secretary.

The political and cultural significance of the *Shan Van Vocht* has tended to be neglected in subsequent accounts of this period,[18] but, despite the fact that it endured for only a little over three years, its influence over a generation of militant Irish nationalists was crucial. Freed from the constraints of editorial interference, Milligan and Johnston were able to create the new paper in their own image, and alongside pieces on literature and folklore it served as a forum for the exchange of ideas and best practice that captures something of the heterogeneous nature of Irish nationalist debate at that time. The effect of this on individuals could be electrifying. Note, for instance, the role it played in the political education of the militant republican Bulmer Hobson, who, with his mother's encouragement, subscribed to the *Shan Van Vocht* while he was a twelve-year-old pupil at the Quaker Friends' School in Lisburn.[19] Hobson would later co-found the Dungannon Clubs, galvanise the IRB and organise the Howth gun-running of 1914.

The paper, then, sought to inspire and educate the individual nationalist and, in return, emphasised the importance of service to the cause and self-sacrifice. In this way, its major achievement was to bind individuals to a developing sense of collective effort. One effect of the Parnell crisis had been to fragment the ideal of Irish nationalism into a series of often disconnected and factionalised movements existing in isolation from one another. As an antidote to this, the 'Notes and news' column of the *Shan Van Vocht* reported on the activities of an often dizzying range of political and cultural nationalist organisations, suggesting implicitly that the rumours of the death of nationalist Ireland as an organised political force were definitely exaggerated. That said, as Robbie Meredith has observed:

> the method may be classically Victorian and bourgeois – an energetic journal forwarding educational propaganda, combined with reading circles celebrating the heroes (and heroines) of the Irish past – but the object was to increase Northern national knowledge and pride, not to incite revolution.[20]

Meredith's observation is astute in that it identifies the manner in which the *Shan Van Vocht* served as a bridgehead between nineteenth-century Parnellism and twentieth-century militant agitation, and recognises the degree to which the paper's editors were alienated from what the

September 1896 issue called 'the fray of party politics which, for some years back, has so bitterly divided the people of Ireland'. It was for this reason that the paper largely maintained the focus on history, poetry and folklore established by its ideological predecessor. A fortuitous event in this context was the centenary of 1798, an anniversary that enabled the journal to combine its obsessions with 'Northern-ness', popular history, martyrology and the role played by Protestants in the struggle for national freedom. Both Milligan and Johnston were elected to the central executive charged with organising the '98 celebrations; the *Shan Van Vocht* propagandised vigorously on its behalf, while Milligan lectured across Ireland on the importance of the event and the lessons modern Irish nationalists could take from it. A significant aspect of this consciousness-raising episode was Milligan's emphasis on the neglected role of women in the events of the period, a distinctive focus that remained with the paper for the rest of its short life. For these reasons, the *Shan Van Vocht* became the conscience of the centenary and it proved to be the paper's defining – and most dynamic – period.

Despite its avowedly sceptical position about the state of contemporary Irish politics, the *Shan Van Vocht* could not remain entirely aloof from emerging events. Indeed, it is unlikely that the combative Milligan would have been able to maintain such a stance for any length of time. Recognising this imperative and seeking to increase the paper's sphere of influence, the November 1896 edition initiated a feature called 'Other people's opinions', a series of articles by nationalist thinkers and politicians 'which we may not necessarily be in agreement with, but which in all cases are worthy of our earnest consideration'. Perhaps to emphasise the innovative nature of this development, the first article to appear was by James Connolly, in which he argued for the necessity of party political mobilisation as a means of achieving revolution. For a paper whose previous consideration of contemporary affairs had consisted of little more than reports on the growth of the Irish language and its continued support for the amnesty campaign, this was an undeniably daring strategy. Its success, though, is indicated by the fact that Connolly contributed a further series of articles for the journal and, while there is little doubt that Milligan held profound reservations about his opinions (usually appending his pieces with a stern warning about their inherent dangers), the relationship between herself and Connolly's fledgling Irish Socialist Republican Party became increasingly cordial.

If the *Shan Van Vocht*'s turn towards the political enabled the articulation of Milligan's and Johnston's burgeoning interests in contemporary affairs, it also led directly to its demise. In the increasingly factional world of Irish nationalist politics, the paper's refusal to declare for any one party left it isolated and with a declining readership. The final issue appeared in April 1899 and noted that 'we conscientiously did our best to steer clear of these sectional differences, and perhaps that contributed to our want of success by depriving us of the backing of any party'. Understood in this context, the end of the *Shan Van Vocht* signalled also the onset of an increasingly organised political system, an environment that the paper had indirectly done much to create. The *Shan Van Vocht*'s obvious successor was Arthur Griffith's *United Irishman*, a new paper which gained the *Shan Van Vocht*'s subscription list and to which both Milligan and Johnston would contribute. While it may have been time for the *Shan Van Vocht* to make way for others – and there appears to have been little bitterness attendant on the decision to cease publication – its absence deprived Ulster of an effective voice in the development of an Irish nationalist consciousness. In itself, this was indicative of a larger silence. Nationalist and republican individuals from the North continued to play a major role in the events leading up to partition, but this was almost in spite of, rather than because of, their origins. In turn, the perception developed that nationalists within Ulster itself were little more than an embattled minority.

The *Shan Van Vocht* did not, however, represent the highpoint of Milligan's life of political agitation. In fact, its demise provided her with the opportunity to increase her efforts on behalf of Irish nationalism in other areas. In the years that followed, she delivered hundreds of lectures on Irish history, politics and mythology, became increasingly involved in the Gaelic League, and wrote much poetry and a significant number of plays, including *The Last Feast of the Fianna* (1900), *The Deliverance of Red Hugh* (1902) and the Abbey-produced *The Daughter of Donagh* (1902). In 1900 she joined Maud Gonne's national women's movement, *Inghinidhe na hÉireann* (Daughters of Ireland) with Johnston (who became vice-president) and continued to emphasise the particular contribution that women could make to the nationalist cause. In 1901 Johnston married Seumas MacManus, the Donegal poet, but she died a year later, at the age of thirty-six, leaving her grief-stricken husband to observe sadly that 'with her, Love was life's resplendent crown'.[21] Under the Ethna Carbery pseudonym, Johnston's major collection of verse, *The Four Winds of Eirinn*,[22] appeared in the same year and was enthusiastically received. It is for this work that she is chiefly remembered. A mythologised figure even in life, after her death she became perceived as one of the Revival's early martyrs; 'Ireland's singing handmaiden' is how the back-cover publicity for an edition of her stories describes her.[23]

Despite the premature loss of her major collaborator and close friend, Milligan's own work continued at an increased pace. Already a well known figure in nationalist Ireland, her poetry was also becoming popular in both Ireland and America. The publication of her collection *Hero Lays*[24] in 1908 struck a distinctly Revivalist note, and embodied her strongly held belief that art, at least in the circumstances of the period, should subordinate its autonomy to the demands of the national struggle – an aspect of her work that 'AE' had already recognised in 1904 when he noted that Milligan was producing 'the best patriotic poetry written in Ireland in my time'.[25] AE's praise was an influential recommendation, and Milligan was soon perceived to be among the first rank of Revival poets. This was no small achievement when one considers that she considered her writing to be only a component part of her many activities, a characteristic that Thomas MacDonagh recognised in an effusive (and now quite famous) commendation of her work in 1914:

> Alice Milligan, Ulster Protestant, Gaelic Leaguer, Fenian, friend of all Ireland, lover of Gaelic Catholics as of her own kith, strong in faith and in hope and in charity, clear of eye and of voice, single-minded, high, inspired and inspiring, humorous and solemn, taking praise and encouragement and blame and rebuff as they come, without thought of herself, with thought always of Ireland's cause – Alice Milligan is the most Irish of living Irish poets, and therefore the best.[26]

MacDonagh, who would later be a signatory to the Proclamation of the Irish Republic and thus knew a few things about the necessity of personal sacrifice, astutely identified Milligan's belief that the only life worth living is that which is given to the national cause. In the years since the cessation of the *Shan Van Vocht* her politics had become increasingly militant and were certainly far from the hesitant Parnellism expressed in the pages of the *Northern Patriot*. Although she spent an increasing amount of time in the South, she maintained her connections with Belfast and remained an enthusiastic member of Bigger's 'Firelight School' at Ardrigh, collaborating in many of his increasingly elaborate ceremonies and commemorations. For instance, in 1913 she delivered a lengthy oration to the 'annual gathering of Gaels around the cairn of Shane the Proud, near Cushendun'[27] and was 'loudly cheered' for her efforts. Through her friendship with Bigger she met many of the leaders of Northern nationalism, including, most significantly, Roger Casement. As I will discuss in greater detail in Chapter 6, in 1916 Milligan attended Casement's trial in London with her companions Alice Stopford Green and Ada McNeill, an event that confirmed her flourishing Anglophobic opinions.

Some sense of Milligan's beliefs about the nature and role of poetry can be gained by consideration of her work 'In answer', from 1910 (and dated, perhaps mischievously, to 12 July). An American publisher in Boston had requested permission to include one of her poems in an anthology of 'Victorian verse', and the necessity of refusal allowed Milligan to develop the theme:

How has this come to be,
That you're writing to me
From the 'Hub of the Universe,' sinker of TEA,
To ask my consent
My poem to include
As 'Victorian Verse'?
My response must be rude.
By George Washington, *No.*
By Abe Lincoln also,
In a book with such name
My verse shall not go.

We in Ireland have reckoned the reign and the years
Of Victoria, in famine, rebellion and tears.
By the chains of John Mitchell,
By the loss of Parnell,
(foulest wrong since the hour
when Tír Chonaill's Hugh fell)
By these griefs, by these wrongs,
I refuse you my Songs,
More in sorrow than anger,
ALICE MILLIGAN, Bangor.[28]

Although undeniably light-hearted, 'In answer' combines humour with uncompromising anger, and illustrates Milligan's characteristic tendency to range across vast historical periods through the deployment of analogies. Her belief that poetry should be written to the moment is a signature aspect of her work, and it is only a small exaggeration to suggest that every significant event in nationalist Ireland during this period gained an immediate Milligan commemoration. Something of this tradition of public poetry has remained in Ireland. Certainly, Seamus Heaney's 'An open letter' from 1983,[29] published in protest at his inclusion in an anthology of British poetry, revisits the territory of 'In answer' in a strikingly similar manner.

As might have been predicted, however, Milligan's poetic reputation collapsed in the very different climate of post-partition Ireland. Priorities had changed, and the absolutist stance of Milligan's verse, its insistence that the value of art could be judged only according to its avowed commitment to a political position, appeared anomalous in an island which, however reluctantly, had been forced to recognise that its future involved learning to live with compromise. Although Cathal O'Byrne, something of a recidivist when it came to these issues, continued to champion her work, declaring in 1946 that 'Alice Milligan, we have no hesitation in saying, is Ireland's greatest living poet. They discovered that in Dublin quite recently',[30] his critical faculties had, like Milligan's, been frozen by the trauma of partition and were incapable of recognising the changed cultural priorities of both the North and the South. A more reliable indication of Milligan's falling reputation is the fact that by 1951 she warranted only a passing (albeit generous) reference in J. N. Browne's survey of the history of Ulster poetry (which formed a chapter of the influential codification of Northern cultural achievement, *The Arts in Ulster*[31]). Milligan's own extraordinary creativity was clearly bound to the circumstances of the period and she produced little work of significance after 1920. Although the University of Ireland awarded her an honorary degree in 1941, her final years were spent as a semi-recluse and she died in April 1953, a largely forgotten figure. Despite this, more notice has been taken of her legacy recently, and it is appropriate that her most well known admirer was to be Bobby Sands, who found comfort in her poetry during the final days of his hunger strike in 1981.

Milligan, then, provided a template for the specific characteristics of Northern Revival poetry. Although she was the most famous and productive of the Northern poets, it is also important to recognise the significant numbers of lesser-known writers who learnt from her example and, to a greater or lesser extent, lived in the shadow of her achievement. In this way, poetry, rather than fiction, became the dominant literary form of the Northern Revival, and the publication of a slim volume of verse was a common stage in the development of a young Revivalist's nationalist consciousness. The example of Cathal O'Byrne, who, as I have already noted, idolised Milligan, is a relevant example of this. While primarily a singer and storyteller – it was claimed at the time of his death that his performance of certain standards such as 'The maid of the sweet brown knowe' or 'The mountains of Pomeroy' 'set up a standard that has not been rivalled all the years between'[32] – he was also a prolific poet and his work illustrates both the possibilities and the shortcomings of the Northern Revival's aesthetic rendering of an idea of nationality. Although now lost, O'Byrne's earliest publication was a short collection of verse, *A Jug of Punch* (the title taken from a famous Ulster folk song), which appeared in 1900, when he was twenty-four. However, it was not until his collaboration with the

Donegal-born Cahir Healy (who would later become a distinguished nationalist politician) five years later that he gained a degree of recognition in the genre. *The Lane of the Thrushes: Some Ulster Love Songs*[33] was a series of lyrics about rural Ulster that sounded the distinctly regionalist note frequently found in the Northern Revival during this period, an agenda clearly signalled by the front cover, which featured a woodcut by John Campbell (the brother of the poet Joseph Campbell) of a peasant woman and a fiddle player. As a whole, *The Lane of the Thrushes* can best be described as a collection of love songs *to* Ulster but, with this, the desire to understand the North as a viable location for a vibrant Celtic peasant consciousness creates an uneasy tension between the recognition of the economic necessities of peasant life and the more stylised tropes of the ballad genre with which O'Byrne usually felt more comfortable. Understood as such, *The Lane of the Thrushes* brings generic convention into the context of geographical and cultural specificity, a task fraught with artistic self-consciousness, as the epigraph to the collection suggests:

> The village folks could never see anything in that lane only brambles and brosna. The brosna was useful for lighting the fires. With the neighbour 'caddies' we trudged there daily for our little bundles of withered sticks. Sometime we lingered behind after the rest had gone. Other things, too, we gathered in the lane as well as the brosna, – things which set alight the fires in which dreams are born.

Dated 'Old Lamas Night, 1905', the description of this moment suggests the organising principle for the collection as a whole. Healy had been a contributor to the *Shan Van Vocht* and, like O'Byrne, was a member of Bigger's Ardrigh coterie. As with the Bigger-organised Glenariff Feis of the previous year, *The Lane of the Thrushes* sought a return to rural Catholic Ulster and did so with the hope that the Gaelic traditions long dormant there could be rekindled. Little wonder, then, that the poets could find dreams among the brosna (from the Irish *brosnach*, or broken wood for kindling), whereas the village folk could see only the harsh imperatives of daily existence.

As David Greer has revealed,[34] O'Byrne contributed many more poems to *The Lane of the Thrushes* than Healy did, although the collection itself gives no indication of individual authorship. What can be asserted with more confidence, however, is that the quality of the poems themselves is variable. For instance, an O'Byrne contribution, 'The hills O'Mourne', illustrates what could happen when Revival sensibilities toppled too far towards vernacular sentimentality:

Och, the pleasant hills O'Mourne.
Though the world is wide between,
Sure I'd sell my heart to see them
With their glint o' gold an' green,
Where there's many a brown stream croonin',
An' in every grey thorn bush,
There's a fairy piper tunin'
Through the dewy evenin's hush.[35]

As with other poems in the collection, the theme of longing found in 'The hills O'Mourne' is generated through the experience of exile and the harsh circumstances of modern city life. In Healy's 'Th' song of th' say' the city is 'lonely' (p. 13), while his 'In exile' finds it to be a place of 'sin and sorrow' where 'the folks are proud and cold' (p. 59). Similarly, O'Byrne's 'A song for the greenwood' castigates the city as a 'babel of meaningless voices' (p. 55) and his 'On a brown bog's edge' sees nothing more in London than 'a dull cold town' (p. 10). In this sense *The Lane of the Thrushes* never actually departs from the fallen present of urban life, as the folklore and customs of rural Ulster that it depicts are always refracted through the lens of a Protestant metropolitan reality. Understood as such, the collection mirrors the characteristics of the Northern Revival as a whole: a Belfast phenomenon invoking rural Gaelic life as a means of contesting the ownership and traditions of the city itself. As John Hewitt has observed of the Belfast Revival poets of this period, so obsessed were they with 'fairies, tramps of both sexes, tinkers, turfcutters, mothers crooning cradle-songs in cabins in misty glens or by lonely shores' that 'from these voluble city dwellers there was not a word about where they lived and the people they lived among'.[36]

In 1908, three years after *The Lane of the Thrushes* appeared, O'Byrne's 'A lullaby' and Healy's 'Dreaming' were set to music by the young composer Hamilton Harty. They were published in London as part of Harty's collection *Six Songs of Ireland*,[37] alongside poems by Moira O'Neill and Lizzie Twigg; this music, according to Philip Cranmer, was 'as good as anything Harty wrote'.[38] Encouraged by this, O'Byrne was to select the best of his contributions to *The Lane of the Thrushes* (which did not include 'The hills O'Mourne') to form the basis for his own collection *The Grey Feet of the Wind*, published in 1917 by the Talbot Press in Dublin. At this stage, there is evidence to suggest that O'Byrne could have looked forward to a career as a poet with some optimism. An anonymous review of the collection for the *Irish Book Lover* noted that:

> Cathal O'Byrne is a true singer, like the lark he sings because he must, and in this volume he has given us of his best. Every note rings true from the opening to the close.

That O'Byrne was becoming well known for activities other than his poetry is also suggested by the reviewer's observation that:

> a note of sadness pervades the volume, and in order to dispel the idea that this is characteristic of the author, we would suggest that his next work should be a selection from his inimitable 'Mrs Twigglety'.[39]

Unfortunately, no such collection ever appeared.

An indication of the increasing readership that O'Byrne's poetry was attracting can be deduced by his appearance in Padric Gregory's *Modern Anglo-Irish Verse*[40] from 1914, Alfred Perceval Graves' *The Book of Irish Poetry*[41] from 1915 and John Cooke's *Dublin Book of Irish Verse 1728–1909*[42] from 1924. Of these, the first two both chose to anthologise 'A silent mouth' (which would subsequently reappear in *The Grey Feet of the Wind*), a work which encapsulates well Hewitt's summary of O'Byrne's poetry as:

> in a style regular, rhythmical and usually rhymed, the imagery and idiom strongly influenced by the early Yeats, with a touch of Northern dialect and a sprinkle of Ulster place names.[43]

As this suggests, the attraction of O'Byrne's work to anthologists is not surprising, as it was at once both expressive of the dominant paradigm of romantic Revival poetics (at that time being codified through anthologies just such as these) while offering, through its expression of lively Ulster vernacular energies, a distinctively different quality derived from its Northern contexts. Indeed, taking into account O'Byrne's habit during this period of performing his work while wearing a saffron kilt, and the romantic image of the young poet that appears in the frontispiece of *The Grey Feet of the Wind*, it is clear that the Yeatsean image of the poet as Gael was an important component of his own self-definition. This emphasis, however, is also misleading, for while the collection is indebted to early Yeats, it also demonstrates in comparison how limited O'Byrne's poetic vision was. Instead, *The Grey Feet of the Wind* reads now as dependent upon an exhausted Celticism, utilising a voice whose historical moment had passed, and regurgitating the tropes of an ideal that was now tired. 'The white road to Ireland'[44] provides an illustration of this:

Och, the weary's on you, London,
With your hot street's all ablaze,
In a rain o' yellow sunshine,
And the drought o' summer days,
Sure I mind me well a white road
That goes westward to the sea,
And the white road to Ireland
Is the right road for me

I'm not minding o' the money,
Here it falls, they say, like rain,
But who'd be thinkin' o' the likes
That longed for home again?
So tie up your kerchief, Maurya,
And we'll foot it to the sea,
for the white road to Ireland
Is the right road for me.

It is revealing to view 'The white road to Ireland' through the lens of Yeats's 'Lake Isle of Innisfree' from 1893, as both poems imagine Ireland from the perspective of a London-based exile. However, while Yeats's poem subverts the expectations of sentimentality it simultaneously sets up, 'The white road to Ireland' finds it more difficult to transcend its inherited forms. The poem's reference to London is the only non-Irish 'elsewhere' in the collection and the homogeneity of this vision mirrors the homogeneity of the united Ireland it gestures towards – a desire reflected in the uniform preoccupations of the collection. As this suggests, *The Grey Feet of the Wind* relies heavily on the incantatory power of place names to map its territory. The pronounced focus on Ulster found in *The Lane of the Thrushes* is less pronounced, and instead the collection's remit encompasses the whole of Ireland. The mythical and mystical are brought into relation with the present in a way that prefigures O'Byrne's later prose work, and vernacular speech rhythms predominate – a skill that he had honed while writing the humorous 'Mrs Twigglety' column for *Ireland's Saturday Night*.

The overall effect of this, however, is uneven. Taken as a whole, the collection draws upon the final glimmers of the Celtic Twilight shortly before it remade itself as something quite different (largely due to Yeats's own restless urge to transform that which was appearing increasingly like an anachronism). If this goes some way towards suggesting why *The Grey Feet of the Wind* is now almost unreadable, one has also to acknowledge the collection's isolation as a key component of its anachronistic status. While the banalities of some of Yeats's early work would be redeemed by their transformation in his later poems, O'Byrne published no subsequent collection through which his early efforts could be read. As such, the poems appear unsure of their own status and become, in turn, hopelessly vulnerable to the threat of parody. Such reservations were well expressed at the time in a review of *The Grey Feet of the Wind* by the Reverend George O'Neill for the journal *Studies*.[45] Indeed, so precise is O'Neill's critique that it deserves to be reproduced in full:

> The publisher's notice introducing this well-printed book tells us that 'the author is thoroughly steeped in the Magic Lore of the Gael, and has the art to reveal the Realms of Mysteries'. The lavish use of capital letters is not the only reason which leads us to regard this notice as an expression of the poet's own mind. We cannot honestly say that the pages which follow 'reveal' to us anything very new or impressive. From an immense number of poets, great and small, we have already heard such ideas as the following, in which the opening poem culminates:-
>
> O Life is bitter and Love is sweet, and only death is kind
> For life is Hope, and Love is Life, and Life is death alway.
>
> For the characteristic sights and sounds of Irish landscapes Mr O'Byrne has an eye and an ear; but 'grey mists', 'grey stones', 'grey clouds', 'grey birds', 'grey raths' and even 'grey winds', are not new to any of us. Hasn't Mr J. C. Squire got them in his *Tricks of the Trade*? In that volume 'Numerous Celts' sing thus:-
>
> There's a grey wind wails on the clover,
> And grey hills, and mist round the hills,
> And a far voice sighing a song that is over
> And my grey heart that a strange longing fills.
>
> In fact, our author has had the singular ill-luck of not only getting parodied, but of getting parodied before his own appearance. To have come too late has been indeed his particular misfortune. Had we never read Yeats, and Ethna Carbery and MacDonagh and Moira O'Neill and a great many others, we should bring a fresher appreciation to the products of Mr O'Byrne's gifts – they are real – of imagery and versification.

O'Neill's perspective is as insightful as it is humorous, and identifies a residual mode of expression within O'Byrne's writing that would reappear throughout his writing career. J. C. Squire was one of the foremost parodists of his generation and his *Tricks of the Trade*,[46] published earlier in 1917, had become a minor phenomenon. With the reading public in Ireland and elsewhere now attuned to the clichés of 'Numerous Celts', subsequent poetry in the form was always going to appear an anachronism, but, from our perspective, O'Neill's accusation that O'Byrne had 'come too late' carries other resonances. Certainly, the innocent longings found in *The Grey Feet of the Wind* may have been appropriate for public consumption when *The Lane of the Thrushes* was published, in 1905, but by 1917 the experience of the slaughter of the Somme and the dangerous and factionalised state of post-Rising Ireland suggest that the expiry date for such poetry had long since passed.

The reasons why O'Byrne effectively stopped publishing poetry after *The Grey Feet of the Wind* are unclear. It may have been because the difficulties highlighted by O'Neill's review were insurmountable or, more prosaically, because the subsequent demands of his freelance prose work provided a more lucrative living, but he did not publish any further collections. However, that he remained proud of his achievement in the genre is testified by Hewitt,[47] who recounts O'Byrne's pride, towards the end of his life, at the imminent prospect of the publication of an edition of collected poems. This volume never in fact appeared, although it is held in manuscript form in the Public Record Office of Northern Ireland.[48] It contains, alongside poems from *The Grey Feet of the Wind*, many later unpublished pieces, including two meditations on the American urban landscape ('Lights of Broadway, New York' and 'The Wrigley Tower, Chicago'), that suggest a widening of both scope and formal approach. It is an interesting, although predictable (taking into account O'Byrne's previous experiences), paradox that he could find beauty in the American cityscape but not in the Belfast version. Ultimately, there are indications that O'Byrne himself realised that his poetry, like his politics, had been left behind by subsequent developments and was, to a large extent, fossilised. In a letter from 1946 to a friend of his later years, Frank Benner (who subsequently gained the copyright to *As I Roved Out*), O'Byrne included some of his recent poetry and commented:

> I am glad you liked [the poems]. There are so few people who appreciate this kind of thing nowadays. One has to keep doing things if only for the pleasure of the achievement.[49]

As O'Byrne's brief excursion into the world of the Celtic Twilight suggests, ultimately the Northern Revival failed to create a distinctive and indigenous poetic form. Overshadowed by the work of Revival poets in the South, apart from Milligan and Joseph Campbell, Northern poets were inclined towards pastiche, self-consciousness and the reiteration of a limited number of 'Cuchulainoid' themes. In these terms, the poetic landscape of Ulster remained colonised by English genres and canons, and the lack of a tradition of artistic autonomy as was developing elsewhere in the island entailed that the enterprise was marked by a debilitating lack of self-confidence. This, however, was far from the case for other forms of Northern cultural activity. The success of the Ulster Literary Theatre

(ULT), founded in 1902 by Bulmer Hobson and David Parkhill (whose pen name was Lewis Purcell[50]), represents the most persuasive evidence for the existence of a distinctively Northern aesthetic in this period, and suggests that drama rather than poetry was the main catalyst in the creation of public support for the idea of a Northern Revival. It is for this reason, perhaps, that the phenomenon of the ULT has received more critical attention than any other element of the Revival in the North, and useful accounts of its history can be found in Sam Hanna Bell's *The Theatre in Ulster*[51] and Ophelia Byrne's *The Stage in Ulster from the Eighteenth Century*.[52] Both agree on the significance of the ULT's intervention and cite it as a precursor for much of the North's subsequent tradition of independent drama. Alongside this, the ULT was the major organisation to advance the idea of a Northern Revival as a coherent entity. This was chiefly because of the vigorous propagandising undertaken on its behalf by W. B. Reynolds as editor of *Uladh*, but in its plays and productions the company also asserted a specific conception of the values and artistic forms that the North could offer to the Revival movement as a whole. As a result, the ULT was to become a talisman for the whole range of cultural activity taking place across the North during this period. As the *Irish News* remarked of the company members in May 1909:

> They have succeeded in kindling a flame in the north of Ireland which promises to survive in spite of the fact that influences inimical to art in any shape are supposed to flourish with peculiar virility in this part of the world, and their reproductions from Ulster life are characterised by a faithfulness to the original and a dramatic excellence that has stamped their work as something more that that of an ordinary amateur company.[53]

The 'influences inimical to art' that the ULT was opposing were indeed significant. Before the company made its entrance, drama in the North could be described, in Denis Ireland's phrase, as:

> a sort of emergency exit from Belfast, a fire-door leading to what our gilt-and-plush Grand Opera House presented as life in London – head waiters, lords in waterfall ties, monocles (no-one on the Malone Road dared to wear one), young women behind ribbon counters who turned out to be daughters of the aristocracy, impoverished earls, comic butlers, and all the other proper appurtenances of the Victorian stage.[54]

As this suggests, the audience for such productions were mainly older middle-class Protestants, a grouping dismissed by Denis Ireland as 'Victorian old ladies'. If Ireland itself was ever to intrude on the stage, then it was the Ireland of Dion Boucicault, whose melodramas were little more than 'plays about beautiful, if cantankerous, Irish colleens'.[55]

Belfast might have been dimly aware of the foundation of the Irish Literary Theatre (ILT) in Dublin in 1899 but, as Ireland observes, such initiatives were regarded with habitual suspicion and mistrust.

In this atmosphere the success of the ULT could hardly be guaranteed. Moreover, the company's early activists had to contend with hostility from quarters that they might have assumed would be sympathetic. Originally founded as the Ulster Branch of the Irish Literary Theatre, Hobson and Parkhill's admiration for the Dublin initiative was not reciprocated, and Yeats, with his inveterate hostility to all things Ulster, refused the company permission to produce his *Cathleen ni Houlihan* as its first play. It was this obduracy that prompted Hobson's now well known, if possibly apocryphal, outburst of 'Damn Yeats, we'll write our own plays!' Authentic or not, Hobson's instincts were surely correct. The recognition that the company had to look to itself for artistic leadership proved to be a crucial factor in the eventual success of the company, giving it regional distinctiveness and a degree of creative freedom. The early desire to stage *Cathleen*, however, remained, and after an intervention by Maud Gonne, who claimed ownership of the play on the grounds that she had been its muse,[56] the company produced it alongside James H. Cousins' *The Racing Lug* (a kind of Ulster version of J. M. Synge's *Riders to the Sea*) in November 1902. The response of the Belfast public was largely indifferent. In 1913 the *Irish News* recalled these early performances and noted that:

> For a long time the young society was forced to fight against the apathy of a populace who regarded the stage as the happy hunting ground of the devil and to whom the words 'literature' and 'art' were as a sounding brass and a tinkling cymbal. As might be expected, neither he nor his sister nor his cousin nor his aunt patronised the early performances of the ULT. Nor did even the ordinary sinful Belfast theatre-goer give it much countenance.[57]

This, then, was clearly a false start, and the company might well have faded into obscurity had not a further act of hostility from the ILT forced it to find its own identity and creative momentum. In 1904 the ILT's secretary informed Parkhill that the company had no right to claim that it was a branch of the ILT, and that royalties should be paid to the ILT for the retrospective performances of its plays. The financial damage that this did to the fledgling company was considerable, but it also led to a change of name, from the unwieldy Ulster Branch of the Irish Literary Theatre to the simple Ulster Literary Theatre and, more importantly, a final recognition that the company had to write its own drama. The ULT was now ready to make an intervention on its own terms. In Hobson's words, this would be to use drama 'as a vehicle of propaganda',[58] and its first manifestation was the performance of Lewis Purcell's *The Reformers* and Hobson's own *Brian of Banba* at the Ulster Minor Hall in December 1904. The contrast between Purcell's realist comedy and Hobson's Yeatsean mix of myth and poetry proved to be more appealing than the company's previous efforts, and the production continued beyond its planned short run into a further week. The critical response was also largely positive. The *Irish News*, which would prove to be an enthusiastic supporter of the company throughout its life, remarked that *The Reformers* was 'brilliant' and described *Brian of Banba* as 'a picture-play and a very beautiful one at that'.[59]

Encouraged by this event, the ULT's next production, in May 1905, staged Purcell's *The Enthusiast* and Joseph Campbell's *The Little Cowherd of Slaigne* in Clarence Place Hall. As Bell has observed,[60] this combination continued the pattern of the first production, in combining a play about modern Ulster life with a dramatisation from Irish mythology. There is no evidence to suggest that this was a deliberate policy, but it was to become a defining characteristic of many of the ULT's subsequent productions. If nothing else, such juxtapositions were in line with the general tendency of the Northern Revival (as is well illustrated by Milligan's verse) to perceive the history of the Ulster as a vast narrative in which Plantation was only a small aberration. It was in this way that the politically treacherous concept of 'Ulsterness' could be understood as a force for national unity rather than potential cause for cultural and political partition.

While the critical reception of Campbell's play was muted, *The Enthusiast* was recognised as a much more substantial piece of drama and one seeking to engage its audience in the practical benefits of political and economic self-sufficiency. Described by Richard Hayward as 'the first play written in Ulster dialect',[61] it was set in County Antrim and was inspired by the ideals of Sir Horace Plunkett's cooperative farming movement, the Irish Agricultural Organisation. Such a theme was timely, not least because Plunkett had visited the Glens of Antrim in July of the previous year in order to open Bigger's inaugural Antrim Feis. In the play, the failure of the 'enthusiast' himself, the young and idealistic James McKinstry, to persuade the country people to set aside their bigotry and embrace the possibilities of communal farming indicates political pessimism, and yet the fact that such a debate could be articulated on a Belfast stage was, in itself, a startling achievement. Indeed, some sense of the pioneering purpose that must have underwritten *The Enthusiast* can be gained by the fact that the ULT performed the play (along with *Brian of Banba*) at a Feis at Toome Bridge in Antrim in the summer of 1905. This event is of added significance to this study because of the involvement of Cathal O'Byrne in providing musical entertainment with his friend and teacher Carl Hardebeck during the interval.[62] O'Byrne would have a lengthy, if sporadic, association with the company during its most dynamic period,[63] and in 1913 formed and managed his own drama company, the Celtic Players, in a manner that was heavily influenced by the ULT's example. The Players' production of Lady Gregory's *The Rising of the Moon*, Seumas MacManus's *The Leadin' Road to Donegal* and O'Byrne's own 'Irish fantasy' *The Dream of Breedyeen Dara* in April of that year taxed Belfast's Alexandra Theatre 'to its utmost capacity'[64] and was anticipated by an overexcited *Irish News* reporter to be 'one of the most artistic and entertaining performances ever given in the city'.[65] Certainly, the success of the event was startling as the packed theatre witnessed 'an "Irish night" in every sense, Irish music, Irish dances, and Irish songs all contributing to make a picture of Irish rural life that left pleasant memories with the audience'.[66] As such breathless testimony suggests, it is hard to think of an occasion that more effectively epitomises the general tone and preoccupations of the Northern Revival as a whole during this period.

Such productions indicate that, contrary to popular stereotype, Belfast was able to support a flourishing theatre culture, and this nascent enthusiasm encouraged the fledgling ULT to intensify its operations. It was, however, through the pages of *Uladh* rather than on stage that the company sought to refine its identity and debate its future.[67] Bigger, who by this stage of his life had invested a considerable proportion of his personal fortune in Northern Revival projects, had provided the initial funding for the magazine's publication and, although it only endured for four issues (between November 1904 and September 1905), it proved to be an important outlet for the dissemination of Northern Revival propaganda. Modelled on *Samhain*, the journal of the ILT, *Uladh* contained poems, essays and dramatic texts, and professed itself to be non-sectarian and non-political in outlook. As with the *Shan Van Vocht*, however, this was always likely to prove an unfeasible aspiration in a province where any form of cultural activity was regarded as inherently political. Moreover, as the first issue's editorial (written by Reynolds) made clear, *Uladh*'s non-political stance was more honoured in the breach than the observance:

> *Uladh* means Ulster. It is still often necessary to state as much; we intend to insist. This Ulster has its own way of things, which may be taken as the great contrast to the Munster way of things, still keeping on Irish land....

> Exactly what that local temperament and artistic aptitude are, *Uladh* wants to discuss. *Uladh* would also influence them, direct and inform them. And as the Theatre is the most essential of all art activities, and the surest test of a people's emotional and intellectual vitality, *Uladh* starts out as the organ of the Theatre, the Ulster Literary Theatre, but proposes to be as irrelevant to that movement and its topics as is deemed necessary. We intend to strike our keynote through the Theatre where our own plays will be produced, and to let that discover our pathway for us and voice those aims and hopes and hatreds and loves best expressed that way....
>
> At present we can only say that our talent is more satiric than poetic. That will probably remain the broad difference between the Ulster and Leinster schools. But when our genius arrives, as he must sooner or later, there is no accounting for what extraordinary tendency he may display. Our business is, however, to plod along gathering matter for his use, practising methods, perfecting technique and training actors....
>
> We do not aim at being sixpence-worth; we aim at being priceless, for honesty and good purpose are priceless. If we do not attain to all this, we shall at least attain to something unique in Ulster, smacking of the soil, the winds on the uplands, the north coast, the sun and the rain, and the long winter evenings.... In any case, our pages will be kept free from the party-cries of mob and clique and market-place. Our contributors are mostly young men, of all sects and all grades of political opinion. The journal will be run on broad propagandistic lines. Propagandism on broad lines, we think, is desirable at this juncture.[68]

This combination of ambiguity and assertion begged more questions than it answered and left open the issue of whether or not the ULT was to be a force for national unity or regional distinctiveness. Seeking to please all parties, Reynolds' obfuscation would satisfy no one. Following the disquiet that the editorial generated both within the company and beyond, he was forced to clarify his position, and stated in his editorial in the second issue that 'we shall have our own way, though the differences will always be within the generous circle of one nationality'.[69] What had originally appeared to be a potentially bold statement of provincial autonomy was now revealed as little more than an awareness of local custom. Furthermore, as events were rapidly proving, nationality in Ireland, whether in its British or Irish manifestation, was anything but 'generous'.

For the ULT, then, the discussion of 'Ulsterness' led only to an ideological cul-de-sac, and in any case there was already a clear distance between Reynolds' declarations of *credo* and what the ULT was actually producing on stage. When *Uladh* ceased production it had already outlived its usefulness,[70] although its departure was marked by a final essay by Seosamh de Paor (James Power) which suggested that the regional question was still troubling its contributors. As he stated:

> North is North and South is South. Ulster has its own way of doing things. Belfast differs as widely from Dublin as Madrid from Seville. It is not merely the admixture of foreign blood that gives a marked personality to this corner of Eirinn; the people of the North differ from the South in every country the world over.[71]

With that unhelpful contribution, the ULT let the matter rest. The cessation of *Uladh*, however, also marked the point at which the ULT became less avowedly nationalist in its concerns. Committed republicans such as Hobson were gradually moving on to other forms of activism and in their place arrived a generation of less politically motivated dramatists. With the closure of Belfast's School of Art Sketching Club in 1904, the drama club there merged with the ULT, bringing to the company a dynamic and diverse range of talents and interests. Of these, the most important was undoubtedly Harry C. Morrow (Gerald MacNamara), who would become, along with Samuel Waddell (Rutherford Mayne), one of the ULT's most significant playwrights. The company now consisted of individuals from a broad spectrum of political backgrounds and with a wide variety of technical skills, and this diversity would lead to the period of the company's greatest dynamism. The ULT would remain committed to Reynolds' often stated vision of the company as essentially satiric in its talents, and yet from this point on it would be a satire willing to attack all factions and inherited beliefs.

With its greater number of members and an increasing degree of popular support, the ULT was now able to stage annual productions, writing and performing such works as Purcell's *The Pagan* and Mayne's *The Turn of the Road* in 1906, MacNamara's and Purcell's *Suzanne and the Sovereigns* in 1907, and, in 1908, Mayne's hugely successful peasant comedy *The Drone*. With Yeats's earlier animosity now seemingly forgotten, in March 1907 the company took *The Pagan* and *The Turn of the Road* to the Abbey Theatre in Dublin. The production was well received and the ULT would become regular visitors to the Abbey, with Yeats eventually declaring that 'the Ulster Players are the only dramatic society, apart from our own, which is doing serious artistic work'.[72] With this success, the ULT's horizons soon stretched beyond Ireland and the Ulster-born actor Whitford Kane organised productions in England in 1910 and 1911 and toured with *The Drone* in Washington, Baltimore and New York in 1912.[73] Despite these excursions, the ULT obviated the danger of spreading itself too thinly by maintaining a diverse cohort of writers and a substantial (and increasingly experienced) production team. For perhaps the first time, indigenous Ulster drama was beginning to have an influence beyond the borders of the province itself.

Above all other considerations, however, the ULT remained committed to its Belfast base, and in May 1909 it performed for the first time at the city's Grand Opera House, previously the home, as Denis Ireland had suggested, of imported middle-class melodrama. The significance of this incursion was not lost on either the ULT or the city's media. The Opera House was by far the largest venue that the ULT had appeared in, and its production, consisting of Mayne's *The Troth* and *The Drone* alternating with Purcell's *The Pagan* and *The Enthusiast*, was suitably ambitious. In a promotional piece advertising the upcoming run, the *Irish News* remarked on the ambition of the ULT:

> to make this city the centre and the home of a form of dramatic art 'racy of the soil', neither Dublin nor Munster nor English in its character and essentials, but Ulster in heart and spirit.... The dramatists and players of the ULT picture an Ulster more real than the home of political and civic strife. They are 'deep observers': and they tell us more of ourselves and of all the people around in 160 minutes than we had learned from all the speeches of the statesmen and the labours of recondite historians.[74]

Considering the struggle that the ULT had endured in order to gain any form of recognition, such praise was overwhelming. The ULT now appeared to symbolise Ulster artistic achievement as a whole, and the piece concluded by proposing that the ILT's '*Kathleen Ni-Houlihan* and even their *Riders to the Sea* were not quite "on the same plane" as Rutherford Mayne's *The Drone*'. The comparison was one that the *Irish News* would become increasingly fond of, and it suggests that regional tensions within the cultural nationalist project were anything but sublimated. Developing the theme, 'Quill' in the *Northern Whig* proposed that:

> the difference between the Ulster and the Abbey plays is the difference between the Ulsterman of practical instincts and the idealist of the South. The Abbey plays take one into Tír nan og; the Ulster into County Down farm kitchens.[75]

Even by 1913, the *Irish News* was still convinced that the ULT was 'not one whit inferior to its contemporary, either in the quality of its productions, in its earnestness to depict life as it is, or in its marked individuality of genre',[76] while, in a similar manner, Hayward, writing from the perspective of 1938, considered that the ULT in this period 'outshone their Southern fellow-artists' in the genre of comedy.[77] Perhaps more telling again are the comments of the Dublin poet and essayist Seamus O'Sullivan in 1946:

> Looking back on those brilliant first years of the Northern Theatre I cannot help feeling that it had in it more of the essential qualities of a national

> theatre than have resulted from the earlier plays of the Abbey. It had, in short, far more in common with the original Irish National Theatre Society than with its successor, the Abbey.[78]

The ULT's run at the Opera House had been a financial and artistic success and it became an annual feature of Belfast's cultural life for the next twenty-five years. As the *Irish News* reported, 'at the end of each act of both plays there were insistent recalls and at the conclusion of *The Enthusiast* the plaudits were redoubled'.[79] A more reflective editorial column three days later praised the company 'on the successful result of a bold experiment' and considered that:

> the Belfast public, on the whole, very generously appreciated the efforts of the brilliant band of writers and players who have done so much to renew Belfast's almost forgotten reputation as a 'Modern Athens'.[80]

There were, however, a few dissenting voices. For Denis Ireland, the ULT's plays were little more than 'an annual *recherché* of the agricultural *temps perdu*' – a brief theatrical excursion away from Belfast's usual metropolitan obsessions consisting of:

> dung, hobnail boots, a clatter of milk pails, talk about hens 'layin' away', china dogs on the mantelshelf, plus highly-coloured pictures of King William crossing the Boyne, complete with mythical white horse.[81]

In a similar, if less flippant, vein, John T. Donovan in 1912 criticised the ULT's playwrights on the grounds that 'the themes selected for their plays were too parochial, too chauvinistic, too partially rural in scope, and altogether too narrowly conceived in their general outlook'.[82] Such reservations suggest that the ULT's influence on Northern drama in general was less profound than the company's advocates were prone to suggest. Certainly, the ULT's annual occupation of the Grand Opera House had a considerable symbolic resonance, but the building continued to gain its real revenue from non-indigenous productions.

The ULT's greatest success was, however, yet to come. In December 1912 the company premiered a new play at the Grand Opera House, MacNamara's *Thompson in Tír-na-nÓg*, and it is for this work that the company is now best remembered. Essentially a brief one-act satirical fantasy, *Thompson in Tír-na-nÓg* represented the culmination of MacNamara's interest in satire developed through his earlier plays *Suzanne and the Sovereigns* and *The Mist that Does Be on the Bog* (1909), a parody of Synge's peasant plays. Originally written for the Gaelic League (who unsurprisingly rejected it), the play depicts the fate of an Orangeman, Andy Thompson, who is killed when his gun explodes during the annual sham battle at Scarva. His soul is transported to the Gaelic land of eternal youth, Tír-na-nÓg, where he is interrogated by mythical heroes from the Fionn and Ulster cycles. The mutual incomprehension that this encounter generates reveals the contradictions in both Orangeism and the Gaelic Revival, the key moment in the play coming with the questioning of Thompson by a previous defender of Ulster, Cuchulain:

Cuchulain: But hast thou never heard of me in Erin?
Thompson: I'll tell you no lies, Mister, I never did. What are ye, or what *were* ye?
Cuchulain: I was of the Red Branch, foremost of the fighting men of Ulster.
Thompson: Ulster! Put it there. *(Shakes hands)* Why didn't ye tell me that before? *(Brings him down stage to front and whispers)* Man, I took you for a luney like the rest....
Cuchulain: *(Bewildered)* Do you still assert that you are Irish?
Thompson: Of course I do.
Cuchulain: And you admit that you do not speak the language of your country?
Thompson: *(Proudly)* The language of my country is English.
Cuchulain: Answer me, sir, can you speak Irish?
Thompson: I told you before that I couldn't and –
Cuchulain: But as you are speaking English, any man might call you English.
Thompson: Well, if he did he would never do it again.
Cuchulain: Why?
Thompson: I'd break his jaw.
Angus: The remarks of the prisoner are most contradictory.[83]

Some of *Thompson in Tír-na-nÓg*'s satire is deeply embedded. For instance, according to Hagal Mengel,[84] the character of Cuchulain was based on the features and political outlook of Bulmer Hobson, the give-away moment being Thompson's peculiar reference to Cuchulain as an 'ould quaker'. The comparison is affectionate, but it does indicate how far the company had moved from its original ideals. While it was feared that the satire of Orange Order dogma undertaken in the play might have caused rioting in the theatre, in actuality it offended no one because, as the *Irish News* pointed out, Thompson himself is portrayed as 'a very likeable person'.[85] In describing a subsequent production of the play at the Opera House, Mayne recalled the manager of the theatre asking 'us not to let off too strong in *Thompson* because he had been told that there were men up there who had been told that this play made fun of a certain Order, and that they were all lined up with rivets and bolts in their pockets'. The manager need not have worried, for 'when *Thompson* came on, instead of bolts and nuts and so forth landing on the stage, I never heard a play receive such acclamation at the end'.[86] As the *Irish News* commented, 'the great good nature which pervades the whole of [MacNamara's] comic and clever perception places it above reach of the slightest taint of partisan suspicion'.[87]

Good natured though *Thompson in Tír-na-nÓg* undoubtedly was, its premiere during the height of the Home Rule crisis in Ulster suggests that it was by no means a risk-free production. Moreover, while Thompson and the Gaelic heroes presented in the play are gentle creations, the play ends with a recognition of absolute difference and an awareness that reconciliation remains an impossibility. Such a message may have pleased most shades of political opinion in the audience, but it also reveals the essentially toothless nature of MacNamara's satire and, more generally, the desire of the ULT to cause no offence to any faction. In this way, the parochialism of the ULT served only to confirm the worst suspicions about Ulster entertained by those from beyond the province. The company's professional expertise had become impressive, but, as a result, in its aims and intentions it now resembled just another regional theatre company. In November 1916 the ULT performed *Thompson in Tír-na-nÓg* and *The Turn in the Road* to an audience of wounded soldiers at the Gaiety Theatre in Dublin – a city still scarred by the Easter Rising seven months previously. The fact that this event appeared to provoke little controversy provides a significant indication of the manner in which the company was no longer understood to be a distinctly nationalist organisation.[88]

Paradoxically, the success of *Thompson in Tír-na-nÓg* and *The Drone* was to contribute directly to the decline of the ULT, in that the overwhelming audience demand for the plays inhibited the company from producing new work. In 1927 Lady Gregory reported a conversation with Mayne in which he told her that: 'the Ulster Theatre languishes, blames the Opera House in Belfast which turns down all new plays and falls back on *Thompson in Tír-na-nÓg*'.[89] This suspicion was shared by Joseph Connolly, an engaged onlooker on the fortunes of the ULT, who believed that:

> the popularity of the company attracted many whose sole interest was to be connected with it and if possible to secure parts in the shows. Warden's [Fred Warden, the manager of the Grand Opera House] interest was purely commercial and, as *The Drone* and *Thompson* could always be relied upon to fill the house, these became almost the only productions that the company staged.[90]

In truth, however, by this stage the ULT's most creative period had long since passed. For reasons that remain vague, the company split in 1916 and many of its most talented actors resigned. From 1920 onwards a clear decline is identifiable in the number and quality of new productions and, after a bad season in 1934, the company was no longer invited to perform at the Grand Opera House. In retrospect, Forrest Reid's suspicion that the ULT's 'happiest period'[91] was in the years leading up to 1912 is surely correct.

There were other reasons for the ULT's later difficulties and its loss of creative momentum. Of its major figures, only MacNamara had remained in Ulster. Following partition, Purcell and Mayne had moved to the South, while the interests of Hobson and Campbell had taken them away from drama and into political life. The ULT remained essentially an amateur company to the end, but its failure to secure a permanent home was also a decisive factor in the waning of its fortunes. Furthermore, there was little possibility that this was going to change in the future, as the new Stormont regime in Northern Ireland was little inclined to prioritise the subsidy of dramatic art. The considered perspective of Mayne on these difficulties is illuminating:

> We never managed to raise enough money to start building a theatre of our own, and besides that, don't forget that even to the end – ten or twelve years ago – we were always a bit of a cloud.... It's the sort of thing that's always happening in Ulster. After all, when you've a flaming Nationalist like Bulmer Hobson, or Joe Campbell or Francis Joseph Bigger as a member of your society, it takes a lot of explaining away. And thus suspicion – although it wasn't always apparent – meant a good deal more than most of us cared to admit. But the suspicion was there – all the time.[92]

Although the ULT's early radicalism had long since been diluted, suspicion about its motives remained and in this regard it became a victim of the increasing polarisation of Northern Irish society. While it was no longer content to remain merely a mouthpiece of the views of the political minority, it was never able to find wider acceptance among the Protestant majority and thus its position became one of increasing isolation. In 1940, the disillusioned remnants of the company merged with two other dramatic companies, the Northern Irish Players and the Jewish Institute Dramatic Society, to form the Ulster Group Theatre, and it ceased to exist in its own right. In the years from its foundation to 1934, the ULT had written and produced forty-seven new plays. Considering its faltering beginnings, this constitutes an extraordinary achievement.

As with many elements of the Northern Revival, the cessation of the ULT's activities left many of those involved quite bewildered. Writing in 1938, Hayward noted that 'drama in Belfast is not in a happy state', a condition quite at odds with the 'happy and vigorous company'[93] that the ULT once was. Hayward had been an active writer and actor for the company and, following its demise, founded the Belfast Repertory Theatre, with the aim of continuing the ULT's work in promoting indigenous drama. As with the ULT, however, Hayward's company struggled to attract finance and it proved to be short-lived. Despite professing himself mystified by the decline of both his own company and the earlier ULT, the experience he gained led him to the realisation that without a permanent home (what he termed 'a clearing house for native dramatic endeavour'[94]) a dramatic movement is always in danger of gradually losing the energies and coherence necessary for its continued growth. This lesson was well learned by those, such as Mary O'Malley, founder of the Lyric Players Theatre in 1951, who followed in the wake of the earlier innovators. While the descendants of Denis Ireland's 'Victorian old ladies' remain, the relatively vibrant state of indigenous drama in Belfast suggests that the ULT's legacy has not entirely disappeared. Considering the extent to which so many aspects of the Northern Revival faded into anonymity or irrelevance following partition, in this regard at least the ULT's achievement in bringing Ulster drama to Ulster stages was by far the most significant manifestation of the movement's cultural ideals.

NOTES

1 James Joyce, *Ulysses* (London: Penguin, 2000, first published 1922), p. 91. All subsequent page references are to this volume.
2 *Irish News*, 16 June 1904, p. 4.
3 Joyce, *Ulysses*, pp. 115–16:

> – How is the concert tour getting on, Bloom?
> – O, very well, Mr Bloom said. I hear great accounts of it. It's a good idea, you see...
> – Are you going yourself?
> – Well no, Mr Bloom said. In point of fact I have to go down to the county Clare on some private business. You see the idea is to tour the chief towns. What you lose on one you can make up on the other.
> – Quite so, Martin Cunningham said. Mary Anderson is up there now. Have you good artists?
> – Louis Werner is touring her, Mr Bloom said. O yes, we'll have all topnobbers. J. C. Doyle and John MacCormack I hope and. The best, in fact.
> – And *Madame*, Mr Power said smiling. Last but not least.

4 Joyce, *Ulysses*, pp. 92–3: 'I hope that smallpox up there doesn't get any worse. Suppose she wouldn't let herself be vaccinated again.'

5 *Belfast News-Letter*, 16 June 1904, p. 3.
6 Joseph Tomelty, Review, *Irish Bookman*, 1.10 (June 1947), p. 90.
7 I am grateful to Declan Long for this perception.
8 It is, of course, possible to argue that the conclusion of the novel implies that the singing tour will not go ahead. If Molly's soliloquy indicates her ultimate rejection of Boylan and a concomitant return to Bloom, then one possible outcome of this would be the recognition that the tour/love tryst was no longer an attractive proposition. Such a reading is, however, dependent on the extent to which Molly's and Bloom's reconciliation can be seen as operating at any level beyond the purely symbolic – a slight possibility at best.
9 Joyce, *Ulysses*, p. 92.
10 Forrest Reid, *Private Road* (London: Faber and Faber, 1940), pp. 35–6.
11 Reid, *Private Road*, p. 38.
12 John Boyd, 'Ulster prose', in *The Arts in Ulster: A Symposium*, eds Sam Hanna Bell, Nesca A. Robb and John Hewitt (London: George G. Harrap, 1951), p. 116.
13 John Wilson Foster, *Fictions of the Irish Literary Revival: A Changeling Art* (Syracuse: Gill and Macmillan, 1987), p. 176.
14 Reid, *Private Road*, p. 36.
15 E. M. Forster, *Abinger Harvest* (London: Arnold, 1936), quoted by Boyd, 'Ulster prose', p. 115.
16 Boyd, 'Ulster prose', p. 113.
17 Seumas MacManus, Foreword, in Ethna Carbery, Seumas MacManus, Alice Milligan, *We Sang for Ireland: Poems of Ethna Carbery, Seumas MacManus, Alice Milligan* (Dundalk: Dundalgan Press, 1950).
18 Happily, the recent work of Robbie Meredith and Catherine Morris has gone some way towards redressing this absence. See, for instance, Meredith's '*The Shan Van Vocht*: notes from the North', in *Critical Ireland: New Essays in Literature and Culture*, eds Aaron Kelly and Alan A. Gillis (Dublin: Four Courts Press, 2001), pp. 173–80; and Morris's 'Becoming Irish? Alice Milligan and the Revival', *Irish University Review*, 33.1 (spring/summer, 2003), pp. 79–98.
19 Bulmer Hobson, *Ireland Yesterday and Tomorrow* (Tralee: Anvil Books, 1968), pp. 1–2. Hobson also notes how his childhood zeal for Irish nationalism was energised by Milligan's loan of a number of inspiring works by Standish O'Grady (p. 1).
20 Meredith '*The Shan Van Vocht*', p. 175.
21 Seumas MacManus, 'A memoir of Ethna Carbery', in *The Four Winds of Eirinn: Poems by Ethna Carbery* (Dublin: M. H. Gill, 1918). See: http://digital.library.upenn.edu/women/carbery/carbery.html.
22 Ethna Carbery, *The Four Winds of Eirinn* (Dublin: M. H. Gill, 1902).
23 Ethna Carbery, *In the Irish Past* (Cork: Mercier Press, 1978, first published 1904).
24 Alice Milligan, *Hero Lays* (Dublin: Maunsel, 1908). David Gardiner's essay 'The other Irish renaissance: the Maunsel poets', *New Hibernia Review/Iris Éireannach Nua*, 8.1 (spring 2004), pp. 54–79, notes that from its foundation by the Belfastman George Roberts in 1905 the Maunsel Press was

unusual in its willingness to publish writers who were from the North of Ireland and women.

25 Russell, G. (AE), ed., *New Songs, Selected by AE from the Poems of Padraic Colum, Eva Gore Booth, Thomas Keohler, Alice Milligan, Susan Mitchell, Seumas O'Sullivan, George Roberts, and Ella Young* (Dublin: O'Donoghue, 1904), p. xi.

26 Henry Mangan quoting MacDonagh in Alice Milligan, *Poems*, ed. Henry Mangan (Dublin: Gill, 1954), p. xi.

27 '"Our Own Ulster", Miss A. L. Milligan's address to the men of Antrim Glens who met at O'Neill's Cairn', *Irish News*, 3 July 1913, p. 6.

28 Milligan, *Poems*, p. 154.

29 Seamus Heaney, 'An open letter', Field Day Pamphlet No. 2 (Derry: Field Day, 1983), reprinted in Roger McHugh (ed.), *Ireland's Field Day* (London: Hutchinson, 1985), pp. 23–9.

30 Cathal O'Byrne, *As I Roved Out* (Belfast: Blackstaff Press, 1982, first published 1946), p. 354.

31 J. N. Browne, 'Poetry in Ulster', in *The Arts in Ulster: A Symposium*, eds Sam Hanna Bell, Nesca A. Robb and John Hewitt (London: George G. Harrap, 1951), pp. 147–8.

32 'Cathal O'Byrne: some reminiscences by "C".', *Irish News*, 2 August 1957, p. 7.

33 Cathal O'Byrne, *The Lane of the Thrushes: Some Ulster Love Songs*, with C. Healy (Dublin: Sealy, Bryers and Walker, 1905). The year of publication was also the year that Healy joined Sinn Féin.

34 David Greer, 'The collaboration of Cathal O'Byrne and Cahir Healy in *The Lane of the Thrushes*', *Irish Booklore*, 4 (1978–80), pp. 109–12.

35 O'Byrne, *The Lane of the Thrushes*, pp. 4–5.

36 John Hewitt, '"The Northern Athens" and after', in *Belfast: The Making of the City*, eds J. C. Beckett, *et al.* (Belfast: Appletree Press, 1988), p. 79.

37 *Six Songs of Ireland: The Poems by Moira O'Neill, Lizzie Twigg, Cahir Healy and Cahal O'Byrne, the Music by Hamilton Harty* (London: Boosey, 1908). Greer ('The collaboration of Cathal O'Byrne and Cahir Healy', n. 5, p. 112) is surely correct in his assertion that the 'Lizzie Twigg' who also appears in the collection influenced O'Byrne in the naming of one of his most famous newspaper characters, 'Liza Ann Twigglety'. More intriguingly again, a 'Lizzie Twigg' appears in *Ulysses* as one of the respondents to Bloom's advertisement asking for a 'smart lady typist to aid gentleman in literary work'. He rejects her on the grounds that her application suggests she might be too literary minded ('My literary efforts have had the good fortune to meet with the approval of the eminent poet A. E. (Mr Geo. Russell)', p. 202). A little later in the day he encounters AE with a young woman, whom he imagines might very well be Lizzie Twigg herself (p. 210). Her literary pretensions and connection with AE suggest that Joyce did indeed have the real Lizzie Twigg in mind.

38 Philip Cranmer, 'Vocal music', *Hamilton Harty: His Life and Music*, ed. David Greer (Belfast: Blackstaff Press, 1978), p. 119.

39 Anonymous, 'Review of *The Grey Feet of the Wind* by C. O'Byrne', *Irish Book Lover*, 11.3 (October/November 1917), p. 34.

40 Padric Gregory, ed., *Modern Anglo-Irish Verse* (London: David Nutt, 1914), pp. 43, 117, 320.
41 Alfred Perceval Graves, ed., *The Book of Irish Poetry* (Dublin: Talbot Press, 1915), pp. 123–4.
42 John Cooke, ed., *Dublin Book of Irish Verse 1728–1909* (Dublin: Hodges, Figgis, 1924), pp. 685–8.
43 John Hewitt, Foreword, in *As I Roved Out*, by C. O'Byrne (Belfast: Blackstaff, 1982).
44 Cathal O'Byrne, *The Grey Feet of the Wind* (Dublin: Talbot Press, 1917), pp. 30–1.
45 Anonymous, 'Review of *The Grey Feet of the Wind* by C. O'Byrne', *Studies*, 6.23 (September 1917), pp. 512–13.
46 J. C. Squire, *Tricks of the Trade* (London: Martin Secker, 1917).
47 Hewitt, Foreword.
48 Public Record Office of Northern Ireland, document ref. T/3306/C1. The manuscript is dedicated to Frank Benner and dated 22 December 1951.
49 Public Record Office of Northern Ireland, document ref. T/3306/A2. Undated.
50 According to Flann Campbell's *The Dissenting Voice: Protestant Democracy in Ulster from Plantation to Partition* (Belfast: Blackstaff Press, 1991), pp. 469–70, Protestant members of the ULT habitually used pseudonyms as drama, let alone nationalist drama, was not considered respectable.
51 Sam Hanna Bell, *The Theatre in Ulster* (Dublin: Gill and Macmillan, 1972), pp. 1–51.
52 Ophelia Byrne, *The Stage in Ulster from the Eighteenth Century* (Belfast: Linen Hall Library, 1997), pp. 37–41.
53 *Irish News*, 18 May 1909, p. 8.
54 Denis Ireland, *From the Jungle of Belfast: Footnotes to History 1904–1972* (Belfast: Blackstaff Press, 1973), p. 26.
55 Ireland, *From the Jungle of Belfast*, p. 27.
56 Despite his initial annoyance at Maud Gonne's intervention, Yeats's attitude to the ULT would eventually soften. He waived any fees payable for the production of *Cathleen* and wrote to David Parkhill on 18 May 1904: 'I am interested in hearing of your work which may go to very great importance'. Cited in W. B. Yeats, *The Collected Letters of W. B. Yeats. Vol. 3: 1901–1904*, eds John Kelly and Ronald Schuchard (Oxford: Clarendon Press, 1994), p. 597.
57 'The Ulster Theatre: an English appreciation of local dramatic work', *Irish News*, 11 April 1913, p. 5.
58 Bell, *The Theatre in Ulster*, p. 2.
59 'Ulster Literary Theatre performance last night: plays by local authors', *Irish News*, 8 December 1904, p. 4.
60 Bell, *The Theatre in Ulster*, p. 19.
61 Richard Hayward, *In Praise of Ulster* (London: Arthur Baker, 1938), p. 33.
62 Bell, *The Theatre in Ulster*, p. 25.
63 In *As I Roved Out* O'Byrne records that he took part in the ULT's outdoor production of Gerald NacNamara's *Thompson in Tír-na-nÓg* at Belvoir

Park in 1913. His memories of the event provide an intriguing glimpse of the ULT's skill in production and staging:

> On one occasion, and how well we remember that particular Saturday afternoon, when, with other members of 'The Ulster Literary Theatre' – then at the zenith of its popularity – we travelled out and in the beautiful Park of Belvoir gave an open air performance of *Thompson in Tír na nóg*. The stage was a level stretch of green sward at the foot of the old Fort where it stands above the Lagan water. The audience was seated in a semicircle on the sloping ground in front, and the actors in their colourful and picturesque costumes came on and made their exits from amongst the bushes on either side. The setting was excellent, as was the staging, and the performance, given in brilliant sunshine, was a unique success. (p. 257)

64 *Irish News*, 8 April 1913, p. 6.
65 'Mr. Cahal O'Byrne's season at the Alexandra', *Irish News*, 1 April 1913, p. 8.
66 *Irish News*, 11 April 1913, p. 8.
67 For further reflections on this see Tom Clyde, 'Uladh, Lagan and Rann: the "little magazine" comes to Ulster', in *Returning to Ourselves: Second Volume of Papers from the John Hewitt Summer School*, ed. Eve Patten (Belfast: Lagan Press, 1995), pp. 145–53. Clyde places *Uladh* in the context of the 'little magazine' phenomenon and notes that such publications 'serve as a unique barometer of the general level, range and vitality of artistic activity in each country and region' (p. 147).
68 *Uladh*, no. 1 (November 1904), pp. 2–3.
69 *Uladh*, no. 2 (February 1905), p. 2.
70 Bulmer Hobson and Roger Casement mooted reviving the journal in 1907, with the latter even submitting an essay on the desirability of entering an Irish team in the Olympics. The plans, however, never came to fruition. See Marnie Hay, 'Explaining *Uladh*: cultural nationalism in Ulster', in *The Irish Revival Reappraised*, eds Betsy Taylor FitzSimon and James H. Murphy (Dublin: Four Courts Press, 2004), pp. 119–131, p. 128.
71 *Uladh*, no. 4 (September 1905), p. 6.
72 Bell, *The Theatre in Ulster*, p. 33.
73 For a fuller account of these tours see Kane's memoir *Are We All Met?* (London: Elkin Mathews and Marrot, 1931).
74 'Native plays and players at Grand Opera House', *Irish News*, 15 May 1909, p. 4.
75 'Ulster literary plays', *Northern Whig*, 15 May 1909, p. 10.
76 'The Ulster Theatre', p. 5.
77 Hayward, *In Praise of Ulster*, p. 33.
78 Seamus O'Sullivan, *The Rose and the Bottle* (Dublin: Talbot Press, 1946), p. 102.
79 *Irish News*, 19 May 1909, p. 5.
80 *Irish News*, 22 May 1909, p. 4.
81 Ireland, *From the Jungle of Belfast*, p. 27.

82 John T. Donovan, 'The possibilities of Irish drama', *Irish News*, 24 December 1912, p. 7.
83 Gerald MacNamara, *Thompson in Tír-na-nÓg* (Dublin: Talbot Press, 1912).
84 Hagal Mengel, *Sam Thompson and Modern Drama in Ulster* (Frankfurt am Main: Lang, 1986), p. 84.
85 'Ulster literary theatre in Grand Opera House: two new plays', *Irish News*, 10 December 1912, p. 6.
86 Bell, *The Theatre in Ulster*, p. 44.
87 'Ulster Literary Theatre in Grand Opera House: two new plays'.
88 See Karen Vandevelde, 'An open national identity: Rutherford Mayne, Gerald MacNamara, and the plays of the Ulster Literary Theatre', *Eire–Ireland: Journal of Irish Studies*, 39 (spring/summer, 2004), p. 52.
89 A. Gregory, *Lady Gregory's Journals: 1916–1930* (London: Putnam, 1946), p. 102.
90 J. Anthony Gaughan, ed., *Memoirs of Senator Joseph Connolly (1885–1961): A Founder of Modern Ireland* (Dublin: Irish Academic Press, 1996), p. 60.
91 Mengel, *Sam Thompson and Modern Drama in Ulster*, p. 108.
92 Quoted in Norah Saunders and A. A. Kelly, *Joseph Campbell: Poet and Nationalist 1879–1944. A Critical Biography* (Dublin: Wolfhound Press, 1988), p. 30.
93 Hayward, *In Praise of Ulster*, pp. 32–3.
94 Hayward, *In Praise of Ulster*, p. 33.

Cathal O'Byrne in Celtic costume, c. 1917.

Cathal O'Byrne, c. 1915.

Roger Casement, 1890. (National Library of Ireland.)

Title page of *Glimpses of Erin*, by Seaton Milligan and Alice Milligan, 1890.

Herbert Hughes (left) and Francis Joseph Bigger making grave rubbings. (National Library of Ireland.)

A performer in costume at the 1904 Feis in the Glens. (Ulster Museum.)

Opening procession, from Cushendall to Glenariff, at the 1904 Feis. (Ulster Museum.)

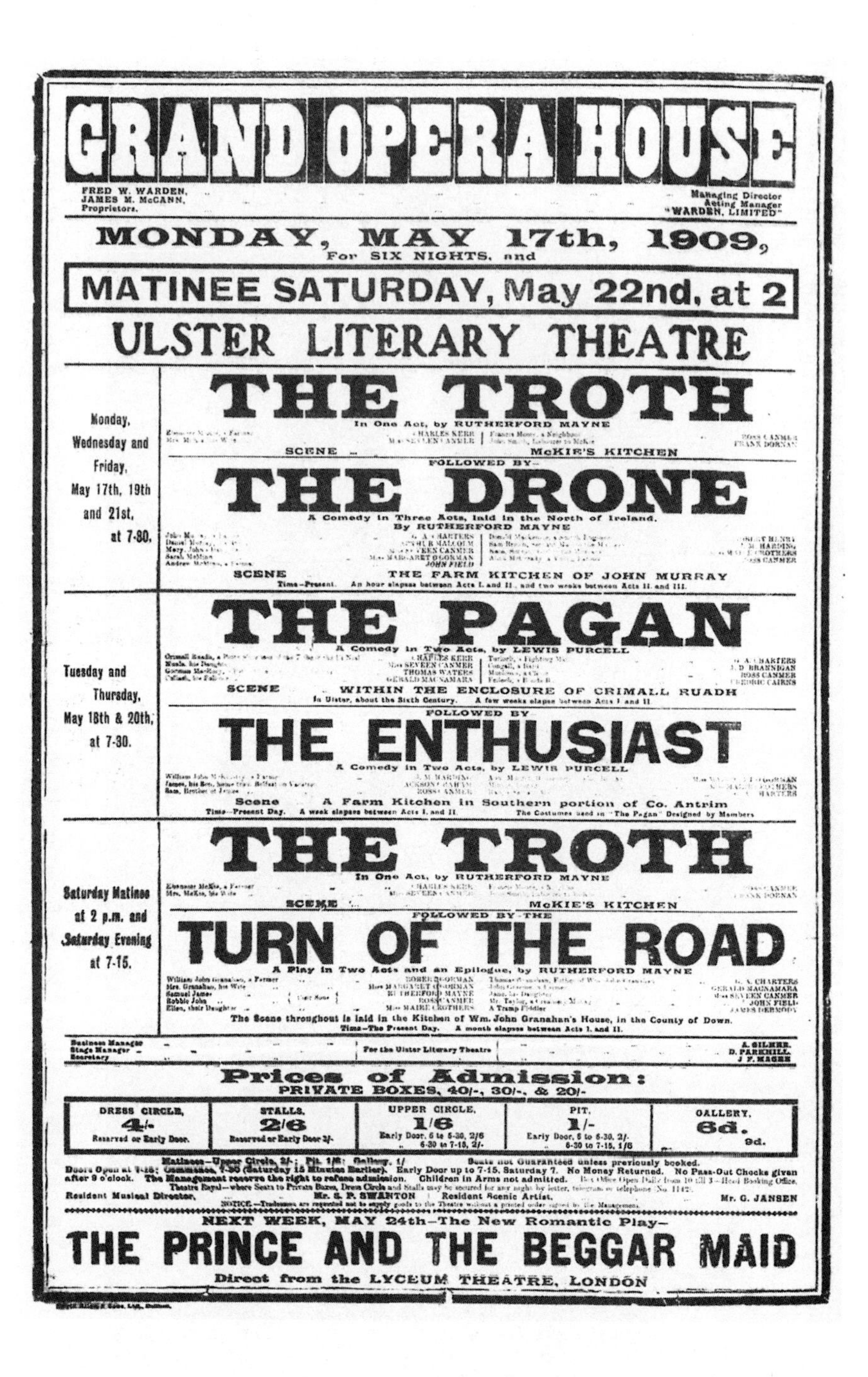

GRAND OPERA HOUSE

FRED W. WARDEN, JAMES M. McCANN, Proprietors. — Managing Director, Acting Manager "WARDEN, LIMITED"

MONDAY, MAY 17th, 1909,
For SIX NIGHTS, and

MATINEE SATURDAY, May 22nd, at 2

ULSTER LITERARY THEATRE

Monday, Wednesday and Friday, May 17th, 19th and 21st, at 7-30.

THE TROTH

In One Act, by RUTHERFORD MAYNE

CHARLES KERR — ROSS CANMER — FRANK DORNAN

SCENE ... McKIE'S KITCHEN

FOLLOWED BY—

THE DRONE

A Comedy in Three Acts, laid in the North of Ireland.
By RUTHERFORD MAYNE

G. A. CHARTERS — ARTHUR MALCOLM — Miss MARGARET O'GORMAN — JOHN FIELD — ROSS CANMER

SCENE ... THE FARM KITCHEN OF JOHN MURRAY

Time—Present. An hour elapses between Acts I. and II., and two weeks between Acts II. and III.

Tuesday and Thursday, May 18th & 20th, at 7-30.

THE PAGAN

A Comedy in Two Acts, by LEWIS PURCELL

CHARLES KERR — Miss SEVEEN CANMER — THOMAS WATERS — GERALD MACNAMARA — G. A. CHARTERS — J. D. BRANNIGAN — ROSS CANMER — CEDRIC CAIRNS

SCENE ... WITHIN THE ENCLOSURE OF CRIMALL RUADH

In Ulster, about the Sixth Century. A few weeks elapse between Acts I. and II.

FOLLOWED BY

THE ENTHUSIAST

A Comedy in Two Acts, by LEWIS PURCELL

William John ..., a Farmer — James, his Son, home from Belfast on Vacation — Sam, Brother of James

Scene ... A Farm Kitchen in Southern portion of Co. Antrim

Time—Present Day. A week elapses between Acts I. and II. The Costumes used in "The Pagan" Designed by Members

Saturday Matinee at 2 p.m. and Saturday Evening at 7-15.

THE TROTH

In One Act, by RUTHERFORD MAYNE

Ebenezer McKie, a Farmer — Mrs. McKie, his Wife

SCENE ... McKIE'S KITCHEN

FOLLOWED BY THE

TURN OF THE ROAD

A Play in Two Acts and an Epilogue, by RUTHERFORD MAYNE

William John Granahan, a Farmer — Mrs. Granahan, his Wife — Samuel James — Robbie John — Ellen, their Daughter

Miss MARGARET O'GORMAN — RUTHERFORD MAYNE — ROSS CANMER — Miss MAIRE CROTHERS — A Tramp Fiddler — G. A. CHARTERS — GERALD MACNAMARA — Miss SEVEEN CANMER — JOHN FIELD — JAMES DERMODY

The Scene throughout is laid in the Kitchen of Wm. John Granahan's House, in the County of Down.
Time—The Present Day. A month elapses between Acts I. and II.

Business Manager, Stage Manager, Secretary — For the Ulster Literary Theatre — A. GILMER. D. PARKHILL. J. F. MAGEE

Prices of Admission:
PRIVATE BOXES, 40/-, 30/-, & 20/-

DRESS CIRCLE,	STALLS,	UPPER CIRCLE,	PIT,	GALLERY,
4/-	2/6	1/6	1/-	6d.
Reserved or Early Door.	Reserved or Early Door 3/-	Early Door, 6 to 6-30, 2/6; 6-30 to 7-15, 2/-	Early Door, 6 to 6-30, 2/-; 6-30 to 7-15, 1/6	9d.

Matinees—Upper Circle, 2/-; Pit, 1/6; Gallery, 1/ — Seats not Guaranteed unless previously booked.
Doors Open at 7-15; Commence, 7-30 (Saturday 15 Minutes Earlier). Early Door up to 7-15, Saturday 7. No Money Returned. No Pass-Out Checks given after 9 o'clock. The Management reserve the right to refuse admission. Children in Arms not admitted. Box Office Open Daily from 10 till 3—Head Booking Office, Theatre Royal—where Seats to Private Boxes, Dress Circle and Stalls may be secured for any night by letter, telegram or telephone (No. 1142).
Resident Musical Director, Mr. S. P. SWANTON | Resident Scenic Artist, Mr. G. JANSEN
NOTICE.—Tradesmen are requested not to supply goods to the Theatre without a printed order signed by the Management.

NEXT WEEK, MAY 24th—The New Romantic Play—

THE PRINCE AND THE BEGGAR MAID

Direct from the LYCEUM THEATRE, LONDON

Handbill for the Ulster Literary Theatre's season at the Grand Opera House, 1909.

Shane's Castle, 1911.

Advertisement for Alexander Hogg's photography service, c. 1911. Note the Celtic design, with shamrock and Irish tower. (Ulster Museum.)

Ardrigh, c. 1912. From left to right on steps: Roger Casement, Father Kelly, Lord Ashbourne, Francis Joseph Bigger, Alice Stopford Green.

Left to right: Eoin MacNeill, Cardinal Logue, Francis Joseph Bigger and the Reverend McNally at the Omeath Irish Summer School, 1912. (Ulster Museum.)

Carl Gilbert Hardebeck.

Alice Stopford Green. (National Library of Ireland.)

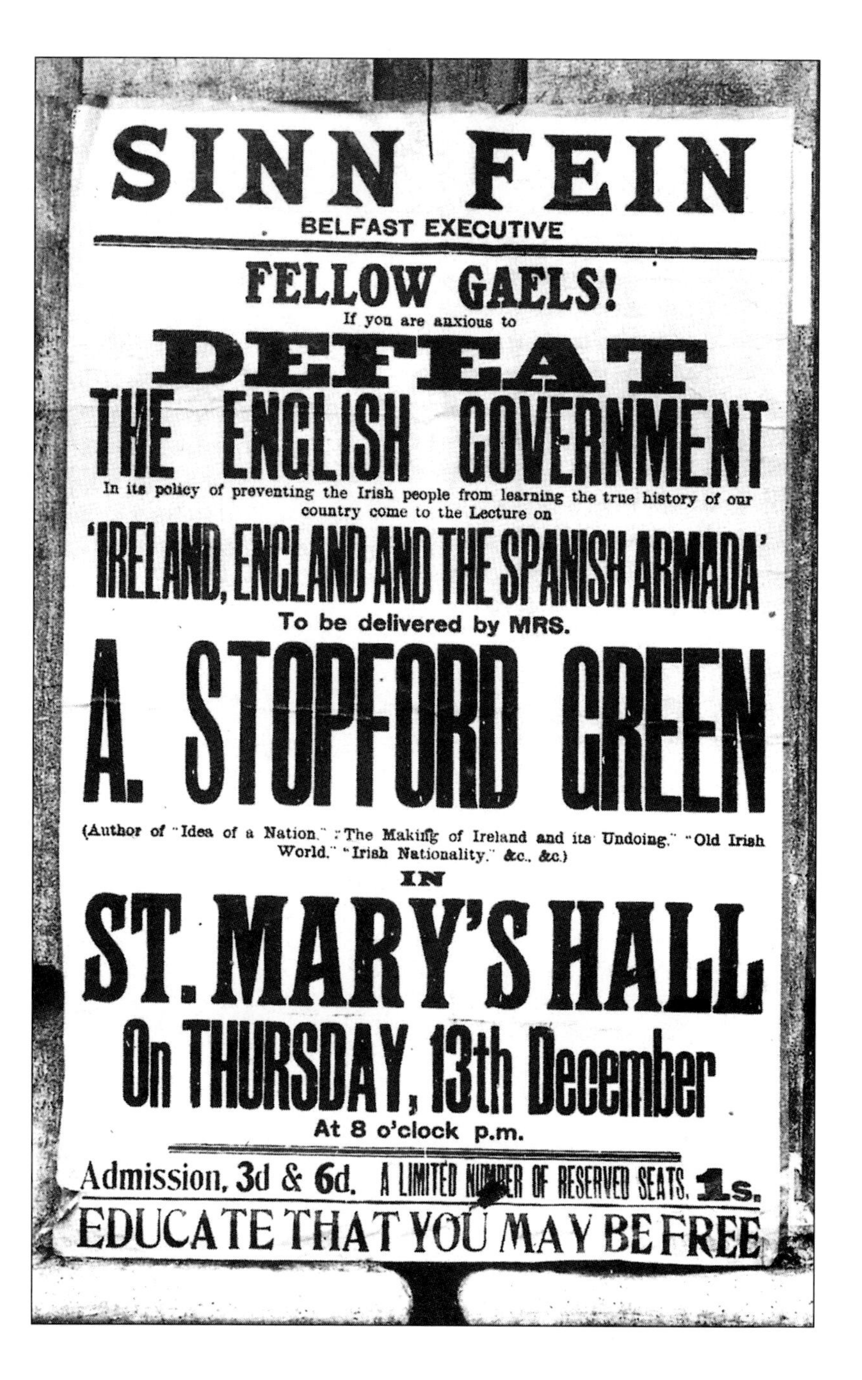

Sinn Féin poster advertising a lecture by Alice Stopford Green, 1917.

Cathal O'Byrne, c. 1946.

CHAPTER FOUR

F. J. Bigger and the Ardrigh coterie

> BIGGER'S GRAVE BLASTED
> Army and police last night searched a cemetery at Glengormley, near Belfast, after an explosion damaged a headstone over the grave of Mr. Francis Joseph Bigger, Irish historian, antiquarian, poet and litterature [*sic*] who died in 1926.
>
> The blast happened in Trench Cemetery and also blew out windows in houses in Hyde Park estate.
>
> Mr. Bigger's grave is near that of Jimmy Hope the Weaver, one of the men of '98.
>
> *Irish News*, 7 April 1971, p. 1

OF the many symbolic acts of violence that took place during the Northern Irish Troubles in the late twentieth century, few were initially as puzzling as the destruction of Francis Joseph Bigger's funerary monument in Glengormley by Protestant extremists in 1971. Bigger was remembered – if he was remembered at all – as a benign solicitor, archaeologist and antiquarian, a man of eccentric tastes and interests who seemingly displayed little interest in the political events of his day, preferring, instead, to inhabit the realms of Gaelic myth and Ulster folklore. He was the author of countless pamphlets and essays,[1] and after his death his collection of some 3000 books and manuscripts was presented to the Belfast Central Library, where it still forms the heart of that institution's special collections. In a province that has long suffered from the effects of historical amnesia and fragmentation, Bigger's dedication to the recovery of Ulster's partial and often discontinuous past was nothing less than remarkable. As his obituary notice in the *Irish News* recorded:

> no man in these parts had given himself more generously to the task of maintaining for this, and for succeeding generations, a continuing interest

> in those fragmentary relics which had survived the violence of human hands and the corroding tooth of time.[2]

Similarly, while Bigger made no secret of his nationalist sympathies, when compared with the positions adopted by many of his contemporaries these were perceived to be of a reasonably tolerant kind, and in his extensive charity work he was always scrupulously even-handed. As his friend John S. Crone noted after his death, 'his great knowledge was distributed as liberally as was his purse to any truly deserving object'.[3]

Why, then, of all the monuments in Northern Ireland, should Bigger's headstone have become a target for terrorist aggression? The answer lies, perhaps, not with the character of Bigger himself, but rather with the people whom he chose to consort with. As will be apparent from this study so far, the politics of Irish nationalism in Ulster during the first half of the twentieth century were overwhelmingly dominated by a small number of individual personalities and the intimacies that developed between them. From its beginnings as a minority faction consisting of a few committed activists to its transformation into a mass movement in the years leading up to 1916, the structure of nationalism in the North, its preoccupations, loyalties and hatreds, owed more to the ineffable processes of coterie and friendship than to the assertion of an abstract political principle. In the tangle of these interpersonal alliances, Bigger was a crucial thread, the figure who gave political nationalism in the North its distinct shape and without whom the Northern Revival would have been an impossibility. As the Casement scholar Jeffrey Dudgeon has argued:

> [Bigger] was the chief promoter of all aspects of Irish culture in the north and as such moulded a generation. No other intellectual force in Belfast as that around him has ever been as strong or as dominant.[4]

In this context, whatever else might be said of those who planned the desecration of his grave, it is clear that they had studied the history of Irish nationalism in Ulster with some diligence.

The reasons why Bigger became this unlikely and yet vital individual at the heart of nationalist political and cultural life in Belfast are remarkable. His house, Ardrigh, overlooked Belfast Lough from Fortwilliam and was, according to Joseph Connolly (later to be a Free State senator and Fianna Fail minister), 'the perfect bachelor's home',[5] a gathering place for 'birds of passage' such as Alice Stopford Green, Roger Casement, Shane Leslie, Alice Milligan, Lord Ashbourne, Patrick Pearse, Bulmer Hobson, Maud Gonne, Joseph Campbell, James Connolly and, of course, Cathal O'Byrne. Described by Leslie as 'the most cultured home in Ireland',[6] many individuals who would otherwise have existed in separate orbits were brought together under its roof. As H. A. MacCartan recalled, 'to walk into that house was a thrilling experience; you were almost certain to meet an established or rising celebrity'.[7] Indeed, Ardrigh was, in Jonathan Bardon's words, 'one of the very few places in Ulster where Protestants, Catholics and sceptics met regularly for social as well as business purposes'.[8] Because Bigger's own interests were orientated towards a mythical, romanticised version of Ireland's past, much that emanated from Ardrigh was inevitably sentimental and remote from contemporary politics, but it also became the centre of revolutionary nationalism in Ulster and the hub of militant republican strategic planning. In fact, the police were so wary of Ardrigh's seditious potential that they kept it under surveillance during World War One, believing that the inhabitants of the house might harbour pro-German sympathies. In the case of Bigger, at least, their fears may have been misplaced, but the general suspicion was surely justified. Certainly, to understand what was happening within the walls of Ardrigh was to understand the preoccupations, strengths and weaknesses of nationalism in Ulster as a whole. For MacCartan, it was nothing less than 'a power-house of knowledge and inspiration'.[9]

The development of Bigger's nationalist consciousness was itself a narrative heavy with symbolism. Born in 1863 and the seventh son of a seventh son, he liked to emphasise his connections to what he saw as an impeccable dissenting Presbyterian heritage. His grandfather, David Bigger, had been a Volunteer during the period of Grattan's parliament, while his father's cousin was the Member of Parliament Joseph Gillis Biggar, Parnell's henchman and the celebrated pioneer of parliamentary obstructionism. His ancestors had resided in south-east Antrim for nearly 300 years and were as dominant in that society as the name of the local village, Biggerstown, suggests. Bigger's obsession with these antecedents was a major component of his identity. According to Leslie, 'in his dreams he was "the O'Neill" returned from a past remote from the politics which clashed around him',[10] and he frequently imagined himself as the guardian and the embodiment of the spirit of the United Irishmen.[11] Bigger was educated at the Royal Academical Institution, a school which his grandfather had founded, and progressed to study law at the Kings Inns in Dublin in 1884. On his return to Belfast, he established a law practice with his friend William Strachan on Royal Avenue and inherited Ardrigh, the family's Belfast home.[12] He developed an abiding passion for archaeology, joined the Belfast Natural History Field Club and began attending P. J. O'Shea's Irish classes there in 1894 – an activity which at that time was not regarded as being particularly indicative of incipient nationalist sympathies. Bigger was ideally placed to explore such pre-occupations for, as John Wilson Foster has observed:

> the North of Ireland was in the nineteenth century a region of scientific and natural scientific achievement, much of it by zealous amateurs. The alliance between science, art, education, business and industry was the chief feature of the Victorian Belfast intellectual scene.[13]

As these biographical details suggest, Bigger's enthusiasms were those of the typical Irish Victorian bourgeois antiquarian, in the mould of such figures as Sir Samuel Ferguson, George Sigerson from Strabane and Dr William Reeves, one time Bishop of Down. Inspired by a vision of a self-sufficient rural Ireland and repelled by what he saw as the brutal disposability of British commercial culture, Bigger's commitment to the cause of Irish Ireland was immense and his achievements considerable. As his brother, F. C. Bigger, remembered:

> 'Home Industries begorrah' was no empty war cry with Francis Joseph. He designed the Irish dress of the Pipers' Bands with their distinctive Saffron and Green. He encouraged Irish games and dances. Presented banners and pipes – gave prizes for Irish stories and lectured at Feisanna all over the country.... Every lecture fired him with fresh enthusiasm and hopes for the future. It mattered not whether the chair was taken by a leading townsman, the Catholic Curate or the Parish Priest, he was always assured of a crowded house.[14]

Such lectures were only a small part of his activities. There is evidence that Bigger's archaeological work was more enthusiastic than constructive,[15] but he did recover the only pre-Reformation statue of the madonna and child in Ulster from a golf club in Ardglass, preserved the fragments of many Celtic high crosses and, in 1901, made secure the reputed grave of Saint Patrick in the grounds of Downpatrick Cathedral. He was certainly more than a 'charlatan historian', the label attached to him by H. C. Lawlor in a vicious attack on Bigger's methods soon after his death.[16] As might be expected from one of his class, Bigger was dedicated to the ideal of the liberal institution and was, at various times, president of the Belfast Natural History and Philosophical Society, editor of the *Ulster Journal of Archaeology* (from 1894 to 1914), a member of *Coisde Gnotha* (the executive council) of the Gaelic League, governor of the Royal Academical Historical Institution and of the Belfast Society for Promoting Knowledge, a member of the Royal Irish Academy, and director of the Ulster Public House Reform Association. The last project sprang from Bigger's desire to promote temperance in Ulster through the refurbishment of some of the province's more disreputable pubs, such as the Ballyvesey Spirit Grocers on the old Antrim Road,[17] and the reforming zeal that this indicates was a major aspect of his identity. Like Dorothea Brooke in *Middlemarch*, he designed plans for improved workers' cottages and even paid for the construction of a row of model houses in Glengormley complete with Celtic decorations. As with Dorothea's scheme, this philanthropy was based on an element of naivety, but Bigger's financial independence meant that he could complete his project without consultation or compromise. Some of Bigger's other philanthropic work was more practical. As Crone describes in his touching obituary of Bigger's life:

> another method, by which he assisted poor persons, was his going security for the cost of a taxi-cab to be paid for by instalments, and helping to pay for it by employing the driver. Many a taxi-cab plying for hire on the streets of Belfast today, the sole property of its proud owner, would never have been there but for his unstinted generosity and his trust – never betrayed – in his fellow-man.[18]

When viewed in the light of these activities, Bigger appeared to be nothing less than a model of liberal Protestant social responsibility. Having accumulated wealth through his successful legal practice, he saw it as his duty to place both his money and his knowledge at the service of wider society. In this way, he became both a figure of the Northern unionist establishment – a solicitor of respectable background with connections to such bulwarks of Protestant power as the Royal Academical Institution and the Freemasons – and yet also a potentially dangerous subversive. As such, his life made manifest the contradictions that were always latent in the ideology of nineteenth-century Protestant antiquarianism. The Irish language, for instance, might well have been a harmless object of study for Protestant unionists in 1890, but by 1910, and thanks to the Gaelic League, it indicated an unmistakable political sympathy. As Roger Dixon has suggested, Bigger remained 'by birth and temperament very much a Victorian',[19] and as such it became ever more difficult to reconcile his essentially amateur enthusiasms with the increasingly political and professional concerns of the twentieth-century Revival.

Perhaps in recognition of this, contemporary accounts of Bigger's life are usually keen to emphasise his lack of interest in contemporary politics. If this is true, it is true to the same degree that the *Shan Van Vocht* professed itself to be non-political while immersing itself in cultural nationalism and urging others to join the struggle. Like Milligan and Anna Johnston, the editors of that paper, Bigger despaired of the factionalised state of nationalist party politics in the years after Parnell, but he was greatly influenced by Douglas Hyde, another visitor to Ardrigh, and began to place his antiquarian interests in the overall context of a general belief in the necessity of de-Anglicisation. As Bigger insisted, 'we may not purify the current from the east, but we can stop it and let it recoil on its own shores'.[20] In a similar manner, while he personally 'never breathed or wrote a word that might incite to force or violence',[21] he inspired revolutionaries such as Pearse, Hobson, Denis McCullough and Casement to dedicate their lives to armed struggle. They, in turn, were careful to keep Bigger remote from some of their plans. Hobson noted how he and Casement would wait until Bigger left for his city-centre legal practice before discussing their 'bold projects' at Ardrigh.[22] Despite this sensitivity, such an ideological balancing act could be maintained only for so long and, as I will discuss in Chapter 6, for Bigger its crisis would come with his near disastrous involvement in the Casement affair of 1916. Fortunately, on that occasion as on others, Bigger's influential connections within the ruling political class of unionism protected him. Despite (or perhaps because of) this insurance, Bigger was always willing to push at the limits of what was politically acceptable. His delivery of a particularly Anglophobic and inflammatory lantern slide lecture (which had the deceptively innocent title 'The hills of holy Ireland') to the members of the Linen Hall Library in January 1907 earned him the formal censure of the Library's committee. More daringly again, during an Ardrigh New Year's Eve party in 1913, he marched a group of Irish Volunteers down the Antrim Road while pipers played 'A nation once again'[23] – an act of some irresponsibility given the political climate of the time. As these events suggest, Bigger's politics could be ferocious in their hatred of England and his claim to be disengaged from contemporary events was entirely deceptive.

The most vivid accounts of Bigger and his work have been provided by the Anglo-Irish novelist and autobiographer Shane Leslie. Leslie's own life was tumultuous: a cousin of Winston Churchill, he had been disinherited by his father because of his increasingly hostile attitude to unionism. As his sympathies for Irish nationalism developed, he joined the Gaelic League in 1905, converted to Catholicism in 1908, stood for election on a nationalist ticket in Derry, and subsequently witnessed at first hand the slaughter of World War One. In the midst of these upheavals, Ardrigh remained an alternative home and an important point of stability, and he accompanied Bigger to the Celtic Congress in Brussels in 1911, taking part in a procession that 'entirely mystified'[24] the watching Belgians. The intense admiration that Leslie felt for Bigger was based on his 'glowing faith in everything and everybody Irish' and his 'lack of bitterness, then a scarce virtue in Ireland'.[25] Leslie's broadly autobiographical novel *Doomsland* from 1923 presents perhaps the most detailed portrait of Bigger available, though in the guise of the incidental character Francis Joseph MacNeill:

> At the critical moment a sturdy figure in an Ulster cape and motor-cap strode through the crowd. 'God bless the work!' came in a northern accent. Richard turned questioning. The stranger was searching, he said, for broken pieces of cross. 'I go through Ulster repairing the High Crosses of Ireland. I have hacked their arms from lintels and out of cowsheds, and put together broken pieces of their circle from drains and the backs of chimneys. Sometimes I am years finding the right piece. But I put them up at the end, and if it's on Protestant ground I leave them in charge of the Orangemen.'... He confided that he had a passion for preserving and cataloguing the memorials of the dead, in Ireland. Even his religion, the easiest thing to guess in Ireland, was mysterious. He turned out to be a Protestant with Franciscan leanings! In politics he was a United Irishman. His chief solution for the Irish problem was to temper the dreary Orange drum with Irish war-pipes. In Belfast he presided over all things archaeological, artistic, and archaic (what an Englishman described as the Aran-Islandish and Arrah-na-poguish side of Ireland)....
>
> They walked back to the Hall together, and in soft decisive undertones Mr. MacNeill laid down two theories (whether practical or fanciful Richard was never to discover) – that everything necessary could be made in Ireland; and that any needed plant could be made to grow in Ireland.... 'I tell you there is no such thing as Scotch-Irish, man or mineral. You might as well speak of a Scotch-Irish potato. What comes to Ireland becomes Irish. Besides, Scotland is an Irish dependency beyond the seas. Her language and literature are links between the Gael of Alba and the Gael of Eire.[26]

Although the plot device that allows this intervention creaks uncomfortably, *Doomsland*'s vision of the hyperactive and naively enthusiastic Bigger describes well his combination of political extremism and individual tolerance, while the perception of him as 'a Protestant with Franciscan leanings' indicates something of the manner in which his beliefs utterly isolated him from the vast majority of his co-religionists. Bigger was little concerned by this. Because he invariably understood religion and politics as forms of theatre, he articulated his identification with the United Irishmen through performance, ritual and commemoration, despite the fact that most contemporary Protestants perceived their ideals as an irrelevance. As he once memorably (if incorrectly) remarked, 'with kilts and pipes you can do anything'.[27]

The most vivid example of Bigger's admiration for the legacy of the United Irishmen came in 1902, when what were believed to be the remains of Henry Joy McCracken were discovered during building work on the site of the old graveyard in High Street, Belfast.[28] McCracken had been hanged for his part in the 1798 rebellion at the Battle of Antrim, and his grave had lain unmarked for many years, since part of the graveyard had been sold for building development. On the rediscovery of the remains in the early twentieth century, Robert May, a local woodcarver and antiquarian, collected the bones and took them to Ardrigh for safekeeping, where they remained for seven years. The significance of this for Bigger was overwhelming. As joint steward of McCracken's remains he was able to combine three of his obsessions: his political passion for 1798, archaeology, and his love of ceremony. Bigger handled the remains with a reverence bordering on the veneration of reliquary,[29] and he invited the leading figures of nationalism in Ireland to Ardrigh in order that they might pay their respects. For Cathal O'Byrne, a writer who would constantly return to the example of McCracken for inspiration, their visit was particularly evocative.[30] In 1909, and after discussions with May, the remains were removed from Ardrigh and reinterred alongside the grave of Mary Anne McCracken, McCracken's sister, in Clifton Street cemetery. The political sensitivity of this operation was such that permission for the reburial was granted only on the condition that McCracken's name was not carved on the headstone. For this reason a sealed phial was placed in the coffin in which was enclosed a parchment bearing the words:

> These bones were dug up in the old graveyard in High Street in 1902, and from several circumstances are believed to be those of Henry Joy McCracken. They were reverently treated and were placed here by Robert May, of Belfast, 12 May 1909, when the monument was placed to the memory of his beloved sister.

There was no other indication that McCracken's remains rested there until 1963, when a new stone was erected by the '98 Commemoration Association with the inscription:

> In this grave rest remains believed to be those of Henry Joy McCracken, born 31st August 1767. Executed 17th July 1798.

As the element of doubt expressed on both the stone and the parchment suggests, the authenticity of the bones was, at best, dubious, with some suggesting they were in fact those of an animal. For nationalists, however, the timing of the discovery could hardly have been bettered, in that it reignited the public interest in 1798 originally created by the centenary celebrations, emphasised the continued importance of the United Irishmen's political beliefs for those few Protestants who continued to subscribe to the increasingly embattled ideals of dissenting radicalism, and provided the antiquarian and historical interests within the Northern

Revival with material of powerful resonance.[31] Bigger himself was well aware of the ways in which the events of '98 continued to impose themselves on modern Ireland and wrote of the United Irishmen in his pamphlet *Remember Orr*:

> They may have lived before their age, but the seed they sowed and nourished with their blood has sprung up and borne fruit a thousand-fold, and their actions will ever continue to influence the life of the people until every creed and party within the four seas of Ireland are welded into a common nation, one and indivisible.[32]

Bigger may have believed in this utopian possibility, but it is unlikely that many others shared his views. Instead, the upsurge of interest in McCracken and his comrades occurred within the highly potent context of a renaissance in predominantly Catholic republican activism and, as a result, the Protestant unionists of the North were further alienated from a key element of their history. Only in 1999, with the decision of Belfast City Council to approve a plaque commemorating the site of McCracken's birthplace, were there signs that his politically explosive legacy was slowly being decommissioned.[33]

Another significant figure in Bigger's life was the poet Joseph Campbell. Campbell had been a frequent visitor to Ardrigh since his adolescence and, like Leslie, he found in Bigger a constant source of emotional and practical support. In August 1903 Bigger had accompanied the musician Herbert Hughes and Campbell's brother John on a trip to north Donegal with the intention of transcribing old songs and photographing the lives of the local people. On their return Campbell provided lyrics for many of the airs that Hughes had collected, the outcome being the volume *Songs of Uladh*,[34] a publication funded by Bigger and illustrated by John Campbell. Strongly regional in emphasis and yet displaying no awareness of the characteristically urban nature of much of Ulster, the collection is an archetypal example of the Northern Revival's preoccupations in this period, a movement that, for these few years at least, was being almost entirely subsidised by Bigger. Although *Songs of Uladh* achieved limited commercial success, it contained settings, such as 'My Lagan love', that have since become so popular as to attain something close to cliché status.

Like O'Byrne, whom he resembled in many ways, Campbell's enthusiasm for the Northern Revival in this period was expressed in a number of directions. Alongside his poetry, he played the part of King Brian in the 1904 production by the Ulster Literary Theatre (ULT) of Bulmer Hobson's play *Brian of Banba* and wrote an almost unperformable piece of his own for the company, *The Little Cowherd of Slainge*, in 1905. Of more significance, however, was the publication of his first collection of verse, *The Garden of Bees*,[35] in the same year. According to the author, the mood of the volume was 'a vespertinal one, and something of the fervour on which we young northern folk were buoyed up in those early days of the Revival infuses the lines'.[36] This description serves equally well as the summary of a collection authored by two other habitués of Ardrigh in this year, O'Byrne's and Cahir Healy's *The Lane of the Thrushes: Some Ulster Love Songs*.[37] In both volumes there is an insistence on the objective reality of the spiritual world of Gaelic folklore and a belief that this realm intervenes in the material world in ways both positive and malevolent. If nothing else, such examples suggest the degree to which Ardrigh was in the grip of a Yeats-inspired mysticism during this period, a mood which Milligan and Johnston also reflected in their poetry.

The title *The Garden of Bees* was inspired by Campbell's love for the garden and apiary at Ardrigh – 'a pleasant blend of order and natural wildness' according to Joseph Connolly[38] – and in the poem 'A character' Campbell was able to express something of the gratitude he owed Bigger as his sponsor and mentor:

I think I see him now, as in his prime –
A short-built, thick-set, brown-faced, eager man,
Born of the seed of fighters,
Who, time of old, had fought for the love of man,
And liberty that is the unpledged birthright of man,
And found their touchstone in the simple words –
'Giving and Forgiving'.
A brown-faced, quiet-mannered, *human* man,
Whose noble mind was mirrored in his eye;
Who loved his people and the land that bore him,
And the lowly peasant-people of the land,
And the ardent poets of the land –
Those chosen souls, those dowered visionaries,
Who dream and dream, and dreaming, do.
A worshipper of good in nature;
A lover of song and music;
Menseful in his tastes and quiet in his dress;
Kind to the poor and hearty in his talk;
Fond of a pleasant story;
Fast in his friendships;
A reader of ancient books, a writer, too;
A prop of institutions, traditions, ceremonies;
Combative ever, but offending never;
A dispenser of gifts and hospitalities;
A diviner of thoughts, a patron and friend of boys;

An urger of native effort – ah, the loveliest soul,
The lordliest type of mortal Irish man
It has been, or will be, my lot to know.[39]

The fulsome praise of this panegyric is troubled not only by its oddly elegiac overtones – Bigger, after all was only forty-two at the time of its composition and still had his greatest achievements ahead of him – but also by its reference to Bigger as a 'patron and friend of boys', a phrase which, in the post-Wilde trial period, carried an unfortunate and unmistakable inference. That said, while Campbell was perhaps naive in remarking on this, as with his friend Casement, Bigger's paederastic tendencies were an open secret in Belfast and, according to W. J. McCormack, provoked police attention.[40] Although there is no evidence that any sexual interest in O'Byrne and Campbell was reciprocated, the ceremonials and festivals that Bigger organised at Ardrigh and elsewhere were often characterised by a strong element of youth worship. This tendency was most fully realised in Bigger's organisation of an eccentric and elaborate youth group called the Neophytes, in the early years of the century. Dominated by rituals, costumes and pseudonyms, it was, in Dudgeon's words, a form of 'intellectual Boy Scout troop'.[41] This aspect of Bigger's character was another reason why his reputation would be greatly threatened by the revelations arising from the Casement trial in 1916, and is a possible factor in his decision to adopt a much lower public profile in the years after partition.

Bigger, then, might have had good reason not to be especially grateful to Campbell for his tribute but, when viewed from another perspective, 'A character' is simply an example of a young poet experimenting with a traditional form of eulogy. Bigger performs the role of the muse and, as such, the listing of his accomplishments becomes gradually less important to the poem than his function in inspiring the verse itself. Alongside this, the poem is uneasily conscious of Bigger's Ulster Protestant lineage, and the reference to him as 'Born of the seed of fighters' contrasts with the instinctive sectarianism that would typify much of Campbell's later work.[42] Although Campbell would always remain on good terms with Bigger and would continue to visit Ardrigh, the poem also constituted a valediction, as Campbell's increasingly republican sympathies and desire for career advancement would eventually take him away from Belfast and sunder him from Bigger's immediate influence.[43] It was left to his son, Flann Campbell, to close the circle some eighty years later with his affectionate portrayal of Bigger and the Ardrigh coterie in his pioneering book *The Dissenting Voice: Protestant Democracy in Ulster from Plantation to Partition*.[44]

As I have already suggested, in a lot of ways Bigger was not party to many of the discussions and decisions that took place at Ardrigh. He imagined his own role as a facilitator, and his house, as Flann Campbell has noted,[45] to be a kind of informal university for any who wished to study Irish Ireland. For this reason, Ardrigh played a number of different roles. For many, it was seen as a place merely of sentimental nationalism, the location from which Bigger would plan his latest commemoration or memorial, and, in Bardon's words, 'the northern focal point for those who turned their backs on their urban, industrial environment and took instead a romantic, almost mystical, view of the Gaelic past'.[46] In these terms, Ardrigh was little more than a refuge for the scattered remnants of the Northern Protestant dissenting tradition: a group who found comfort in each other's company and who enjoyed dwelling endlessly on the betrayal of the ideals of the United Irishmen. In the midst of this nostalgia, however, other contacts and plans were forged. For republican and nationalist activists such as Eoin MacNeill, Joseph Connolly, Denis McCullough and Bulmer Hobson, Ardrigh was a safe meeting place, and it was also one of the few locations where agitators from the South, such as Maud Gonne and Patrick Pearse, could encounter their Northern counterparts. For Connolly, especially, Ardrigh was primarily important because of the 'interesting contacts and associations it gave us'.[47] Bigger may not necessarily have supported the substance of some of the discussions that took place under his roof, but he was seemingly quite happy to let them take place, and the general perception in Belfast of Ardrigh as a home of harmless eccentrics suited everybody's purpose.

Bigger termed the gatherings that he held at Ardrigh on Saturday and Sunday evenings his 'firelight school'. These informal meetings were attended at various times by nearly all the major figures of nationalist Ireland and Connolly's memoirs provide a detailed account of an evening's typical activities:

> It was customary for the 'intimates' to gather inside the house after the garden party was over and the passing guests had dispersed, and in the big library and on the landing adjoining it have a real céilidhe until midnight or later. The library was what a friend of mine aptly described as a 'noble room'. It ran the full length of one side of the first floor. It was lined from floor to ceiling with books with occasional 'breaks' for pictures, sketches, and memorials and mementoes of historical interest. There was a big wide fireplace and hearth and on this blazed the heaped up fire of turf and logs. With the rugs rolled back and the polished floor cleared there was ample space for forty or fifty people to dance comfortably and still have plenty of room for the less active to sit around and talk and argue and joke to their hearts' content. We enjoyed many big evenings and nights in 'Ardri', and

> almost equally the innumerable quiet evenings with the wonderful library at our command or the quiet talks with some of those whose shadows must still hover around the corners of that grand room.[48]

The range of performers and guests at these gatherings was often impressive. Flann Campbell records in *The Dissenting Voice*[49] that a typical evening would consist of music by the famous *uilleann* piper Francis McPeake[50] and a recital by Joseph Campbell, while the audience might include such figures as Casement on leave from the Congo or Douglas Hyde visiting from Dublin. O'Byrne's involvement in the night's entertainment was always significant and another account of the 'firelight school', probably again by Joseph Connolly, demonstrates the magnetism of his personality:

> I think of him in the library at Ard Righ. Our genial host, Frank Bigger, in his armchair at the big table. Roger Casement is deep sunk in his favourite armchair. There are a few of the boys up from Dublin, Con O'Friel is there from Ballymoney. Carl Hardebeck is rolling his pebble in his restless fingers and Frank McPeake has brought his pipes. There is good talk and gay laughter and then we have music. Everybody takes his turn but above all there is Cathal. There is no end to his repertoire. Gay songs and sad songs and, of course, his stories. We have all heard his 'Battle of Scarva' but we insist and Cathal tells it again. One night he sang the 'Ballad of Barbara Allen'. It was the first time we had heard it but I remember that Roger asked him to sing it again.... It was good to be alive and to be young then and there were countless happy evenings and week-ends spent in Bigger's hospitable home and garden.[51]

The 'Battle of Scarva' was not a song but rather an extended piece of storytelling based on the 'sham fight at Scarva', an anecdote that had first appeared in Eleanor Alexander's *Lady Anne's Walk*, from 1903.[52] Described in that novel as 'a veritable passion play', it describes a series of farcical events taking place during the annual commemoration of the Battle of the Boyne from the perspective of 'Tummus', a Protestant labourer on Alexander's estate. O'Byrne's version of this became his most requested performance and he records delivering it and gaining a hysterical reaction at the Abbey Theatre in Dublin and many times at the Ulster Hall (which was 'crammed to the doors [and] rocking with laughter'[53]) and the Old Museum in Belfast. It is likely that it was one of the sources of inspiration for Gerald MacNamara's play for the ULT *Thompson in Tír-na-nÓg* from 1912,[54] and so closely did O'Byrne become associated with the piece that he continued to perform it well into the 1930s.[55]

O'Byrne, however, was more than just Ardrigh's court jester and, like Connolly's accounts, his recollections of the 'firelight school' are haunted by an awareness of the anguish that many of its members would subsequently endure. While *As I Roved Out* describes a 'great gathering of Gaels' at Ardrigh, including Lord Ashbourne, Alice Stopford Green, William Bulfin, Shane Leslie and Kuno Meyer,[56] he provided a more detailed record of a particularly emotional Ardrigh evening in an article for the *Capuchin Annual*, 'Roger Casement's ceilidhe'.[57] The ceilidh had been planned by Bigger as a homecoming party for Casement, who, still suffering from the malaria he had contracted in the Putamayo Basin, was placed 'close to the warmth of the blazing hearth, on a heaped-up pile of cushions'. Written from the perspective of 1946, the essay attempts to recall him as he was 'before the clouds began to gather above the heads of the true men of Erin, and before their shadows fell to darken our own particular pathway', but the hope remains chimerical. Instead, Casement is presented as a figure who had already begun to make the transition from life into death and whose actions could be understood only in the context of his later execution:

> Thus, on that wintry night, in the great library at Ard Righ, to the music of the harp, and in the ruddy glow of the peat fire, we sang the old songs that Roger Casement loved, songs telling of the cruelty of hard-hearted 'Barbara Allen', and particularly the lovely old lullaby 'The Castle of Dromore', which was his favourite of all the songs, the one he was to recall, with the memory of our singing of it, on his last night on earth, and to mention in his last letter from his prison cell.

O'Byrne's perception that Casement's journey to the gallows began long before 1916 is one that Casement himself also shared. As Leslie remarks, even during his Ardrigh years, Casement was a 'sad and goaded figure',[58] prone to bouts of melancholy and self-imposed isolation. Certainly, Casement's thoughts frequently turned to Ardrigh during his final days in Pentonville Prison and he placed his memories of that time within the overall narrative of an unyielding destiny.

As O'Byrne's account indicates, his friendship with Casement was significant and was based on his attempts to convert Casement to Catholicism. 'Roger Casement's ceilidhe' describes the ultimate success of this proselytising, but can say little else about Casement's unhappy post-Ardrigh life. For O'Byrne, the ceilidh remains a 'hoarded' memory, an appropriate term for a writer who, even after twenty-five years, was still unable to adjust to the failure of the Ardrigh coterie's aspirations to national unification, the existence of the Northern Irish state and the deaths of his friends. The mnemonics of O'Byrne's remembrance were shared by Connolly, who, in his obituary tribute to O'Byrne in 1957, recalls meeting O'Byrne in Chicago during the 1920s at a house-warming party for a priest. As 'JC' records:

> We had songs and talk and argument and everything that made for happiness, but when Cathal sang 'The Gartan Mother's Lullaby' and 'Barbara Allen' my mind went back to Ard Righ and our great friend and very gallant gentleman whose bones were buried in the prison grave at Pentonville.
>
> Cathal has gone and we will pray for him but I like to think that already he has met and embraced all his old associates and friends and that he may even be repeating the ballad of 'Barbara Allen' for one whom we all loved.[59]

Even when commemorating the life of O'Byrne it seems that, for Connolly at least, the ghost of Roger Casement continued to beat at the door.

Despite Bigger's emphasis on culture and socialising, in the years leading up to partition Ardrigh could not remain separate from the increasingly tense political atmosphere of the city it overlooked. One frequent visitor to the house was Denis McCullough, a member of the Gaelic League and the Gaelic Athletic Association, co-founder (with Bulmer Hobson) of the Dungannon Clubs and, for a short period from 1915, president of the Supreme Council of the Irish Republican Brotherhood (IRB). Bigger had helped McCullough establish his musical instrument manufacturing business in Belfast in 1909 and the pair had developed a strong friendship. McCullough also found a close confidant in O'Byrne, who was the best man at his wedding in 1916 and was converted by McCullough to a belief in the necessity of armed insurrection. Despite a period of imprisonment under the Defence of the Realm Act from August to November 1915, McCullough had presided over the IRB meeting at which the decision to hold the Rising had taken place, but because of poor communications and the growing impatience of Pearse and James Connolly, he became increasingly removed from the planning of the operation. It was partly for these reasons, and because of the general uncertainty that surrounded the days leading up to the Rising, that he returned in disarray with his men to Belfast on the Sunday before the Rising (see Chapter 5): an occurrence that may not have adversely affected the overall outcome of the operation in Dublin but which bore unfortunate symbolic overtones. He was arrested on the following Friday and endured a lengthy period in prison. On his release he resumed his activities on behalf of the IRB and used Bigger's home as a safe house. As Dixon has described, it was as a result of this that security forces searching for McCullough raided Ardrigh:

> Bigger, however, with his wide circle of contacts, was tipped off and was able to telephone his home from his office and warn Bridget, his housekeeper, to get McCullough out. This she accomplished with her usual efficiency, hauling the young man out of bed, bundling his clothes in a bag and then literally pushing him through a hole in the hedge on to Fortwilliam golf course as the security forces arrived at the front door.

> McCullough successfully made his escape, and Bigger had the hole in the hedge made into a little archway, and in the archway he placed a wooden cross in memory of Denis McCullough's delivery.[60]

Had Bridget not acted so promptly the consequences for Bigger and for Ardrigh's fragile cultural freedom would have been extremely serious. As it turned out, McCullough managed to escape to Dublin and Bigger gained another opportunity to indulge his fondness for memorials and ceremony. However, the anecdote illustrates the extent to which Bigger was always able to remain at one remove from the revolutionary violence that his commitment to the ideal of Irish Ireland inspired in others. In this way he provides a vivid example of the manner in which the cultural preoccupations of the Revival became, whether directly or indirectly, inevitably connected to the possibility of armed insurrection.

The most tangible way in which Bigger enabled such activity was through his membership of the Gaelic League and it was as one of the major Northern representatives of that organisation that he exerted a powerful influence over the generation of nationalist revolutionaries who would lead Ireland into rebellion. The Gaelic League had been founded in 1893 and one of its founders, Eoin MacNeill,[61] an Antrim-born historian, was a frequent visitor to Ardrigh. The League was – at least in its early years – a predominantly urban and lower-middle-class phenomenon committed to the revival of the language and wary of aligning itself with any political faction. Its first president, Douglas Hyde, scrupulously maintained this position and it was not until a concerted effort by the IRB to infiltrate its committee structures in the first decade of the new century that it became more readily associated with an unequivocally nationalist political position, a development which led to Hyde's resignation as president in 1915. Belfast's first Gaelic League branch was inaugurated in August 1895 with Bigger as one of the founding patrons and a Protestant unionist, Dr John St Clair Boyd, as its first president. Others present at the first meeting included Milligan (who supported the League through the pages of the *Shan Van Vocht*[62]) and MacNeill himself. The branch had developed as a logical result of the interest in the language generated by the Irish classes held at the Belfast Naturalists' Field Club and statistics suggest that its growth across Ulster was impressive and swift. Roger Blaney records that there were 13,025 people attending Irish classes in Ulster by December 1903,[63] while Padraig Ó Snodaigh's research[64] indicates that the number of Irish-speakers in the territory that is now Northern Ireland doubled during the period 1891–1911. In Belfast itself, Ó Snodaigh states that there were nine branches of the League in 1899, while Gerry Adams places the total at twenty-six, with a strong concentration around the area of the Falls Road.[65]

Bigger could certainly have taken much of the credit for this growth. His energy on behalf of the League's activities was seemingly inexhaustible and the rationale and objectives of the organisation provided a focus for his disparate range of enthusiasms and beliefs. He served on the committee for the second Gaelic League *Feis Ceoil* (music festival), held in Belfast in 1898, acted as patron for the Belfast College of Irish, founded in 1905 and based in St Mary's Hall, became president of the Belfast branches of the League (*Coiste Ceanntair*) and was a member of the *Coiste Gnotha* (the executive committee) of the national organisation. According to O'Byrne, it was during his term as Belfast president that Bigger 'decided that the Gaels had stayed quite long enough in the lanes and back streets, and, as nothing was too good for the Gaelic League, they should have a "big show" in the Ulster Hall'.[66] O'Byrne acted as organiser, stage manager and chief attraction for the event and subsequently judged it to have been 'a great success'. With his combination of commitment to the movement and private wealth, Bigger funded a number of such eye-catching initiatives and his presence in the movement became increasingly significant. He was, for instance, an important influence on Pearse during the early years of the century and in 1907 the pair toured the Gaeltacht areas in Donegal, Sligo, Leitrim, Mayo and Galway in Bigger's touring car under the title 'Gaelic League motor party'.[67] Driven by Bigger's faithful chauffeur Tommy, according to Bigger even the car itself was 'burnished like Cuchulainn's Chariot'.[68] Bigger inspired Pearse's commitment to the Irish language and the institutional necessity of the Gaelic League, and it was through him that Pearse became aware of the extent of Northern nationalist radical activism.

Some examination of the range of Bigger's other work on behalf of the Gaelic League reveals the different fronts on which the organisation was fighting in order to bring popularity and respect to the language. Along with the novelist and fellow member of the central governing body James Owen Hannay (who used the pseudonym George Birmingham), in 1906 he addressed Queen's University in Belfast, an institution which, in Hannay's words, 'seemed an unlikely place for Gaelic League propaganda to succeed'.[69] Both were respectable members of the Protestant community and Hannay's perception of his own role – that he could best 'serve the League by writing in its defence and speaking (though only in English) in places where perhaps other members would scarcely have got a hearing'[70] – was surely true for Bigger as well. The men had much in common, and it was appropriate that Hannay dedicated his novel about

James Hope and the 1798 uprising, *The Northern Iron*, to his Belfast colleague.[71] Perhaps encouraged by his foray into Queen's, in May 1909 Bigger formed part of a deputation to the University to lobby for a chair in Gaelic language and literature.[72] Despite its wariness about such subjects, Queen's eventually agreed and a suitably qualified candidate, the Reverend Canon Feardorcha Ó Conaill, was appointed. The League offered to pay half Ó Conaill's salary for five years if he was, in turn, made a full professor. Queen's initially agreed to this but later reversed the decision – an act which provoked Ó Conaill into publishing a long satire on the subject (written, devastatingly, in the meter of *Hiawatha*) in the *Ulster Guardian*.[73]

As well as taking the League's work into the institutions of civil society, Bigger was also mindful of its role in providing popular and improving entertainment to the people of Ulster and it was in this area that the Belfast branches of the League were most active. As the diary columns of the *Irish News* during the first fifteen years of the century indicate, the League provided not just weekly and fortnightly branch meetings but a whole range of concerts, talks and day trips. These were often only tangentially connected to the language question, as an advertisement for an *Aonach* to be held at St Mary's Hall in December 1912 reveals.[74] Organised by a sub-committee of the Belfast League, the event was to be opened by Bigger, while Milligan had responsibility for 'promoting the special historical tableaux and Irish plays' that formed a major part of the entertainment. Alongside this, 'a number of very interesting competitions have been arranged, some of which include best seed cake, best sultana cake, best griddle cake, and most artistically dressed doll'. As this suggests – in Belfast at least – the social function of the League and its role in promoting the ideal of Irish Ireland became an important aspect of its activities. Indeed, fluency in the language was by no means an essential prerequisite for membership and some of its most energetic advocates (such as O'Byrne) remained essentially monolingual. It can be argued that this was, if anything, of benefit to the Belfast branches of the League if only because the tensions between those who wished to promote the Ulster variety of Irish and those who resisted this regional emphasis often threatened to cause a schism within those elements of the League's membership that focused solely on the language issue itself.

Bigger's most important achievement on behalf of Gaelic Ireland – and perhaps the most significant Northern Revival event of all – was the June 1904 Feis in the Glens of Antrim. Funded by Bigger, organised in part by Casement (although hardly 'Casement's Feis', as it has sometimes been termed) and attended by such figures as Milligan, Green, Hobson,

MacNeill and Joseph Campbell, the Feis was by far the biggest such event that Ireland had ever witnessed, and an event that, according to the *Irish News*, 'promise[d] to be unique in the annals of the Irish revival'.[75] Competitions were held in such diverse areas as recitation, essays on history, antiquities and cottage industries, Gaelic conversation and poetry, Gaelic names of places and things, leaping and whistling; there were over 700 entries. The *Irish News* supported the event with enthusiasm and reported with feverish anticipation:

> In almost every Glen men who understand the scope and breadth of the revival movement have gone amongst the people. Everywhere they have succeeded in drawing the attention of the people to a movement that aims at the development of the intellectual powers of the people, making for them a happier and more elevated life, a life charged with restless energy and much thought.... A day of promise for the people of the Antrim Glens is at hand, a day that marks the beginning of an era in the development of native thought and effort, and one that must exercise a remarkable influence in the life of the Glens people. A movement brimful of great good for every section in the community has been brought to the very eve of victory.[76]

Such evangelical sentiments might have served as the Northern Revival's general manifesto. As the newspaper expressed it in a later piece, 'the organisers of the Feis have united the sentimental and the practical sides of the revival movement in a way that commands admiration and could not fail to secure support'.[77] However, the Feis also encapsulated some of the enduring tensions also found in the movement. Funded with Protestant money but with minimal Protestant participation, the Feis self-consciously asserted the Glens as a Gaelic location to rival the west of Ireland (despite suffering from what was termed 'an annual infliction of Lancashire tourists'[78]) – although many of the actual inhabitants of the Glens appeared to need some tuition in, what was termed, 'the ways of the Gael'. At the same time, the Feis maintained what was perhaps a more distinctly Northern emphasis on economic regeneration (the full title of the event was 'The Gaelic and Industrial Festival') and it was significant that the event's most celebrated guest was Sir Horace Plunkett, the pioneer of agricultural and rural industrial cooperation in Ireland. After all, as the *Northern Whig* reported of the event, 'there is no reason why a man should not be keen in business *and* an admirer of Oisin and the tales of the Red Branch Knights'.[79]

It appears that nearly every aspect of the event was shaped by Bigger's instinct for symbolic detail. The land on which the Feis was held belonged to Ada McNeill, a member of a prominent unionist family and one of the organisers. It was:

> well selected on the spacious flat grounds lying at the foot of one of the most beautiful Irish valleys under the shadow of the castle of *Uaim Dearg*, the great red bay stronghold, held by the McDonnell's in the days of their struggle for supremacy on the wild Antrim seaboard.[80]

The competitors, perceived by the *Irish News* as the 'Irish of the Irish',[81] were drawn from the nine surrounding Glens – an area inhabited by about 1000 native Irish-speakers – and were supplemented by a steam-tug load of Rathlin Islanders, whose travel expenses were paid for by Casement. What awaited them on arrival was, by any measure, remarkable:

> At the entrance to the village where the road leads over the old stone bridge towards the hall a streamer bearing an inscription in Gaelic, of which the translation is, 'May the Gaelic live in the Glens', stretches between the summits of two tall poles, wreathed with ribbons of yellow and green, and bearing shields and other devices. Over the entrance to the hall itself artistically executed lettering proclaims that 'Tá na naoi nGleanna dúisithe ag an bPíbereacht' (the nine glens are awakened at the piping). It was fitting that as the eye rested on this inscription the ear should be saluted with the sound of 'the pibroch in the glen' but one was not prepared on turning a corner of the building to find two pipers and a drummer of the time of Seaghan an Diomais marching up and down the green field stirring the sunlit air with the war march of 'O'Dhomnaill abu'. To all intents and purposes that was the sight which presented itself. The costumes were of a cut and colour which must often have greeted the eyes of the proud O'Neill, and the three stalwart wearers suited the attire and looked the parts to perfection.[82]

On the Thursday morning, the Feis began with a procession from Cushendall to Waterfoot. Led by pipers in sixteenth-century costumes designed by Bigger,[83] it consisted of hurling teams, banners of old family clans with inscriptions in Irish, a number of choirs and, finally, the bulk of the competitors. That said, as the increasingly exasperated *Irish News* correspondent observed, the procession 'might have been better organised', and the choirs' attempts to sing songs in the native language 'were few and faint-hearted'[84] – a sign, perhaps, that the Feis's motto, 'May the Gaelic live in the Glens', was an expression more of hope than of expectation. Despite this, over 4000 people attended the Feis and the listing of the winners of the various competitions extended over a number of issues of the *Irish News*. Although the people of the Glens may have forgotten something of their Gaelic inheritance, the Feis did reveal the extent of the area's industrial and craft movement. As Plunkett declared in a speech at the Feis's evening concert, 'there was scarcely a cottage in the whole countryside that could not find something which it could do, and something in which it could succeed'.[85]

The Feis, then, succeeded because its characteristics and emphases were closely matched to the talents and needs of the community in which it was based. Although in Belfast, as the *Northern Whig* suggested, it was 'regarded as more of an experiment than anything else',[86] its practical benefit to the Glens was considerable. If this suggests the event was a distinctly Northern phenomenon, in other ways it shared anxieties found in the Irish Revival movement as a whole – particularly an acute sensitivity about the way its activities might be viewed by outsiders. In this regard, the one 'unpleasant incident' that took place during the festival was significant. As the *Irish News* reported:

> There could not have been less than 4,000 persons present at mid-day when the Feis was at its height, and despite such a great attendance everything passed off quietly. There was only one unpleasant incident during the whole day and it, after all, was very trivial. After an item in the dancing competition, whilst the platform was bare and the piper still playing a drunken woman, one of a band of thimble-riggers in the vicinity, got upon the platform and proceeded to caper grotesquely about. A frock-coated individual in the crowd was proceeding to snap-shot the scene, when some of the Gaels near by objected. The woman was ejected, much to the disgust of the 'camera fiend' who explained that he merely 'wanted a snap shot for an English magazine.' It turned out afterwards that he had paid the woman to give a stage Irish exhibition so that he might be able to supply the readers of the 'English magazine' according to what he considered to be their requirements.[87]

The vulnerability of the Revival movement's identity politics is evident, as is the extent to which the ideal of the Gael had to be carefully policed. The Feis had sought to find in the Glens the essence of a Gaelic tradition it had already declared to be pre-existent, so it was beholden on the people of the Glens to maintain the perception that the Feis was merely a confirmation of their own lived folk practices and beliefs. This, of course, was no longer the case; indeed, if it had been then there would have been little need for the Feis in the first instance and the very concept of a revival would have been problematic. Understood in these terms, the Feis revealed one of the central paradoxes within nationalist identity formations: the fact that they need constantly to reaffirm that which they must assume is already securely lodged in the hearts of their adherents. It was into this delicate system of compromises that the drunken thimble-rigger capered. In making a deal with the English photographer, the woman was certainly demonstrating the skills of initiative and local enterprise the Feis more generally was hoping to promote, but this, in itself, was clearly not where the insult lay. Instead, it was her act of mimicry that caused offence: the fact that the stunt took place within the same space as those accepted versions of Irishness that the Feis wanted to promote. For this reason, perhaps the dilemma encountered was one too sensitive for the *Irish News* to approach directly: the possibility that the 'stage Irish exhibition' required by the English magazine was uncomfortably close to the staged Gaelicism of the Feis's ratified competitions. The irony of this is, of course, unavoidable. The Feis went to the Glens to find authenticity, but in this instance, at least, the authentic refused the definition. At such moments it is possible to see how the performance of identity politics in this period could so easily turn into a mode of self-referential camp, a fraught and implausible procedure more appropriate to the music hall than to Bigger's earnest hopes for cultural renaissance.

Despite this, and as the *Irish News* commented, the incident 'after all, was very trivial'. The Feis in the Glens was, perhaps, the high-water mark of Northern Revival activity and also constituted the most successful extension into the social realm of Bigger's Ardrigh coterie. In turn, the event had a galvanising effect on many of those responsible for its organisation. For instance, Casement, who along with Hobson was staying at Ada McNeill's Cushendun House for the duration of the event, had served on the organising committee, funded and distributed some of the prizes (including one of ten shillings or a pair of gloves for the winner of the 'best dressed boy'), and was inspired by the celebrations to a much greater involvement in Irish culture and politics. Joseph Campbell also played a full part in the running of some of the competitions and it was at the Feis that he first met the poet Padraic Colum, his lifelong friend and a significant influence on his work.[88] Moreover, the Gaelic League (in whose name the Feis was held) gained considerable credibility in Ulster from the event, persuading even the often sceptical *Northern Whig* to recognise that although 'the Gaelic League has been guilty of some absurdities, these are incidental to every new movement, and are probably more indicative of healthy growth and vitality than staid and dull respectability would be'.[89] The Feis, then, was proof that the League could still operate, in the words of Plunkett, as 'a common platform upon which every man who wished well to Ireland, and was ready to help Ireland, could meet and work shoulder to shoulder',[90] while the *Irish News* commented:

> to make the people of Ireland self-respecting and to teach them to know themselves is the work of the Gaelic League, and the success of the Feis of the Nine Glens is only another proof from amongst many all over the country that the work of the League is bearing fruit.[91]

Such idealism would become ever more difficult to uphold as the century progressed. From this point onwards, the League became increasingly aligned with uncompromising nationalist politics and Plunkett's dream of the organisation as a 'common platform' was sacrificed. However, the major beneficiaries of the event remained the people of the Glens themselves. In subsequent years the Feis was maintained by the Gaelic League, and it has been an annual event to this day. That the Glens are now recognised as a centre for traditional music has much to do with Bigger's original vision and constitutes one of his more enduring legacies.

If the founding of the Feis was one of Bigger's greatest achievements, another was undoubtedly the restoration of Shane's Castle at Ardglass in 1911, a project that, by its very magnitude, demonstrated Bigger's considerable personal wealth and influence. Described in his memorial volume, *In Remembrance*, as 'one of the most notable of his many laudable deeds and the one of which he was proudest',[92] the venture came to symbolise the aspirations of the Northern Revival in its entirety and was a potent statement of historical and cultural rebirth. A four-storey fifteenth-century tower-house, the castle had been built and owned by the Jordan family, from which it took its original (and now restored) name, Jordan's Castle. While under the ownership of Simon Jordan, a merchant, it had withstood a three-year siege during the Tyrone Rebellion in Ulster, which was lifted only with the sea-borne arrival of the Lord Deputy Mountjoy in 1601. This aspect of the castle's history would hardly have been pleasing to Bigger and, according to O'Byrne, on taking possession of the property, 'the first thing he did was to change its name from Jordan's Tower – as it had been called by some English upstart – to Castle Seaghan'.[93] The repossession was complete when Bigger subsequently inserted the O'Neill badge into the masonry above the castle's main entrance, an act which led a puzzled Richard Hayward to observe in 1938:

> but Shane O'Neill never had anything to do with Jordan's Castle, and even a more powerful O'Neill, the great Earl of Tyrone, failed in his attempts to dislodge the courageous Jordan.... It seems curious that a keen antiquarian like Francis Joseph Bigger should have sought to obscure the well-authenticated origins of this interesting structure.[94]

Lawlor, a long-term detractor of Bigger and his methods, was more forthright still in his condemnation, describing Bigger's restoration as an 'ill-advised attempt to falsify history', which deserved no less than to be 'relegated to oblivion'.[95]

As Bigger intended the castle's function to be, in the words of O'Byrne, 'a hosting place for the Gaels of the North',[96] his elision of much of its history was scarcely surprising and, indeed, the whole project was imagined as an act of reclamation, an attempt to assert a benign Gaelic authority on the village over which it loomed. Before Bigger owned it, the castle had been sold under the Land Purchase Act and was earmarked for demolition to make way for a row of shops. It had lain in a derelict (if not entirely ruined) state for a considerable period and 'was roofless, doorless and windowless, the haunt of rooks and jackdaws, with all the winds that blow echoing through its four walls'.[97] This, however, did not discourage Bigger and his own (anonymous and third-person) account of the restoration indicates something of his motivation for undertaking the project:

> And so it came that the old walls must go to the hammer. Their ghosts and past history were not reserved by the conditions of the sale, and so went to the purchaser. He speedily roofed and floored the 'pallace', as an old record calls it, and made it habitable and fit for plenishing, after the big wood fires had been lighted for some time. Gaily the sparks chased each other up the wide stone chimneys to the topmost tower, as if there had never been a break since Norman baron or Irish Chieftain had warmed his limbs under the cross tree.... Life had come back to the old castle: plants and flowers and birds and insects recognised this first with their truly natural instinct.[98]

The historical amnesia displayed in this description is significant. In imagining the castle as a symbol of continuity, Bigger overlooks its previous function as a centre of English and Anglo-Irish power.[99] Rather, he dreams that his ownership restores the building to its proper 'natural' relationship with the surrounding landscape. This was a typical element of the Revivalist imagination; the castle's restoration became an exercise in the recovery of a submerged collective memory and an attempt to make whole that which had become increasingly fragmented. Inspired by the Irish Ireland movement and Plunkett's belief in the need for indigenous crafts and industry, Bigger insisted that the materials used in the rebuilding were all of Irish provenance. Within three months the castle was made habitable and filled with locally built furniture and fittings. O'Byrne's overawed account of this refurbishment records in breathless detail such features as the rush-strewn floor of the banqueting hall, 'a great circular iron candlestick, made to hold at least a dozen candles', the huge kitchen table made from 'an immense oaken log', the ancient firearms and weapons hung on the walls, the retirement room 'exquisitely furnished with Donegal rugs and hangings, costly furniture, antiques and rare pictures', a life-size painting of 'Seaghan the Proud' by Harry Morrow, and, bizarrely, a chair from the old Downpatrick Gaol, upon which condemned prisoners would sit before their execution. Appropriately, the flag of O'Neill flew from the high battlements.

The habitués of Ardrigh were all frequent visitors to the castle[100] and were clearly inspired by the symbolic resonance of Bigger's act. Alongside O'Byrne's and Bigger's articles about the project, an extraordinary account of the building's essentially Gaelic heritage and its restoration appears in Alice Stopford Green's work of nationalist history *The Old Irish World*.[101] This constitutes by far the fullest record of the events in Ardglass during 1911 and its description of the celebrations to mark the castle's opening betrays a feverish excitement:

> There was no moon, and a gale was blowing down the Irish Sea – a wind from the North. A little platform was set against the west wall of the castle. A beacon flamed on one of the towers, and the ceremony began with a display of limelight pictures on the wall. I was in the middle of an audience packed as tight as men could stand in the castle yard and across the wide street.... It seemed as if thousands had gathered under the resplendent stars. 'I do not mean to show you,' said Mr Bigger, 'China or Japan; I mean to show you Ardglass'. The audience went wild with delight to see their fishermen and women, their local celebrities, the boats laden with fish, the piles on the pier, the Donegal girls packing them, the barrels rolled out to the tramp steamers. But the delight reached its utmost height at views of the sea taken from a boat out fishing, the dawn of the day, the early flight of birds, the swell of the great waters. The appeal of beauty brought a rich answer from the Irish crowd.[102]

Even when judged by Bigger's high standards, the strategy of this ceremonial was ingenious. In reflecting Ardglass back at itself, Bigger's technology recast the familiar landscape as a place both strange and yet more beautiful; this was an act of aesthetic distancing that cleared an imaginative space for his determined attempt to reassert what he insisted was the essentially Gaelic character of the community. In this he had a willing ally in Green, whose energetic propagandising on his behalf explicated the emblematic significance of the unfolding events. After the picture show, the crowd was presented with a display of Irish dancing and singing, 'but the great moment of all came when a huge Irish flag was flung out on the night wind from the Columba tower'. She continues:

> I have never seen so magic a sight. Lights blazed from the castle-roof, rockets flamed across the sky, and in the midst suddenly appeared like a vision among the host of stars (for no flag-staff could be seen against the night-sky) a gleaming golden harp hanging secure in immensity, crossed and re-crossed by balls and flames of fire, so that it seemed to escape only by a miracle.[103]

As with Bigger's Feis in the Glens seven years previously, according to Green the inhabitants of Ardglass responded enthusiastically to Bigger's ceremonies, entering the castle to pray in the oratory and to sing 'songs of famine, emigration, lamentation and woe' in the old guardroom. The next day the parish priest preached twice on the subject of the restoration and reminded the villagers 'to hold it sacred, and to act with courtesy and good breeding when they entered it'. The castle remained open to the villagers afterwards and the moral of their symbolic occupation was unavoidable:

> they had been given that which every Irishman lacks – something of their own. No Englishman can picture to himself that lack. He has never had it. But with us it is an old story.[104]

For Green this constituted nothing less than a moment of revolutionary potential, and her account concludes with an overheard prophecy of national liberation uttered by an Ardglass fisherman: 'It's comin'.... We're too long held in chains'.[105] Her optimism was, at least in the short term, misplaced. Indeed, by 1913 the Ardglass branch of the Gaelic League had ceased its activities, a state of affairs that, as the *Irish News* censoriously commented, 'was not creditable to them'.[106]

In the years that followed the restoration, Bigger remained keenly aware of Shane's Castle's emblematic significance, and encouraged nationalist organisations to visit Ardglass to inspect his work. The Gaelic League held regular summer schools there while the Belfast Field Club studied the castle's antiquarian artefacts.[107] One such trip took place in 1913, when the 'Dawn of Freedom' branch of the United Irish League (UIL) visited the castle on an excursion. Bigger was unable to receive them there because of a prior engagement, but he did leave a letter which was read to the meeting as they gathered on the battlements:

> The restoration of this old castle and its capture from destruction and unworthy hands has been a symbol of our race and country at this time. I have tried to preserve all that is worthy of the past, and utilise it to the advantage of the present. A people without a past and without a language cannot be a nation in the full sense of that term, as our Irish people claim to be. We have both. We should treasure and preserve them and hand them on to posterity.... I hope that you will be pleased to say that, in re-claiming and re-edifying these old historic walls of Castle Shane, an effort has at least been made on the right lines for the encouragement and education of our people on full national ideals.[108]

The thought progression here is typical of Bigger's political imagination, in that his purchase and rebuilding of the castle is contextualised both within the public realm and as part of an Irish narrative of dispossession and restoration. In this Bigger himself remains both a facilitator of the public good – a reminder of his nineteenth-century liberal Protestant antiquarian inheritance – and, more curiously, a living embodiment of the continuity of a historical ideal. To condense what is an inevitably complex argument, nineteenth-century antiquarianism was ultimately dependent on the distance between the scholarly method employed and the cultural material investigated, as this distance meant the whirl of contemporary politics could remain separate from the historical fragments under scrutiny. As a result, many of the key antiquarians in Ireland during this period (and thus the prophets of the Revival itself) could remain resolutely unionist in their personal politics. Traces of this dissociation are certainly apparent in Bigger's apprehension of the past, but at the same time the increasingly evident contradictions of that position forced him to recognise the continuities between cultural loss and contemporary calls for reparation. What can be witnessed in Bigger's own work, then, is an often bewildering mix of historical, aesthetic and political discourses as he moves from observation to incarnation, or, to put this in more concrete terms, from the objectivity of a scholarly investigation of Ardglass's ruins to having himself photographed in the rebuilt castle dressed as the great O'Neill. That this created an influential and galvanising form of popular history, however, cannot be doubted, and Bigger's work can be seen as providing the kind of 'individualised' history demanded by Charles Gavan Duffy in 1893.[109] Certainly, the effects of Bigger's vision on individuals could be quite intoxicating. Observe, for instance, the thoughts of a 'Dawn of Freedom' UIL branch member who lingered at the top of the tower on that afternoon in 1913 after his colleagues had departed:

> As I gazed at the entire scene a subtle rapture filled me. Here alone on the shattered battlements, hallowed with holy phantoms and illustrious shades, and around which the winds of heaven sing a perpetual requiem, I began to think of Ireland, her martyrs, and her cause. I felt as I never did before the unutterable pathos of Ireland's long exile from the temples of justice. On every stone around me decay had written defeat. Was I in the midst of a nation's tombs? Were we as a nation dead? My brain throbbed as I asked myself these wild questions, and gradually I dropped into a profound and solemn reverie. I became wrapped up in sacred and inspiring communion with the immortal shades of Ireland's departed. These shades became manly forms, instinct with life, warm with feeling.[110]

As with Green's reminiscences, this nationalist reverie gains its momentum from its preoccupation with visions of death and rebirth, and in this reasserts the often overwhelming sense within contemporary Irish nationalism of being haunted by previous betrayals and disappointments. Crucially, this disquiet arises not so much a result of English perfidy, but indicates instead a much more troubling sense of individual shame and powerlessness. Because the Irish nation remains spiritually unfree, it is humiliated by a guilty failure to inherit the possibilities bequeathed to it by generations of Irish martyrs and for this reason its psychological state remains vulnerable to hauntings and apparitions. Only independence, it is assumed, can restore the unity of the Irish and exorcise the restless dead, but in the meantime their insistent calls for reparation echo in the minds of the living, a condition of disquiet perhaps best illustrated in the Northern context by O'Byrne's collection of stories *The Ashes on the Hearth*[111] from 1948.

Eventually Shane's Castle was presented to the government of Northern Ireland with the condition that it ensured that O'Neill's red banner was flown from the tower on 17 July each year, the anniversary of Bigger's birthday. O'Byrne professed himself mystified as to why Bigger gave away the castle in this manner, and his final visit there in the 1940s ('we paid sixpence for the privilege'[112]), long after Bigger's death, revealed that 'it had gone back to the rooks and the jackdaws'. As he noted glumly: 'the rooms were empty, its walls were bare, and Harry Morrow's great picture lay in a corner, its frame in splinters and its canvas in tatters'. Searching for consolation, the only comfort that O'Byrne could arrive at was to suggest that the castle had reverted once again to its status as a symbol of future Irish freedom. Under partition its history was half-forgotten and its condition neglected, but:

> some day, when the Gaels of the North come into their own, the old place may become again a haven of Gaelic culture, when its old walls may re-echo to the stories told of Ireland's heroic past, and its rafters ring anew to the light-hearted lilt of her matchless songs.

The restoration of Shane's Castle was the last of what can be termed Bigger's spectacular projects. Although he remained active within Irish cultural nationalism,[113] he was disillusioned by the partition of the island and his faith in the Irish Ireland movement was shaken. His hatred of the border was so intense that he refused to cross it; as J. S. Crone records, 'he who had hitherto been free to roam at will all over Ireland, resented the petty inquisition there, and the obstacles placed in his way'.[114] While his interest in Ulster (or rather the parts of Ulster that constituted Northern Ireland) continued, the scope of his historical and archaeological enquiries narrowed and was less frequently attached to an explicit nationalist agenda. As Dixon has identified, it is significant that nearly all the articles he published after 1920 appeared in Belfast unionist newspapers.[115] In July 1926, the final year of Bigger's life, he received an honorary MA from Queen's University for his services to local history – a sign, perhaps, that at least some Northern Irish institutions were prepared to forgive his earlier nationalist excesses – and in December he died at Ardrigh, in what had been his mother's bed.[116] Rather like the satin banner bearing the arms of medieval Ulster that was folded around his coffin at his funeral, by this period Bigger had become an anachronism, the embodiment of an idea of Irish Ireland whose moment had passed. He was buried with his ancestors at Mallusk in County Antrim, close to the grave of one of his heroes, James Hope.

Just as partition effectively ended Bigger's aspirations, so it marked the end of Ardrigh's political and cultural significance. The days when it had hosted glittering gatherings of nationalist leaders were over. Of those who used to belong to the 'firelight school', some, like Casement and Johnston, were dead and others, such as O'Byrne, fled abroad to escape both the political climate of the new Northern Irish state and the possible danger of retribution, while figures like Milligan retreated into what can only be described as a kind of internal imaginative exile. In this, the fate of the Ardrigh coterie enacted in microcosm what Flann Campbell has described as the 'haemorrhage of talent among writers and artists who found it virtually impossible to make any sort of living in their native province'.[117] After Bigger's death, Joseph Devlin, the great leader of Catholic nationalism in Belfast, purchased Ardrigh but any hopes that he might have entertained that Ardrigh's great days could be resurrected soon proved illusory. The house had a number of owners after Devlin's death in 1934, but was eventually demolished in 1986 to make way for new properties and an apartment block named Ardrigh Court. During Bigger's occupation Ardrigh had been in many ways an experiment in living, and it is a tribute to his restless creative energy that it was, for a brief period at least, both the most culturally dynamic location in Ulster and the heart of Northern nationalist insurgency. Despite its proximity, however, Ardrigh remained politically isolated from Belfast, and Bigger's failure ever fully to appreciate the determination of Ulster unionism entailed that the values that it sheltered were always vulnerable. That said, for O'Byrne Ardrigh always remained as much a state of mind as a physical location and, indeed, in the years to come it would be the place his memory would always flee to whenever he was confronted with despair or danger.

NOTES

1 According to Roger Dixon, Richard J. Hayes's bibliography *Sources for the History of Irish Civilisation* credits Bigger as the author of an extraordinary 387 articles and essays. Roger Dixon, 'F. J. Bigger: romantic, enthusiast and antiquary', *Causeway: Cultural Traditions Journal*, 1.2 (spring 1994), pp. 5–7.
2 'Death of Mr. F. J. Bigger', *Irish News*, 10 December 1926, p. 8.
3 John S. Crone, 'Necrology: Francis Joseph Bigger', *Journal of the Cork Historical and Archaeological Society*, 32 (1927), p. 115.
4 Jeffrey Dudgeon, *Roger Casement: The Black Diaries* (Belfast: Belfast Press, 2002), p. 182.
5 J. Anthony Gaughan, ed., *Memoirs of Senator Joseph Connolly (1885–1961): A Founder of Modern Ireland* (Dublin: Irish Academic Press, 1996), p. 76. The euphemism here is carefully lodged.
6 Shane Leslie, 'Dedication', *The Irish Tangle for English Readers* (London: MacDonald, 1946).
7 H. A. MacCartan, 'Belfast: some backward glances', in *Capuchin Annual* (Dublin: Capuchin Franciscan Fathers, 1943), p. 177.
8 Jonathan Bardon, *A History of Ulster* (Belfast: Blackstaff Press, 1992), p. 421.
9 MacCartan, 'Belfast: some backward glances', p. 177.
10 Shane Leslie, *The Film of Memory* (London: Michael Joseph, 1938), p. 385.
11 To this end, Bigger planned a series of pamphlets on the lives of the United Irishmen to commemorate the rebellion of 1798. For once, the task proved to be beyond him and only one appeared in print: F. J. Bigger, *Remember Orr* (Dublin: Maunsel, 1906).
12 For many years Bigger shared Ardrigh with his widowed mother Mary Jane and their relationship was particularly close. In John S. Crone and F. C. Bigger, eds, *In Remembrance: Articles and Sketches by Francis Joseph Bigger* (Dublin: Talbot Press, 1927), p. viii, his brother recorded that: 'the inner life of Francis Joseph reveals two beautiful and distinctive qualities. His steadfast love for Ireland and his ardent devotion to his Mother and her memory.' Elsewhere Crone ('Necrology', p. 113) has described Bigger's mother as 'a woman of great force of character, nimble fingered, well-informed, skilled in all house-wifely arts, and a never failing source of information in family history'. After her death, Bigger left her favourite armchair unused in the dining room and placed fresh flowers under her portrait every day. As Cathal O'Byrne was to find out, unwittingly taking a seat in the vacant chair was not to be recommended.
13 John Wilson Foster, 'Natural history, science and Irish culture', in *The Poet's Place: Ulster Literature and Society: Essays in Honour of John Hewitt, 1907–1987*, eds Gerald Dawe and John Wilson Foster (Belfast: Institute of Irish Studies, 1991), p. 126.
14 Crone and Bigger, *In Remembrance*, p. x. This description is plagiarised by T. J. Campbell in his *Fifty Years of Ulster: 1890–1940* (Belfast: Irish News Ltd, 1941), p. 281.

15 According to Dixon, 'F. J. Bigger', p. 6, professional archaeologists in Ulster would refer to sites previously excavated by Bigger as being 'well and truly Biggered'.

16 H. C. Lawlor, 'Bun-na-Mairghie Friary: Ballycastle's great Franciscan link', *Glensman*, 1.3 (1931), pp. 26–32. Following this attack, others sprang to Bigger's defence. In the correspondence column of the *Glensman*, 1.5 (1932), Joseph Allen described Lawlor's actions as 'neither manly nor gentlemanly' (p. 29), while a contributor writing under the name 'Senior' concluded that Lawlor 'hates F. J. Bigger so much that he can't bear that he should lie quiet in his grave' (p. 31). Despite this, Lawlor refused to retract his comments. In truth such arguments were by no means out of the ordinary and, indeed, the world of Ulster local historical studies continues to be typified by sporadic outbursts of internecine bloodletting.

17 Perhaps the most well known beneficiary of this organisation's efforts is the Crown and Shamrock public house outside Glengormley. The scheme had its successes but was always constrained by Bigger's declaration that customers were allowed to consume a maximum of only two drinks per visit. For more information on this peculiar aspect of Bigger's activities see Dixon, 'F. J. Bigger', pp. 5–7.

18 Crone, 'Necrology', p. 116.

19 Dixon, 'F. J. Bigger', p. 6.

20 Campbell, *Fifty Years of Ulster*, p. 281.

21 Crone and Bigger, *In Remembrance*, p. xi.

22 See R. B. McDowell, *Alice Stopford Green: A Passionate Historian* (Dublin: Allen Figgis, 1967), p. 81.

23 Dudgeon, *Roger Casement*, p. 413. It was not uncommon for such events to get out of hand. One Belfast anecdote I have encountered a number of times recounts Bigger and O'Byrne celebrating St Patrick's night on the Ardrigh balcony overlooking Cavehill. Bigger had recently taken possession of a restored eighteenth-century pistol he fondly assumed had belonged to one of the United Irishmen. As part of the celebrations, Bigger, dressed in his bottle-green kilt and robes, delivered a dramatic speech declaring his willingness to free Ireland or to die in the attempt. As his polemic reached a climax, he waved the pistol above his head, at which point it slipped from his grip. As he fumbled to catch it, the pistol discharged and shot him in the arm. If this incident is true, it is perhaps no surprise that Bigger did not record it.

24 Leslie, *The Film of Memory*, p. 385.

25 Leslie, *The Film of Memory*, p. 384.

26 Shane Leslie, *Doomsland* (London: Chatto and Windus, 1923), pp. 171–2.

27 McDowell, *Alice Stopford Green*, p. 81.

28 There are three almost identical accounts of the discovery and reinterment of McCracken's remains: Edna C. Fitzhenry, *Henry Joy McCracken* (Dublin: Talbot Press, 1936), pp. 155–7; Richard Hayward, *Belfast Through the Ages* (Dundalk: Dundalgan Press, 1952), pp. 43–4; and Fred Heatley, *Henry Joy McCracken and His Times* (Belfast: Belfast Wolfe Tone Society, 1967), pp. 45–7.

29 Roger Dixon, 'Heroes for a new Ireland: Francis Joseph Bigger and the leaders of the '98', in *From Corrib to Cultra: Folklife Essays in Honour of*

Alan Gailey, ed. Trefor M. Owen (Belfast: Institute of Irish Studies, 2000), pp. 29–38, describes in detail Bigger's persistent use of the language of Christian martyrdom to describe the executions of many of the leaders of '98.

30 Cathal O'Byrne, *As I Roved Out* (Belfast: Blackstaff Press, 1982, first published 1946), p. 66.

31 Traces of this fervour can still be identified. See, for instance, Tom Paulin's poem 'Under Creon', in *Liberty Tree* (London: Faber and Faber, 1983, p. 13):

> The daylight gods were never in this place
> and I had pressed beyond my usual dusk
> to find a cadence for the dead: McCracken,
> Hope, the northern starlight, a death mask
> and the levelled grave that Biggar traced....

32 Bigger, *Remember Orr*, p. 7.

33 Jacqueline Hogge, 'Joy as City Council honours McCracken – after 201 years', *Irish News*, 1 October 1999, p. 1.

34 Joseph Campbell and Herbert Hughes, *Songs of Uladh* (Belfast: W. J. Baird, 1904).

35 Joseph Campbell, *The Garden of Bees* (Belfast: Erskine Mayne, 1905).

36 Norah Saunders and A. A. Kelly, *Joseph Campbell: Poet and Nationalist 1879–1944. A Critical Biography* (Dublin: Wolfhound Press, 1988), p. 31.

37 Cathal O'Byrne and Cahir Healy, *The Lane of the Thrushes: Some Ulster Love Songs* (Dublin: Sealy, Bryers and Walker, 1905).

38 Gaughan, *Memoirs of Senator Joseph Connolly*, p. 76.

39 Campbell, *The Garden of Bees*, pp. 56–7.

40 W. J. McCormack, *Roger Casement in Death or Haunting the Free State* (Dublin: University College Dublin Press, 2002), p. 77.

41 Dudgeon, *Roger Casement*, p. 186.

42 See, for instance, his later poem 'The planter', in *Irishry* (Dublin: Maunsel, 1913), p. 50, which contains the uncompromising lines:

> The Celt, I say,
> Has shown some artistry
> In living; you, the Planter, none.
> Under moon or sun
> You are the same, a dull dog, countryless,
> Traditionless and letterless.

43 For more on Campbell's turbulent post-Ardrigh life, and especially his period of imprisonment during the Civil War, see Eiléan Ní Chuilleanáin, ed., *As I Was Among the Captives: Joseph Campbell's Prison Diaries 1922–1923* (Cork: Cork University Press, 2001).

44 Flann Campbell, *The Dissenting Voice: Protestant Democracy in Ulster from Plantation to Partition* (Belfast: Blackstaff Press, 1991).

45 Campbell, *The Dissenting Voice*, p. 374.

46 Bardon, *A History of Ulster*, p. 420.

47 Gaughan, *Memoirs of Senator Joseph Connolly*, p. 77.
48 Gaughan, *Memoirs of Senator Joseph Connolly*, pp. 76–7.
49 Campbell, *The Dissenting Voice*, p. 375
50 Bigger had in fact paid for McPeake to receive lessons from the blind piper John O'Reilly. He also provided McPeake with instruments and organised recitals and concerts for him.
51 JC, 'Cathal: an appreciation and a memory', *Irish News*, 6 August 1957, p. 6.
52 Eleanor Alexander, *Lady Anne's Walk* (London: Edward Arnold, 1903), pp. 37–44.
53 O'Byrne, *As I Roved Out*, p. 258.
54 This play is discussed in more detail in Chapter 3. MacNamara and O'Byrne were friends and met frequently both at Ardrigh and through O'Byrne's involvement in the ULT. Like O'Byrne's story, MacNamara's play is based on events at Scarva taking a disastrous turn. Similarly, it features a Protestant protagonist, and is reliant on the humorous possibilities of Ulster vernacular speech for its comic effect. O'Byrne would subsequently take part in an open-air production of *Thompson in Tír-na-nÓg* at Belvoir. See O'Byrne, *As I Roved Out*, pp. 257–8.
55 See 'Armagh fundraiser', *Irish News*. 26 January 1932, p. 3:

> There was a large and appreciative audience in Armagh Parochial Hall at a concern organised by Armagh Young Ireland's football club in aid of the hall. The 'star' turn of the programme was Mr Cahal O'Byrne (the Belfast writer) who contributed various items, responding to repeated encores with his characteristic generosity. His marvelous interpretation of some of the old folklore ballads and lullabies was thoroughly appreciated, as were his humorous character recitals and sketches, especially 'The Battle of Scarva'.

56 O'Byrne, *As I Roved Out*, p. 170.
57 Cathal O'Byrne, 'Roger Casement's ceilidhe', in *Capuchin Annual* (Dublin: Capuchin Franciscan Fathers, 1946–47), pp. 312–14.
58 Leslie, *The Film of Memory*, p. 385.
59 JC, 'Cathal'.
60 Dixon, 'Heroes for a new Ireland', p. 36.
61 The best account of MacNeill's astonishing role as 'architect, organizer and philosopher' of the Gaelic League is John Hutchinson, *The Dynamics of Cultural Nationalism: The Gaelic Revival and the Creation of the Irish Nation State* (London: Allen and Unwin, 1987), pp. 120–7.
62 According to Brighid Mhic Sheáin, *Glimpses of Erin. Alice Milligan: Poet, Protestant, Patriot* (Belfast: Fortnight Educational Trust Supplement, undated), p. 12, Milligan's experience of this historic event was not entirely happy:

> she recorded her displeasure with the chairman who was from Cork, and who had expressed doubt if 'Belfast could be considered to be in Ireland at all,' and, by way of refutation, she made a point of informing her readers that she had had to leave the meeting early in order to catch the boat to Scotland where she

> had been asked to: 'enlighten the representatives of the six Celtic races about the great work done by Belfast for the saving of the Irish music and language'.

63 Roger Blaney, *Presbyterians and the Irish Language* (Belfast: Ulster Historical Foundation, 1996), p. 175.
64 Padraig Ó Snodaigh, *Hidden Ulster: Protestants and the Irish Language* (Belfast: Lagan Press, 1995), p. 85.
65 Gerry Adams, *Falls Memories* (Dingle: Brandon Books, 1983), p. 46.
66 O'Byrne, *As I Roved Out*, p. 175.
67 Pearse records his gratitude to Bigger for the trip in a letter of 31 July 1907. See Séamus Ó Buachalla, ed., *The Letters of P. H. Pearse* (Gerrards Cross: Colin Smythe, 1980), pp. 110–11.
68 McDowell, *Alice Stopford Green*, p. 81.
69 George Birmingham, *Pleasant Places* (London: Heinemann, 1934), p. 185.
70 Birmingham, *Pleasant Places*, p. 185.
71 George Birmingham, *The Northern Iron* (Dublin: Maunsel, 1907). The frontispiece reads:

> My Dear Bigger, This story, as you have already guessed, is the fruit of a recent holiday spent in County Antrim.... I remember a time – full of interest and delight – spent with you when I mention Donegore, Antrim and Templepatrick.... You told me what I wanted to know, you corrected patiently my manuscript, and you have helped me to enter into the spirit of the time.

72 *Irish News*, 18 May 1909, p. 5.
73 Ó Snodaigh, *Hidden Ulster*, p. 89.
74 'The coming Aonach: interesting function', *Irish News*, 12 December 1912, p. 5.
75 'Report of the upcoming Feis at Glenariff', *Irish News*, 25 June 1904, p. 5.
76 'The coming Gaelic and Industrial Festival', *Irish News*, 27 June 1904, p. 6.
77 'The Antrim Glens Feis', *Irish News*, 28 June 1904, p. 4.
78 'Preparations at Glenariff', *Irish News*, 30 June 1904, p. 8.
79 'The Feis of the Nine Glens: preparing for the event', *Northern Whig*, 30 June 1904, p. 8.
80 'The coming Gaelic and Industrial Festival'.
81 'Preparations at Glenariff'.
82 'Preparations at Glenariff'. Flann O'Brien's later satire *The Poor Mouth*, trans. Patrick C. Power (London: Grafton, 1986, first published 1941), pp. 54–5, on the obsessive discourses of the Revivalist Feis tradition highlights the unwitting anxiety that was always seemingly attendant on such protestations of inherent Gaelicism:

> Gaels! He said, it delights my Gaelic heart to be here today speaking Gaelic with you at this Gaelic feis in the centre of the Gaeltacht. May I state that I am a Gael. I'm Gaelic from the crown of my head to the soles of my feet – Gaelic front and back, above and below. Likewise, you are all truly Gaelic. We are all Gaelic Gaels of Gaelic lineage. He who is Gaelic will be Gaelic evermore.

> I myself have spoken not a word except Gaelic since the day I was born – just like you – and every sentence I have uttered has been on the subject of Gaelic. If we're truly Gaelic, we must constantly discuss the question of the Gaelic revival, and the question of Gaelicism. There is no use in having Gaelic, if we converse in it on non-Gaelic topics. He who speaks Gaelic but fails to discuss the language question is not truly Gaelic in his heart; such conduct is of no benefit to Gaelicism because he only jeers at Gaelic and reviles the Gaels. There is nothing in this life so nice and so Gaelic as truly true Gaelic Gaels who speak in true Gaelic Gaelic about the truly Gaelic language. I hereby declare this feis to be Gaelically open! Up the Gaels! Long live the Gaelic tongue!

83 The description in the *Belfast News-Letter*, 1 July 1904, p. 43, of these extraordinary costumes is noteworthy:

> The doughty pipers were gorgeously apparelled: they were in full Elizabethan costume, cross-gartered like Malvolio, with flowing cloaks and tight hose of brightly coloured materials, but, sad to relate, they wore painfully yellow boots of the most unartistic pattern.

84 'First Gaelic meeting at Glenariff', *Irish News*, 1 July 1904, p. 5.
85 'Speech by Sir Horace Plunkett', *Irish News*, 1 July 1904, p. 5.
86 'The Feis of the Nine Glens'.
87 'After Feis Na Ggleann', Editorial, *Irish News*, 4 July 1904, p. 7.
88 See Saunders and Kelly, *Joseph Campbell*, pp. 21–2, for more information about Campbell's experiences at the Feis. Although the authors misdate the Feis to 1902, it is clear from their description that they can only be referring to the events of 1904.
89 'The Feis of the Nine Glens'.
90 'Speech by Sir Horace Plunkett'.
91 'The Feis in the Glens', *Irish News*, 1 July 1904, p. 4.
92 Crone and Bigger, *In Remembrance*, p. xxvii.
93 O'Byrne, *As I Roved Out*, p. 372.
94 Richard Hayward, *In Praise of Ulster* (London: Arthur Baker, 1938), p. 32.
95 H. C. Lawlor, *Ulster: Its Archaeology and Antiquities* (Belfast: Carswell and Son, 1928), p. 145.
96 O'Byrne, *As I Roved Out*, p. 371.
97 O'Byrne, *As I Roved Out*, p. 371.
98 'Ardglass and its haunted castle', *Northern Whig*, 18 November 1911, p. 8.
99 Hayward, *In Praise of Ulster*, p. 126, in his history of the castle, identifies Ardglass as 'the chief link between the English pale in Dublin and the English settlement at Strangford'.
100 For instance, O'Byrne, *As I Roved Out*, pp. 372–3, records a gathering at the castle that included Green, Kuno Meyer, William Bulfin and Casement.
101 Alice Stopford Green, 'A castle at Ardglass', in *The Old Irish World* (Dublin: M. H. Gill, 1912), pp. 130–67.

102 Green, 'A castle at Ardglass', p. 152.
103 Green, 'A castle at Ardglass', p. 153.
104 Green, 'A castle at Ardglass', p. 156.
105 Green, 'A castle at Ardglass', p. 157.
106 'Gaelic ideals preached at stirring Ardglass meeting', *Irish News*, 3 July 1913, p. 7.
107 The Field Club responded enthusiastically to the castle, noting that:

> the greatest attraction at present to this famous old stronghold is the manner in which it is furnished, from cellar to beacon tower. Pre-historic implements and more recent old-world plenishings are called into service for present-day use, giving a practical lesson in the study of antiquarian objects. (*Irish News*, 12 June 1913, p. 6)

108 J. H. Campbell, 'A visit to Ardglass', *Irish News*, 26 June 1913, p. 7.
109 'Big books of history are only for students, they are never read by the people. But they will read picturesque biographies, which are history individualised, or vivid sketches of memorable eras, which are history vitalised.' Charles Gavan Duffy, *The Revival of Irish Literature* (London: T. Fisher Unwin, 1893), p. 24.
110 Campbell, 'A visit to Ardglass'.
111 Cathal O'Byrne, *The Ashes on the Hearth* (Dublin: At the Sign of the Three Candles, 1948).
112 O'Byrne, *As I Roved Out*, p. 374.
113 For instance, the *Irish News* records that in March 1926, the last year of his life, Bigger presented an Irish banner to Mrs J. B. McAllister, president of the butterfly stall of Ballymena Bazaar and organiser of a ceilidh held in the town ('Irish banner for Ballymena', *Irish News*, 23 March 1926, p. 5). The gesture could not have been more typical of Bigger and his life work.
114 Crone and Bigger, *In Remembrance*, p. xxxv.
115 Dixon, 'Heroes for a new Ireland', p. 37.
116 Although Bigger had to face a number of disappointments in his final years, it is worth recording that his financial status remained healthy. According to his will, his personal estate at the time of his death was over £10,000 (*The Times*, 28 April 1927, p. 17).
117 Campbell, *The Dissenting Voice*, p. 394.

CHAPTER FIVE

1916, partition and the end of the Northern Revival

The only long-term cure for the latent savagery, both in Ireland and in Germany, is better education and fuller mingling with other races.

Maurice Headlam, British civil servant in Ireland, 1912–20[1]

IN Belfast on New Year's Day 1916 there were few causes for optimism but many reasons to feel despair. Reports of the appalling slaughter of the trenches dominated Ulster daily life and whatever cause had once underwritten its necessity appeared now to be no more than a futile aspiration. The Great War had become, to all intents and purposes, a monotonous endgame and, for those at home, there was little that could be done other than to observe its vast, mechanical progress. The memoirs[2] of the *Irish News* reporter James Kelly provide a vivid picture of the atrophied condition of the city at this time. The street lamps were painted black for fear of Zeppelin raids, planes flew over West Belfast dropping recruiting leaflets, and injured soldiers from the Front, housed in the Belfast War Hospital on the corner of Grosvenor Road, 'all looked alike, cadaverous, dull-eyed, unsmiling and silent'.[3] The *Irish News*' New Year editorial saw clearly the pointlessness of the struggle and, more painfully perhaps, recognised its own powerlessness to do anything other than record the endless advances and retreats:

> A year of woe and suffering for the peoples of the European Continent has ended; a New Year has opened, and there is no visible prospect of an early end to the terrible strife. Armies bigger than those on the field on the 1st of January, 1915 confront one another all over Europe on January 1st, 1916. The struggle is practically at a standstill along the ghastly Western frontier: neither side has improved materially upon its position twelve months ago.[4]

The horrified clarity of this analysis captures in miniature the peculiar, almost paralysed, state of the paper and its readership at this time. The usual activity on which it had become reliant for its news – the endless reports of Revival meetings, concerts, day excursions and clerical matters – had seemingly dried up (particularly in Belfast itself) and been replaced by lengthy wire reports from the Western Front and the other theatres of war, morale-boosting stories of individual heroism, accounts of the latest Zeppelin raids in Britain and, most pressingly for many of its readers, opinion pieces on the increasingly complex Irish conscription debate. As this indicates, the war had brought the momentum of the Northern Revival to a sudden halt and it would never regain its vitality. Indeed, the despairing tone of the *Irish News* editorials in this period closely reflected a more general impasse in nationalist political opinion, an impasse that would be broken only by the spectacular and unexpected eruption of the Easter Rising later in the year.

For contingent reasons, then, the *Irish News* threw itself into the war effort with commitment if not enthusiasm. If by 1916 its sense of hopelessness about the struggle reflected the marginalised status felt by many regional papers across Britain and Ireland, in a period when local concerns were entirely subsumed into the vast dynamics of geo-political conflict, at the same time we have to recognise the unique position of the paper, and the Northern Catholic constituency it spoke for, in relation to events in continental Europe. Although disillusionment and betrayal were the dominant notes sounded in Britain – the logical outcome of early and misleading government propaganda – for both communities in Belfast the engagement with the war was a much more strategic affair. At the beginning of the war, in 1914, the prolonged, often painful, journey towards Home Rule appeared to be reaching some kind of conclusion. After intense and usually bitter negotiations, various retractions and emendations, a bill was on the statute book but, according to the prime minister, Herbert Asquith, it was not to be enacted until after the conclusion of the conflict, a date which, it was assumed, would not be far distant. Although the war prevented the achievement of Home Rule, it also almost certainly prevented (or, perhaps it should be said, postponed) the outbreak of civil war. In April 1914 Edward Carson's Ulster Volunteer Force (UVF) had successfully landed a huge arsenal of guns and ammunition at Larne, Donaghadee and Bangor, and its plans for a unilateral declaration of Ulster independence were well advanced. Appalled by this prospect and fearful of losing influence among his own predominantly Catholic constituency, John Redmond, the leader of the constitutional nationalist Irish Parliamentary Party (IPP), assumed control of the Irish

Volunteers, a nationalist force dedicated to supporting the Home Rule cause. Although large in number, in comparison with the UVF the Irish Volunteers were poorly armed and unsure of their objectives. Certainly, the organisation's gun-running venture at Howth in July 1914 (which used a yacht owned and piloted by Erskine Childers, an occasional visitor to Ardrigh) yielded only a small amount of obsolete equipment and was of greater symbolic than operational significance. Moreover, Redmond's leadership of the Volunteers was not guaranteed and could hardly be compared to the military structure of Carson's UVF.

As this suggests, by 1914 the preconditions for prolonged and organised violence in Ireland were securely in place and it was only in this unreal context that World War One could have appeared to be a unifying force. This in any case was an appearance which would soon prove to be illusory, as the conflict ground on into a realm of unimaginable horror. Carson's response to the outbreak of war was immediately to pledge the UVF to the service of the king, a declaration of loyalty to crown rather than government which unionism has often found useful at such moments of conditional allegiance. As a reward, the UVF was kept together as a single unit and was reconstituted as the 36th (Ulster) Division, which was posted to the Western Front in 1915. The Division was at Thiepval on the opening day of the Battle of the Somme (1 July 1916), one of the most brutal and wasteful episodes of the entire conflict, in which 5500 of its men were killed in two days of fighting. As Kelly recalls of the aftermath of the battle in Belfast, 'everywhere throughout the city that day there was the sound of weeping as the dreaded telegrams, "Killed in Action" flooded into the little houses'.[5] The Battle of the Somme was to become the pre-eminent symbol of sacrifice for subsequent generations of Ulster Protestants and continues to be a potent force in shaping what has been termed the Northern Protestant imagination.

If Carson's response to the outbreak of war had within it a certain inarguable logic, this could hardly be said of Catholic opinion, which was more obviously, and dangerously, divided. Redmond's uncertain control of the Irish Volunteers reflected a more general instability in nationalist attitudes to Home Rule and with the outbreak of the war these tensions would rapidly surface. In an act that matched Carson's immediate deployment of the UVF, Redmond initially offered the Irish Volunteers to the service of the crown, proposing that they could be given the responsibility of guarding Ireland and thus free other troops for the war effort. This had the startling, if temporary, effect of uniting the Irish Volunteers with Carson's Ulster Volunteers and, in the North especially, it was lauded as a historically portentous moment. Whether

Redmond could have maintained the unity of the Irish Volunteers under such circumstances is debateable, but this was a question that ultimately required no answer as, at Woodenbridge on 20 September 1914, he further pledged that the Irish Volunteers would fight wherever they were required, whether in Ireland or not. If the chances of a split within the Irish Volunteers had always been great, Redmond's declaration made it a certainty. Around 10,000 Volunteers, under the leadership of Ardrigh habitué and Gaelic Leaguer Eoin MacNeill, left the organisation but retained the title Irish Volunteers, while the much larger majority (around 160,000) stayed with Redmond and the IPP and became the National Volunteers.

The division within nationalist opinion that Redmond's actions had made explicit was clearly pre-existent and, for the most part, occurred along the fault-line between constitutional and radical nationalist ideologies that had existed at least since the fall of Parnell. That said, both positions were marked by contradictions, and for Redmond especially events were to prove the impossibility of his stance. As the war showed no sign of conclusion and the reports from the Front became increasingly appalling, recruitment among the National Volunteers declined markedly, while the Irish Volunteers, now determinedly anti-recruitment and increasingly militant, grew steadily. In Belfast this tendency was encouraged by Francis Joseph Bigger, who had begun to print and distribute anti-recruitment leaflets from his Ardrigh base. As he remarked to Alice Stopford Green with a *frisson* of excitement, 'think of me here in this respectable suburban residence writing such articles'.[6] This, then, was the beginning of the end for the once great IPP as an effective force within Irish politics. Weakened, perhaps fatally, by the ongoing postponement of Home Rule, the Easter Rising would deliver its *coup de grâce*. Certainly, while the contradictions of Redmond's stance can now be seen as unavoidable, many Irish nationalists at the Front must have been bewildered about the arcane turn of events that had led them to a position where they were expected to give their lives in support of an imperial power that was hostile to their interests and responsible for the oppression of themselves, their community and, it can be argued, their religion. In 'Easter 1916' W. B. Yeats tentatively observed that the Rising may have been unnecessary, 'for England may keep faith/For all that is done and said'.[7] It was with a commitment to this expectation that many Irish soldiers died at the Front. More blunt again was Blanche Mary Kelly, an Irish-American poet and friend of Cathal O'Byrne, who commented as follows in her poem 'The Irish at the Front' from 1916:

Because of the bush and the gallows,
The felon's cell,
Because of the fire and the famine,
'Connaught or Hell:'

For these we have left the boreens,
The Irish sky,
These are the things, O England,
For which we die.

For there are the fields of Flanders
With our blood wet;
O England, let you remember
What we forget![8]

As usual, however, things looked a little different when viewed from the perspective of Belfast. Joseph Devlin, MP for West Belfast, had maintained nationalist enlistment at a level that defied the trend for Ireland as a whole, and out of 32,000 Irish Volunteers in Belfast only 120 had defected to the more militant faction (led in Belfast by Bigger's confidant Denis McCullough) following Redmond's Woodenbridge declaration. After the split, Devlin, who was determined to reduce any residual independent power within the National Volunteers, deliberately demilitarised their activities. The manoeuvre was classically Devlinite in its strategy. By influencing and gradually assuming control of those nationalist or Catholic institutions in the North that might have posed a threat to his power base, Devlin exercised a degree of influence over Catholic Belfast that was far in excess of what nationalist leaders could achieve elsewhere in Ireland. As I observed in Chapter 2, at various times Devlin could mobilise to his cause such organisations as the Ancient Order of Hibernians (AOH), the United Irish League (UIL), the National Volunteers and the *Irish News*. Ultimately, the demise of the IPP was due to forces outside Devlin's reach, but no one fought harder or with greater imagination for its survival – even when it had reached the point where it was hardly worth saving.

Despite Devlin's remarkable control over his constituency, his support for nationalist enlistment still proved to be highly inflammatory and a policy that was to ignite the continually simmering tensions in Belfast between pro-Devlinite Hibernians and profoundly anti-Devlinite republicans. The terms of the split were intractable, as James Connolly's bitter fury at Devlin's stance, voiced through the pages of his newspaper *Workers' Republic* in 1915, indicates:

As I think of the hundreds of good men I have known, fathers of families, husbands, sons with aged parents, etc., who have been enticed to leave

> their homes and dear ones and march out to battle for an Empire that never kept faith with the Irish race, and think that it was Wee Joe's influence that led them to their folly, I think things that the Defence of the Realm Acts will not permit me to print.[9]

It is possible to glimpse the impotent frustration that hides behind this polemic. While the anti-enlistment agitation of individuals like Connolly and Countess Markievicz was gaining advocates across Ireland, in Ulster Devlin was still delivering recruits for the war effort in significant numbers. Connolly could attack Devlin as nothing more than 'a recruiting sergeant luring to their death the men who trusted him and voted him into power',[10] but he knew that on the Falls Road he had little answer to Devlin's charismatic appeal. Ultimately, however, Devlin's work would come to nothing as the IPP's policy of support for the war was entirely undermined by an increasingly desperate British government. Its decision to introduce conscription in Ireland in 1918 led to a wave of protest in Ireland so overwhelming that even the IPP, now led by John Dillon, felt obliged to withdraw its MPs from Westminster. Not only did the initiative fail in its primary objective, but it also further marginalised the increasingly embattled proponents of constitutional nationalism and helped prepare the ground for the Anglo-Irish War of 1919–21.

It is worth considering in more detail the *Irish News*' response to these developments. The paper's editorial line was inextricably linked to Devlin's politics and, indeed, from its beginnings as a pro-clerical, anti-Parnellite paper in 1891, its own success had mirrored his personal rise to power. Devlin had been one of the paper's first journalists, he had joined its board in 1905 (at which point the paper began supporting calls for Home Rule) and he would become managing director of the company in 1923. The *Irish News*, then, disseminated and encouraged Devlinite opinion in all its variety: it was staunchly IPP in its editorial line, carried exhaustively detailed reports on the affairs of the then resurgent AOH, supported enlistment, and fiercely attacked those shades of nationalist opinion that sort to gain advantage for Ireland from Britain's incapacitation. One figure who had invested much hope in this latter aspiration was, of course, Roger Casement, a member of the Ardrigh coterie for whom 1916 would bring intrigue and espionage, adulation and opprobrium, accusations of treason and, ultimately, execution. At the start of 1916 Casement was in Berlin and although only a few republican activists (and, unfortunately, British military intelligence) were aware of his plans to smuggle German arms into Ireland for the use of the Volunteers in the Rising, his pro-German sympathies had become a matter of public record. The *Irish News* cast more than a cold eye on these activities and in February 1916, in an editorial entitled 'If the Germans came?', addressed what it saw as the naivety of Casement's stance – particularly the belief that Germany's own imperialistic desires were compatible with the attainment of an independent Irish Republic. What, the piece asked, would in fact happen if the Germans were invited to invade Ireland on behalf of Irish nationalism?

> would the Germans, who realise that the possession of Ireland means dominance over the Atlantic, proclaim an Irish Republic, establish Sir Roger Casement as President, and withdraw their troops to Holyhead and Portpatrick? The question does not invite discussion.[11]

Having posited this unlikely scenario, the piece concluded:

> The fact, of course, is that the small group of Irishmen like Sir Roger Casement (in Berlin) and Mr McGuire (in New York) who chatter about 'our friends in Berlin' and the few Irishmen at home who have done nothing for their country and who seek to justify their lack of patriotism to their own consciences by whispering nonsense about the 'liberation' of Ireland at Germany's hands never trouble themselves to look the facts straight in the face. They talk – but they do not think.

This would not be the last time in 1916 that Casement would be accused of fundamentally misunderstanding political reality, and the belief that he made his way by instinct rather than reflection would become an enduring aspect of his legacy. The *Irish News* was not alone in speculating about Casement's presidential credentials. According to the memoirs of the novelist Shane Leslie, Bigger, Casement's friend and confidant at Ardrigh, had also 'dreamed of him as a possible President of a United Ireland', on the grounds that 'as a Sinn Féiner in arms he appealed to the South and while still a Protestant he might have appealed to the old Radical and Republican North'.[12] As with many other issues relating to contemporary politics, Bigger's judgement on this issue was fantastically perverse, but it indicates something of his belief that the spirit of '98 was still a meaningful element within contemporary Protestant opinion – a perspective that required considerable myopia. Leslie's own opinion of Casement's activities in Germany was tempered by a greater awareness of political reality and was more in line with the *Irish News*' scepticism. For Leslie:

> [Casement] was an Irish Quixote mixing some brave qualities with a bubbling vanity.... He was suddenly seized with the idea that he was Wolfe Tone returned to life and that it was his duty to stage an invasion of Ireland, whether Ireland summoned him or not. Certainly he met Tone's fate.[13]

Whatever else it may have signified, for the *Irish News* Casement's misaligned loyalty was just another symptom of what it saw as the general hysteria gripping radical nationalist opinion. After all, despite the many who regarded him as a hero, there were plenty of other nationalists who, according to Sean O'Casey, suspected that he might have been a British spy.[14]

No other member of the Ardrigh coterie would have as high a profile as Casement during the tumultuous events of 1916. Certainly, Bigger and Cathal O'Byrne, figures whose activities before the war had frequently been reported in the pages of the *Irish News*, were now conspicuous by their absence. This was partly because of the general reduction in Revival activity that the war caused, but it also indicated a more profound divergence of beliefs. In general, the Ardrigh coterie was hostile to enlistment and had, individually and collectively, cultivated friendships with such militant nationalists as Patrick Pearse (with whom Bigger had undertaken a motoring tour in Donegal in 1907), Maud Gonne (who would prove to be an enduring friend of O'Byrne) and Denis McCullough (whose daughter, Úna, had O'Byrne as a godfather). Ardrigh, then, became a focal point for militant republican activity in Belfast and was deemed to constitute such a threat to national security that the police were to keep it under surveillance for the duration of the conflict. Previously viewed as an eccentric if essentially harmless centre of Irish Ireland in the North, Ardrigh was now perceived as nothing less than a potential threat to the state itself.

As this suggests, those at Ardrigh who followed Casement's stance were faced with a double isolation, for while they remained exotic and dangerous figures to the unionist community, they were also becoming increasingly alienated from the Devlinite pro-Hibernian constituency of Northern nationalism. For O'Byrne in particular this must have been a painful sundering. A Hibernian by instinct and temperament and a childhood friend of Devlin, O'Byrne's career as a writer and performer had received crucial encouragement from such Devlinite organisations as the *Irish News* and the AOH. His work had, in turn, adapted itself to the preferences and prejudices of those institutions and while such a connection may have been artistically limiting (it is hard to think of an Irish artist from this period more distant from Joyce's uncompromising demand for aesthetic autonomy) it did at least guarantee full houses and favourable reviews. As a result, by 1914 O'Byrne had become a popular figure in the North, both as an entertainer and as a writer. Although the outbreak of the war led to a general reduction in Revival activity, he continued to perform at concerts in Ireland and abroad, but it was as the author of 'Mrs Twigglety's weekend letter', a weekly column for the pro-union paper *Ireland's Saturday Night*, edited by 'Franc' Williams, that he gained his most startling success. A carnivalesque celebration of Ulster daily life reporting the (usually mundane) adventures of characters such as Liza Ann Twigglety, Margit Bella, Wee Mrs McCrum and Squib McCall, the column parodied the vernacular language of female working-class Belfast speech and became a phenomenon, appealing to all ages and sections of the community. Young boys of the time such as John Hewitt and Denis Ireland[15] were transfixed by her activities and letters published in *Ireland's Saturday Night* from soldiers at the Front (usually consisting of bitter condemnations of conscientious objectors or requests for footballs and other gifts) often concluded by sending 'special regards to Liza Ann and Margit Bella'. The column's appeal was understandable for, as the paper asserted in an obituary tribute to O'Byrne, the characters were 'drawn with such sympathy and subtle cunning that they appear to step right into print from the everyday life of the Falls and the Shankill'.[16]

Ulster society, then, was clearly in need of the reassuring celebration of domesticity that Mrs Twigglety provided. Indeed, that fact that very little ever appeared to happen to her or her friends was surely attractive in the context of a province straitened by international conflict and threatened by the outbreak of civil war. Nothing of these affairs would ever intrude into Mrs Twigglety's universe. Instead, to cite a typical example, in the column published immediately after the Easter Rising Mrs Twigglety is preoccupied by the visit to her home of a French polisher, and is puzzled in turn by the realisation that such craftsmen need not necessarily be French.[17] In another piece, Mrs Twigglety expresses her bewilderment at Margit Bella joining an 'amachure dramaticks' society and asserts her belief that 'people what goes in fur dramaticks, speshall amature dramaticks – isn't rite in the head'.[18] O'Byrne himself must have realised that the strain of camp vernacular tweeness in the Twigglety formula strongly appealed to elements within Irish culture, for he was to recreate her in 1934 as 'Mrs Farrell', a middle-class housewife from the South, for a Catholic Truth Society of Ireland pamphlet, *Mrs Farrell's Fancies*.[19] Mrs Farrell, however, entirely lacks Mrs Twigglety's vernacular riotousness and, although her 'delight … in making her own names for things and twisting and turning the names that things already have into all kinds of shapes' resembles Mrs Twigglety, the comparison serves to underline only how genuinely bizarre the Twigglety world could be. Moreover, the fantastical nature of her voyages through quotidian life was heightened by the manner in which the column was juxtaposed with the news stories that surrounded it on the tightly packed page. In January 1917, for instance, Mrs Twigglety's lengthy discussion of modern husbands and their general purpose in the household was placed next to a report about the death of Private Donald Sloane at the Front. As the paper commented:

> The family of which he was a member made a splendid response to the clarion call of the Empire, and, alas, yet more pathetic and more immortal are the sacrifices they have been called on to make, as Donald was the fourth brother to lay down his life on the battlefield.[20]

In this chaos of incompatible discourses can be glimpsed something of the emotional confusion that the war created in Ulster.

The fact that homesick Ulster soldiers serving at the Front held Mrs Twigglety in such affection was profoundly ironic for, during the period of the war, the author of her column was becoming ever more committed to militant republican revolutionary politics and was actively seeking to make a tangible contribution to the struggle. In this O'Byrne was swayed fundamentally by his close friend McCullough, a charismatic figure whose ideas about the necessity and practice of republican insurrection were proving to be highly influential. McCullough had been sworn into the Irish Republican Brotherhood (IRB) outside Donnolly's public house on the Falls Road in 1901 and was so appalled by the slovenly manner of the initiation that he immediately recognised that the movement required restructuring. His intervention was to prove a crucial factor in the events that led to the Easter Rising. Prior to his involvement the IRB had become a largely ineffective force, still dominated by the Fenian tradition from which it had emerged, and unable to respond to the increasingly complex political situation with anything more effective than sentimental rhetoric and unconvincing promises of violent reprisal. This was particularly true of its activities in Ulster, despite the attempts of the IRB organiser P. T. Daly to reform the branch in March 1903 and the fact that quarterly meetings of the IRB executive of Great Britain and Ireland were usually held in Belfast.[21] In order that the IRB might be able to meet the challenges now facing militant republicanism, McCullough, along with his friend Bulmer Hobson (whom McCullough swore into the organisation in 1904), began reshaping the organisation, losing those members who were past usefulness – including McCullough's own father – and tightening the movement's internal security. As Roy Foster has observed, the pair 'represented a tiny, but highly disciplined tradition: puritanical, anti-alcohol, highly selective'.[22] It was, perhaps, no coincidence that the saviours of the organisation came from the increasingly factionalised and embittered political climate of early-twentieth-century Ulster, but their uncompromising approach was to alienate many within the organisation. For Sean O'Casey, an IRB member during this period, Hobson was a 'Protestant shit, exploiting his Protestantism in the National movement',[23] and the two were to come into direct conflict over the direction the organisation was taking. As O'Casey recalled:

> at a general meeting of the IRB in Dublin, I criticised its workings, I was howled at by a lot, and supported by some; Bulmer, on the platform drew a gun, and there was pandemonium. So, afterwards, with some others, I left the IRB, and flung myself into the Labour Movement.[24]

Despite these defections, under McCullough's influence, and with the aid of Hobson, Sean MacDermott and Thomas Clarke, the IRB became both a more professional and a more militant organisation. The movement's internal balance of power was now weighted towards Belfast and the traditional simplicity of its message – an uncompromising demand for an Irish Republic – was allied to a political and military structure capable of delivering it. As a result, by the time McCullough became president of the Supreme Council of the movement in December 1915, the IRB's position was stronger than it had been for many years; the removal of the old and ineffective veterans had been largely completed and its dedicated membership stood at approximately 2000. Moreover, the IRB now had significant influence within the Gaelic League at both branch and executive level and, more importantly, had infiltrated the leadership of the Irish Volunteers to the extent that it was able to shape the policy of that much larger organisation. This was, perhaps, the most impressive aspect of the IRB's strategic thinking: although its members remained a tiny minority within the spectrum of Irish nationalism, they exerted a degree of control over the agenda of the wider nationalist struggle that was out of all proportion to their small numbers.

It was at this point that the possibility of an armed insurrection against the British became a viable prospect. However, although the IRB had taken the decision to plan a wartime rising against the British as early as September 1914, it was, ironically, precisely in the execution of this event – its keynote moment in history – that the IRB was to demonstrate both its own internal divisions and the manner in which Ulster remained ideologically distinct from the rest of Ireland. In the summer of 1915 the Military Council of the IRB had been formed; this was a tightly knit grouping consisting of Pearse, Joseph Mary Plunkett, MacDermott, Eamon Ceannt and Clarke, who immediately assumed authority for the planning of the Rising. McCullough remained entirely unaware of their plans and possibly did not even know of the Military Council's semi-autonomous existence – and this despite the fact that they had manipulated the IRB's Supreme Council into making him president in the first place. Events were clearly moving beyond McCullough's control and he, along with Hobson, would soon find himself entirely marginalised within the organisation. The ideological compass of militant republicanism was again shifting away from the North.

The implications of this for subsequent events were serious and, to an extent, are still being felt.[25] Because the IRB represented the most extreme elements of Irish republicanism, it tended to move as quickly as its most militant members wished. As a result, control of the organisation's destiny passed from individual to individual and cabal to cabal with often confusing speed. As this suggests, there was probably no deliberate strategy to exclude Northerners from the planning of the Rising, although the fact that many Northern republicans were kept under close surveillance by the security forces would have entailed a clear risk to the secrecy of the operation. That said, the extent of McCullough's ignorance – an ignorance shared to varying degrees by Hobson and MacNeill – remains surprising. Even when James Connolly (who could mobilise his Citizen's Army on behalf of the uprising) and Thomas MacDonagh were voted onto the Military Council in 1916 and the date for the Rising was confirmed as Easter Monday (24 April), McCullough and Hobson remained unaware of the manner in which events were being forced to a crisis or the degree to which their own more pragmatic views on the use of revolutionary violence were being overlooked in favour of a sacrificial ideal.

It was, then, practically inevitable that the minor roles played by McCullough and Hobson in the actual events of Easter 1916 would appear in retrospect to be something close to farcical. This was due in part to the IRB's poor communication network but it was also the result of deliberate obfuscation by Plunkett and MacDermott (who, according to Hobson, learnt his skills of 'intrigue and wire-pulling behind the scenes'[26] from the AOH in Belfast) and the manner in which they persistently misled MacNeill about the Military Council's real intentions. When MacNeill eventually discovered the truth he issued a countermanding order to the Volunteers via the press on the Saturday before the planned assault, stating that, 'owing to the very critical position all orders given to Irish Volunteers for Easter Sunday are rescinded, and no parades, marches, or other movements of Irish Volunteers will take place'.[27] MacNeill had recognised that the Volunteers were entirely unprepared to undertake an operation on the scale intended, but with this act his position as a leader of Irish nationalism was effectively over. Hobson was another whose period of influence was rapidly coming to an end. Only three years previously he had been the most powerful republican organiser in Ireland but his consistent opposition to the Rising and his belief that all military action against the British should be postponed until the war was over meant that he was now little more than a liability to the ever more determined Military Council. He had discovered the extent of the Council's plans before MacNeill and in the week prior to Easter had begun issuing alternative orders. For this reason he was arrested on Good Friday by the very forces he had once commanded, and was detained for the crucial final period before the Rising took place. The world-weary manner in which his autobiography describes this moment indicates that Hobson knew at the time that history was running ahead of him:

> On the afternoon of Good Friday I was asked to attend a meeting of the Leinster Executive of the IRB at Martin Conlon's house in Phibsboro. I was reluctant to go, and did not see any purpose to be served. At the same time I yielded to the importunities to attend, and was not greatly surprised when, as I entered the house, a number of IRB men who were armed with revolvers told me that I was a prisoner and could not leave the house. I felt that I had done all I could to keep the volunteers on the course which I believed essential for their success, and that there was nothing further I could do. My principal feeling was one of relief. I had been working under great pressure for a long time and was very tired. Now events were out of my hands.[28]

Disillusioned and bitter, Hobson had come a long way from the Ulster Literary Theatre (ULT) and *Brian of Banba*, but his involvement in revolutionary Ireland was now over and he would never again seek such a role. As MacNeill said to him while the events of Easter week unfolded around them, 'we would have no political future if we were not arrested'.[29] The prophecy was correct and in future years Hobson would think of 1916 as nothing less than a 'personal tragedy'.[30]

At least MacNeill and Hobson were close to the centre of events. McCullough's role in the Rising, by contrast, brought him no nearer than Tyrone and was perhaps the most frustrating of all. Having been informed of the plans in their full extent only a few days prior to their enactment, he was ordered by the Military Council to mobilise his Volunteers in Coalisland, rendezvous with other local troops and then head to Galway with the intention of creating diversionary activity. With very little time available to him and his men poorly equipped, he purchased supplies from a shop usually patronised by the UVF and headed south. McCullough's sense that the expedition was little more than a futile exercise was compounded when some of his men were arrested on the way and the expected reinforcements did not arrive. Realising that the expedition was in total disarray, he decided to return to Belfast with his men on the Sunday evening and thus his involvement in the Rising came to a premature and unsatisfactory end. He was arrested five days later as part of a security clampdown on republican activists and endured a protracted period of imprisonment. McCullough remained committed to militant republican activity and in 1918 became a Sinn Féin councillor in Belfast, but he was never again to enjoy the level of influence that he exercised in the years before the Rising.

Concentrating on these essentially peripheral figures is not to suggest, of course, that Northerners played no role in the momentous events taking place in Dublin. Indeed, the final decision to go ahead with the Rising following the disastrous news of Casement's arrest in County Kerry by the Royal Irish Constabulary and the failure of his attempt to land German arms was taken by two men with very strong Ulster connections, MacDermott and Clarke. Moreover, although it is clear that individuals in the IRB had very different perspectives on the role of the Rising and its potential as a sacrificial gesture, these tensions cannot be equated to a simple distinction between the stereotypes of Northern hard-headed pragmatism and Southern dreamy idealism. However, the transformation of the Rising from what was originally intended – a national event with the mass of Volunteers participating – to its final manifestation – a Dublin rebellion involving only a tiny number of combatants – did have the effect of fundamentally isolating the republican movement in Ulster. Considering that revolutionary nationalist politics in the North was always vulnerable to being neglected, the perception of its lack of involvement in the Rising was little short of calamitous and it has been argued that it was in this way that the Rising helped create the conditions necessary for the eventual partition of the island. Certainly, in the years that followed the Rising, what remained of the IPP's political strength became concentrated in Devlinite Ulster, while the rest of Ireland embraced the more radical politics of Sinn Féin. Alongside this, it is important to recognise the Rising's specifically Catholic character. As the historian George Boyce has observed:

> [its leaders] thought in terms of the special nature of the Irish Catholic people who, as MacDonagh put it, were like the Jews, a people who bore much and suffered much for their religion, harbouring a 'black passion' of anger for centuries of English persecution.[31]

This does not mean that they were particularly sectarian in their vision of a future Ireland, but it did further marginalise what remained of the dissenting Protestant revolutionary tradition in Ulster, as embodied by

Hobson and, to a lesser extent, Casement. Joseph Connolly's perception that, for Bigger, who remained safely ensconced in Ardrigh, 'the whole period must have been a nightmare of shock and apprehension'[32] in itself indicates the extent to which Northern Protestant radicals were unable to comprehend the possibility of an outbreak of political violence so devastating that it would cost 450 lives, injure 2614 and leave much of Ireland's major city in ruins.

While there were ideological reasons why Northern nationalism appeared removed from the events in Dublin, there were also more obvious, geographical factors. In the years leading up to 1916, and thanks mainly to the railway system, new roads and the telegraph, communications in Ireland had vastly improved and it became increasingly possible to visualise the island as a coherent entity. This, in itself, was an important factor in the rise of cultural nationalism, and wealthy figures such as Bigger (alongside his chauffeur Tommy) were able to traverse large areas of the country disseminating Revival propaganda with a speed that had hitherto been unimaginable. Easter 1916, however, was a startling reminder that Belfast remained a long way from Dublin, as the news of the Rising that filtered north combined conjecture and rumour with an overwhelming sense of disbelief that such an event could have taken place at all. It was in this context that the *Irish News* attempted to explicate the significance of the ongoing insurrection. Because the paper was heavily committed to the war effort and the promise of Home Rule, its gaze had become firmly fixed on continental Europe. While it was able through press agencies and its own staff to provide frequent and detailed reports on the latest progress (or lack of it) of the campaigns at the Front, by comparison its awareness of events taking place locally verged on the myopic. For instance, the arrest of Casement at Banna Strand on 21 April was unconfirmed by a definite report in the paper for four days,[33] while, more significantly again, the tumultuous events in Dublin a few days later entirely bewildered the paper's editorial staff. Its earliest report on the Rising, on 25 April (the day after the event), was headlined 'KEEP COOL!' and attempted to downplay the importance of what was taking place:

> We trust sincerely that Rumour has magnified the story of the occurrences which has been borne Northward on its wings. But it is certain that evil has been done – irreparable evil from the personal point of view of many unhappy families, but not irreparable from the National standpoint if the people of this country hold firmly to their principles, cleave to the leaders who brought them to the verge of victory – who sought to save the humblest and most credulous of them from the consequences of suicidal folly.[34]

At this early stage, and as the story's headline suggests, the paper was probably most anxious to prevent the outbreak of a similar event in Belfast, but its construction of the Rising's leaders as irresponsible charlatans would remain a constant feature of its subsequent, highly negative coverage. The paper's obsession with rumoured German plots to invade Ireland led it to overestimate the significance of the IRB's German connections and, as such, the Rising became a 'wicked German plot' and its leaders nothing more than the 'unhappy instruments of German duplicity and treachery who have fought Germany's battle in the capital of this country'.[35] Slowly, but perceptibly, it was becoming clear that the actions of the IRB's Military Council had unravelled the complex narrative towards the peaceful attainment of Home Rule that the paper had championed.

It was primarily for this reason that the *Irish News* was slow to admit the significance of what had taken place. With its Devlinite connections it was able to mobilise such organisations as the AOH in a united condemnation of the Rising, but the paper's overwhelming allegiance to the IPP prevented it from acknowledging that, foolish or not, the bravery of the Rising's leaders had stirred patriotic feelings in many of its core readers and could not merely be dismissed as insanity. It would, though, be unfair to be overly critical of the *Irish News* for the rigidity of this stance. It was certainly not the only paper in the North to be caught out by the speed of events – *Ireland's Saturday Night*, for instance, saw those who took part in the Rising as nothing more than a 'mob'[36] – and by the start of May, as the executions of the leaders began, its editorial gave some perspective on the lessons that could be drawn:

> There was not a 'national uprising' in Dublin. It was not even a sectional 'uprising'. The whole sad business was conceived and planned, and carried into fatal effect without the knowledge or the sanction of the Irish Nation. Had it been possible to take a vote of the people of this country on the issue, 99 per cent of them would have declared against such an attempt without hesitation and with all the power of protest they could muster. In due time we shall discuss the varied influences that operated on the minds of the ill fated leaders, who have paid the dread penalty of their own rashness, folly and credulity. But on the morrow of their doom, and while the fate of so many other victims is still undecided we hope the charity of silence, will be extended to the dead. Ireland has already suffered bitterly through the ghastly events of the last days of April; but the hearts of her people are strong and their minds have been disciplined by trials and disappointments that would have made the men of any other nation despair of their country's future and their own.[37]

The analysis here is largely correct. Prior to the Rising the majority of Irish nationalist opinion would clearly have been appalled had it known of the Military Council's designs, but the bloody retribution enacted by the British was transforming Ireland's political landscape and the old certainties that the paper was clinging to were already becoming an irrelevance. On 6 May the *Irish News* was the first Home Rule paper in Ireland to call for a halt to the executions of the Rising's leaders – a stance that was a credit to both its compassion and its regained political acumen – but by this stage eight men had been killed and it was obvious that the protracted nature of the vengeance was becoming more significant than the event that had originally triggered it. With even Carson calling for an end to the executions, the government finally intervened to halt the process when the total stood at fifteen. This figure was to rise when the final conspirator, Casement, was hanged at Pentonville Prison on 3 August, an outcome that surprised the *Irish News*, as it had (perhaps naively) been convinced that the British would not execute a figure whom they had previously so lauded.

With the transformation of Irish politics in the Easter Rising period, the *Irish News*' determined adherence to the Home Rule cause was becomingly increasingly difficult to maintain. Although Devlin's personal support in east Ulster remained strong, areas to the west and south embraced the politics of full separatism and with that abandoned the *Irish News*, and switched to local papers produced by Herald group, which supported Sinn Féin. Twenty-five years after the Parnell crisis, nationalist opinion in the North was again dangerously split and, as events would prove, vulnerable. In the three years of intense political activity that followed the Rising, support for Sinn Féin spread rapidly through rural Ireland and was bolstered by the regular release from prison of the veterans of Easter week, including Eamon de Valera, who became president of the party in October 1917. In comparison with the simple and yet obviously appealing message of Sinn Féin, the IPP appeared bereft of ideas and, in its obsession with Home Rule, increasingly open to manipulation by the British, a perception seemingly confirmed by its disastrous involvement in Lloyd George's scheme for temporary partition of the six counties in June 1916. Seen as the only viable way to secure immediate Home Rule, Redmond supported the plans, but was unaware that Lloyd George had promised Carson that exclusion would be permanent. Ultimately the scheme collapsed due to the opposition of implacable unionists in the south, but the damage it did to the IPP's profile among nationalist voters proved terminal.

For John Dillon, the new leader of the IPP after Redmond's death in March 1918, it must have appeared that the British government was doing all in its power to radicalise Irish nationalists and to marginalise the IPP's constitutional position. Seemingly oblivious to the threat posed by the resurgent Sinn Féin, in April 1918 the government's desperate shortage of troops for the final stages of the war led it to introduce measures for conscription in Ireland, a decision that effectively wrecked what was left of the IPP's tattered wartime strategy. Thanks to a universal coalition of protest, which included Sinn Féin, the IPP, the Catholic Church and the trade unions, the proposal was never enacted, but it further confirmed the growing sense in Ireland that only the Sinn Féin ideology of full independence could provide an adequate means of resisting continued British duplicity. This perception gained tangible form in the post-war general election of 1918, when Sinn Féin gained a landslide victory, claiming 73 of the 105 seats available. The IPP, by contrast, was all but destroyed and held just six seats, mostly in Ulster. If this was not bad enough, three of its victories were practically guaranteed as a result of a 'green pact' initiated by the Catholic Church. The only comfort for the Home Rule party came with Devlin's convincing victory over de Valera in the Falls Division, but this result, if anything, merely confirmed the increasingly anomalous position of nationalists in Belfast when viewed in the national context. That said, the Devlin personality cult remained strong and, as Gerry Adams has sardonically observed, his party machine was still capable of bringing out the vote:

> The *Irish News* coverage of the election makes interesting reading, for that paper appears to have acted as an election periodical for the Irish Parliamentary Party. Nowhere in its coverage of the election for the Falls Division was one Republican statement, speech or election manifesto reported and reporting of Republican election activity was minimal. Exposure of Joe Devlin went to the other extreme, and pages were filled with details of his sponsors, expansive reports of his meetings, parades, election addresses and statements.[38]

Following Devlin's victory thousands of his supporters held a joyful impromptu rally in the city centre but the truth was that Devlin, for all his charisma, was now largely a political irrelevance and the republican agenda in Ireland was moving forward with or without Ulster.

The stunning election success of 1918 not only gave Sinn Féin a clear electoral mandate, it also rejuvenated the military campaign. While there was little desire to repeat the grand sacrifice of Easter 1916, the Irish Volunteers had continued to recruit members and, thanks to continuing infiltration of its ranks by the IRB, reformed itself in 1917 as a much more disciplined fighting force. In 1919, the meeting of the first Dáil Éireann in Dublin declared independence – or rather confirmed Pearse's 1916 proclamation of the Republic – and the Volunteers subsequently became known as the Irish Republican Army (IRA) (although the term was already in informal use). The IRB, meanwhile, continued to lead a semi-autonomous existence both within and outside its ranks, under the presidency of the young Michael Collins. With a coherent political and military strategy to follow, the example of the 1916 martyrs as inspiration, and the concomitant collapse of the Home Rule movement, membership of the Sinn Féin/IRA movement increased dramatically, particularly among young lower-middle-class Catholic men. One such individual was O'Byrne, a figure whose journey from the essentially Devlinite politics he had espoused in the early years of the century to his later membership of the IRA was paradigmatic of many similar conversions.

The extent of O'Byrne's influence in the organisation is difficult to assess; although Bruce Stewart has proposed that he was possibly a member of its Military Council[39] there is a lack of documentation to corroborate this. What is clear, however, is that under the influence of his friends McCullough and Tom Cullen, a leading member of Collins's Intelligence Section in Dublin and an extremely talented urban guerrilla, O'Byrne became an increasingly active IRA volunteer and was involved specifically in the movement of arms from the North to Dublin during the years 1918–19. Cullen was assistant quartermaster at the IRA headquarters in Dublin at this time and it is from him[40] that we have the best example of O'Byrne's ingenuity in ensuring that weapons were safely delivered. Ordered to transport a number of handguns in two leather bags to the Volunteers in Dublin, O'Byrne arrived at Amiens Street Station to find that British troops were searching all the passengers at the platform exit gate. Rather than risk an interrogation, he presented himself to the young officer in charge, announced that he was going to the Castle (the centre of British administrative rule in Ireland) and requested that a soldier help carry his bags to the cab rank. The officer immediately ordered his sergeant to carry out the request and saluted O'Byrne for good measure. As the cab drew away from the station and headed the horse towards the river, O'Byrne ordered the cabby to turn in the opposite direction and make instead for the Castle Hotel in Gardiner Row, a location that was known as a key rendezvous point for republicans during this period. The guns were delivered safely.

The fact that many accounts of O'Byrne in his later years draw attention to his pacifist beliefs indicates either that he was fundamentally to change his opinions about the ethics of armed insurrection or that he was particularly skilled at concealing the dual life he led at this time. The uncompromising and embittered politics revealed in his final books (especially *As I Roved Out*, from 1946) suggest the latter option, but it is interesting to observe that while O'Byrne was ultimately quite happy to describe the extent of his intimacy with Roger Casement[41] at a time when he deemed it safe to do so,[42] he was never to write about his own role as an IRA activist. This could be because, despite his often-professed nationalism, O'Byrne did not want to compromise the affection with which he was held by many in the Protestant community in the North. As I have already described, at the time of O'Byrne's militant activism he was also the revered author of the 'Mrs Twiggelty' column for the pro-union paper *Ireland's Saturday Night*, and there is evidence that his contemporaneous collection of poems, *The Grey Feet of the Wind*,[43] appealed to readers from both communities. Such a balancing act would become increasingly difficult to maintain after partition, as the cultural lives of the two communities retreated behind sanctioned expressions of political identity.

By 1919, it was clear that some form of partition in Ireland was inevitable. For Northern nationalists, who now appeared largely powerless to shape their own destiny, the anxiety was over what guise it would finally assume. In December, Lloyd George's Government of Ireland Bill appeared to provide an answer. Proposing two parliaments, one in a six-county Ulster and the other for a twenty-six-county South, the Bill made provision for a Council of Ireland which could, eventually, become a parliament for the whole of the island. With Sinn Féin's ongoing abstention from Westminster, Irish opposition to the Bill was inevitably weak and haphazard, and the Bill was enacted in December 1920. For nationalists in Ulster the insult was twofold, for not only was the settlement disastrous in itself but the manner in which it had been achieved indicated the extent to which they had become politically marginalised. In the subsequent negotiations that would lead to the Anglo-Irish Treaty of 1921 there was no representative to speak for the interests of Northern Catholics, and the one significant concession on partition that emerged from it – the proposal to establish a boundary commission to investigate the viability of the border as it had been drawn – was, at best, a vague promise. Divided on the border question and with many of its most able leaders now domiciled in the South, the nationalist movement in the North could find no adequate means of challenging the new settlement.

The immediate effect of this abandonment was to ensure that the Catholic minority in the North was even more vulnerable than it had appeared previously, and in this context the brutal pogroms enacted against Catholics in Belfast between July 1920 and June 1922 can be understood merely as the inevitable expression of the new political order. The attacks were chronicled by the curate of St Mary's Church in Belfast, Father John Hassan, and the devastating document that he produced (under the pseudonym G. B. Kenna), *Facts and Figures: The Belfast Pogroms 1920–2*,[44] detailed a high level of complicity between the security forces and violent loyalist mobs. Of the 557 people killed in this period, 303 were Catholics while, as Thomas Hennessey has recorded,[45] between 8700 and 11,000 Belfast Catholics lost their jobs and 23,000 became homeless. Although often appearing random and incoherent in execution, the overall effects of the violence were, in fact, highly precise: by the time the pogroms finally came to an end with the IRA's assassination of a local unionist politician, the economic base of Belfast's Catholic working class had been destroyed and the sectarian geography of the modern city was securely in place. In May 1921 Sir James Craig become the first prime minister of Northern Ireland, but any possibility that the new state might gain the allegiance of its minority population had disappeared even before it was properly established. With the British government reluctant to intervene in the settlement it had effectively imposed, Craig put in place increasingly draconian security measures and the alienation of the Catholic community was complete. Despite the pogroms, the social infrastructure of the Catholic North – defined by Eamon Phoenix as consisting of 'church, schools, hospitals, Gaelic sports and the sectarian Ancient Order of Hibernians'[46] – remained and through this the minority population became partially self-governing, in Phoenix's term, 'a state within a state'.

To adapt the famous remark about the effects of the French Revolution often attributed to Chairman Mao, it is still too early to tell what is the full legacy of 1916 and its immediate aftermath for the North of Ireland. It is possible, however, to trace some of the passing symptoms it gave rise to. With the annihilation of the Home Rule argument and the subsequent disappearance of the IPP, Devlin's power base in Belfast became an increasingly anachronistic phenomenon and one that he held together purely by force of character and political acumen. The *Irish News* continued to support him through the 1920s and in its growing insularity it reflected the general political life of the community it claimed to represent. As this suggests, nationalism in the North was, to use a phrase that had become much in vogue during this period, shell-shocked by the rapid turn of events, and it would be many decades before it regained any kind of political energy. Memories of the Great War suggest that it, too, remained a divisive and bitter legacy. The impossibility of reconciling the sacrifice of the Somme with the sacrifice of the Rising led to what Fran Brearton has referred to as 'the eventual stalemate of Easter 1916 versus July 1916',[47] two contesting commemorations demanding, as Edna Longley has put it, 'their incompatible due'.[48] More starkly still, for Shane Leslie – who had experienced the horrors of the Front at first hand – the war was nothing less than 'the suicide of a civilisation called Christian'.[49]

Already battered by the effects of the Great War, the Rising effectively killed off what was left of the Northern Revival, with the mass of cultural activity taking place in Belfast in, for example, 1909, vanishing almost completely. Although classic narratives of the Irish Revival as a whole usually describe it as lingering into the 1920s, this can be accounted for by recognising the much greater extent of Anglo-Irish involvement in the Revival in the South. While the Anglo-Irish were hardly insulated from the political turmoil of the period, they could at least occupy imaginative spaces beyond the often bitterly sectarian and factionalised reality of the time. Moreover, with the final removal of the remnants of Anglo-Irish political influence during this period, there was a concomitant increase in their engagement in the cultural realm as new roles and vocations were sought – often in a particularly determined and self-conscious manner. The Revival in the North was, by comparison, a more profoundly Catholic affair and was typified by a delicate series of cultural negotiations between constitutionalism and separatism. It was in this way that it maintained, at least for a short period, the unity of nationalist opinion in the North after the Parnell split – a crisis that struck in Ulster with particular venom. The Rising, then, brought to the surface divisions that had been deliberately sublimated and the expression of cultural nationalist unanimity (in Belfast especially) became an immediate impossibility.

A number of other factors should also be recognised in this decline. The (Ardrigh-dominated) Protestant dissenting tradition in the North was both alienated from the overtly Catholic character of the Rising and yet marginalised by the increased polarisation of Protestant society in Ulster. Certainly, the new, militant versions of loyalist identity inspired by Carson were no longer willing to perceive the eccentric activities of renegade sons such as Bigger as merely harmless manifestations of their religion's underlying love of liberty. Alongside this, the other major staple of the Northern Revival's cultural programme – Catholic lower-middle-class popular entertainment, as typified by the events and concerts organised by such bodies as the UIL and the AOH – was similarly disrupted. In part this was due to practical necessity, as wartime Belfast was unable to provide either the locations or the audience for such gatherings, but it is important to recognise that the collapse of Home Rule nationalism led also to the contraction, or even the termination, of many of the nationalist societies and clubs that had flourished under its sponsorship.

Finally, of course, one has to recognise the overwhelming sense of shock caused by the violence of the Rising. While for activists such as Hobson cultural activity was always intended to be no more than a precursor for direct political or military action, even less militant participants in the Northern Revival (including the *Irish News*, the movement's main organ of propaganda) could see that the Rising indicated that there was a clear correlation between cultural nationalism and military engagement. Whether they were right in this assumption is largely beside the point: what matters is the degree to which the force of the association was a felt reality. The effective cessation of Bigger's Revival activities after 1916 provides, perhaps, the best example of this anxiety, but it was also shared by many of those who once gathered at his home, with individuals such as Alice Milligan unable to adapt either temperamentally or artistically to the transformed structure of Irish politics. In these terms, the Rising provided nothing less than a harsh lesson in the realities of cultural politics, while the eventual partition of the island converted the optimistic energies of the Revival in the North into a mode of endlessly cyclical nostalgia. It was this form that O'Byrne would spend the rest of his artistic life perfecting.

NOTES

1 Maurice Headlam, *Irish Reminiscences* (London: Robert Hale, 1947), p. 231.
2 James Kelly, *Bonfires on the Hillside: An Eyewitness Account of Political Upheaval in Northern Ireland* (Belfast: Fountain Publishing, 1995), pp. 2–3.
3 Kelly, *Bonfires on the Hillside*, p. 28.
4 'Old Year – New Year', Editorial, *Irish News*, 1 January 1916, p. 4.
5 Kelly, *Bonfires on the Hillside*, p. 3.
6 R. B. McDowell, *Alice Stopford Green: A Passionate Historian* (Dublin: Allen Figgis, 1967), p. 81.
7 *Collected Poems of W. B. Yeats* (London: Macmillan, 1982), p. 204.
8 Blanche Mary Kelly, *The Valley of Vision* (New York: Encyclopaedia Press, 1916), pp. 49–50.
9 James Connolly, 'Wee Joe Devlin', *Workers' Republic*, 28 August 1915, p. 2.
10 Connolly, 'Wee Joe Devlin', p. 2.
11 'If the Germans came?', Editorial, *Irish News*, 17 February 1916, p. 4.
12 Shane Leslie, *Long Shadows* (London: John Murray, 1966), p. 188.
13 Leslie, *Long Shadows*, p. 187.
14 Sean O'Casey in a letter to Robert Monteith, 31 December 1954. See David Krause, ed., *The Letters of Sean O'Casey. Vol. 2: 1942–54* (New York: Macmillan, 1980), p. 1136.

15 See John Hewitt, Foreword, in Cathal O'Byrne, *As I Roved Out* (Belfast: Blackstaff Press, 1982), and Ireland's appreciation of O'Byrne, Denis Ireland, 'Prince of storytellers: Cathal O'Byrne', *Belfast Telegraph*, 26 May 1956, p. 5. In the latter article, Ireland recalls:

> Every Saturday night, hail, rain or shine, I was lurking somewhere about the hall door, waiting for the newsboy to come darting up the street shouting the *Pink 'Un* or the *Tallig* so much so that it wouldn't have seemed to me like Sunday the next day if I hadn't had my previous night's ration of the adventures of Margit Bella and Mrs Twigglety.

16 'The man who created Mrs Twiggelty', *Ireland's Saturday Night*, 30 August 1957, p. 1.
17 *Ireland's Saturday Night*, 29 April 1916, p. 4.
18 *Ireland's Saturday Night*, 22 April 1916, p. 4.
19 Cathal O'Byrne, *Mrs Farrell's Fancies*, Catholic Truth Society of Ireland pamphlet no. 879 (Dublin: Veritas, 29 December 1934).
20 *Ireland's Saturday Night*, 27 January 1917, p. 4.
21 Austen Morgan, *Labour and Partition. The Belfast Working Class 1905–23* (London: Pluto, 1991), p. 199.
22 Roy F. Foster, *Modern Ireland: 1600–1972* (London: Penguin, 1989), p. 474.
23 Sean O'Casey, letter to Saemas O'Sheel, 26 May 1951. See Krause, *The Letters of Sean O'Casey. Vol. 2*, p. 800.
24 Letter to Horace Reynolds, 6 February 1938. See D. Krause, ed., *The Letters of Sean O'Casey. Vol. 1: 1910–41* (London: Cassell, 1975), p. 697.
25 Foster, *Modern Ireland*, pp. 486–7, has argued that the leaders of the Rising were to some extent responsible for the eventual partition of Ireland, in that their obsession with a 'pure and visionary republic of IRB tradition' led them to overlook the political complexity of Ulster and the manner in which their actions would be interpreted in that province. His thesis is persuasive but cognisance should be taken of Seamus Deane's coruscating attack on Foster's reading of the event in his essay 'Wherever green is read', in *Revising the Rising*, eds Máirín Ní Dhonnchadha and Theo Dorgan (Derry: Field Day, 1991), pp. 91–105, which argues that Foster's scepticism about the Rising and its significance is a direct result of his uneasiness about the extent to which it has since given ideological reinforcement to contemporary violent republicanism in Northern Ireland.
26 Bulmer Hobson, *Ireland Yesterday and Tomorrow* (Tralee: Anvil Books, 1968), p. 8.
27 'The Easter manoeuvres unexpectedly cancelled', *Irish News*, 24 April 1916, p. 4.
28 Hobson, *Ireland Yesterday and Tomorrow*, pp. 76–7.
29 Foster, *Modern Ireland*, p. 491.
30 W. J. McCormack, *Roger Casement in Death or Haunting the Free State* (Dublin: University College Dublin Press, 2002), p. 49.
31 George Boyce, *Nationalism in Ireland* (London: Routledge, 1991), p. 310.
32 J. Anthony Gaughan, ed., *Memoirs of Senator Joseph Connolly (1885–*

1961): A Founder of Modern Ireland (Dublin: Irish Academic Press, 1996), p. 96.

33 The headline of the story, 'Sir Roger Casement really arrested!', captures the paper's sense of incredulity that a figure it had previously seen as an incorrigible dreamer was capable of such an act that led to his arrest, *Irish News*, 25 April 1916, p. 5.

34 *Irish News*, 25 April 1916, p. 4.

35 *Irish News*, 1 May 1916, p. 4.

36 *Ireland's Saturday Night*, 29 April 1916, p. 4.

37 *Irish News*, 4 May 1916, p. 4.

38 Gerry Adams, *Falls Memories* (Dingle: Brandon Books, 1983), p. 54.

39 See the entry for O'Byrne in Bruce Stewart's extraordinary online dataset of Irish literature, the Princess Grace Irish Library (Monaco) Electronic Irish Records Dataset, at www.pgil-eirdata.org/.

40 Personal correspondence from Richard Madden (Cullen's son-in-law), 24 August 2000.

41 Cathal O'Byrne, 'Roger Casement's last will', *Irish Monthly*, 65 (October 1937), pp. 668–72; and 'Roger Casement's ceilidhe', in *Capuchin Annual* (Dublin: Capuchin Franciscan Fathers, 1946–47), pp. 312–14.

42 The key event in this was the publication of W. J. Maloney's *The Forged Casement Diaries* (Dublin: Talbot Press, 1936). Maloney's (now discredited) thesis initiated the long-running belief that the diaries were inauthentic and enabled individuals such as O'Byrne to publicise their memories of Casement without the taint of association. That O'Byrne's first published memoir of Casement appeared only a year after Maloney's book is surely significant. For a detailed consideration of the Maloney phenomenon, see McCormack, *Roger Casement in Death or Haunting the Free State*.

43 Cathal O'Byrne, *The Grey Feet of the Wind* (Dublin: Talbot Press, 1917).

44 G. B. Kenna, *Facts and Figures: The Belfast Pogroms 1920–2* (Belfast: Donaldson Archives, 1997, first published 1922).

45 Thomas Hennessey, *A History of Northern Ireland* (Dublin: Gill and Macmillan, 1997).

46 Eamon Phoenix, ed., *A Century of Northern Life: The Irish News and 100 Years of Ulster History 1890s–1990s*, ed. Eamon Phoenix (Belfast: Ulster Historical Foundation, 1995), p. 67.

47 Fran Brearton, *The Great War in Irish Poetry: W. B. Yeats to Michael Longley* (Oxford: Oxford University Press, 2000), p. 14.

48 Edna Longley, 'The Rising, the Somme and Irish memory', in *Revising the Rising*, eds Máirín Ní Dhonnchadha and Theo Dorgan (Derry: Field Day, 1991), p. 39.

49 Shane Leslie, Preface, in *The End of a Chapter* (London: Constable, 1916).

CHAPTER SIX

Roger Casement

I made awful mistakes, and did heaps of things wrong, confused much and failed at much – but I *very near* came to doing some big things ... on the Congo and elsewhere. It was only a shadow they tried on June 26; the real man was gone.

Roger Casement, 1916[1]

Poor Casement, the recent publication of his secret diaries has at last revealed the man as the worst of sinners, a bore.

Oswell Blakeston, 1960[2]

ON 23 February 1965, nearly fifty years after his execution, the remains of Roger Casement were returned to Ireland by Harold Wilson's new Labour administration. With great ceremony, the tricolour-draped coffin was led through the crowded Dublin streets to Glasnevin cemetery, where, at the graveside, the eighty-two-year-old president of Ireland, Eamon de Valera, delivered the oration. According to various reports, the president, an old, blind and infirm man who had risen from his sickbed against the advice of his doctors, was urged to cover his head from the swirls of snow blowing across the site. 'Casement', he replied, 'deserves better than that'.[3] While it may have been hoped that Casement's reinterment would place a full stop at the end of an unhappy sentence in Anglo-Irish relations, in actuality, and as the *Irish Press* editorialised, his work and legacy were 'not yet complete':[4] the national territory was still partitioned and unlikely to be unified in the near future, while the imminent fiftieth anniversary of the Easter Rising only cast in sharp relief the many frustrated aims and desires of the new state. De Valera's oration drew attention to this rupture and expressed the hope that Casement's example would provide its own inspiration:

> This grave ... will become a place of pilgrimage to which our young people will come and get renewed inspiration and renewed determination that they also will do everything that in them lies so that this nation which has been one in the past will be one again in the future.[5]

Such wishful thinking apart, it was perhaps appropriate that Casement should have returned when he did. In his death as in his life, Casement again came to embody that strange combination of frustrated good intentions and tragic outcomes that has remained the unhappy fate of his legacy since. As a symbol of unification or the coherency of national destiny, it is difficult to think of a more unsuitable figure for martyrdom.

Despite the reburial, the Casement affair has continued to be a troubling presence within Anglo-Irish relations. This has derived largely from lingering bitterness at the manner in which the British used his so-called 'Black Diaries' – journals purporting to be by Casement that describe a promiscuous homosexual lifestyle – in a campaign of defamation against him while he was imprisoned in 1916. Because the British government consistently refused to grant an independent enquiry to determine the authenticity of these texts, suspicions that they were forged have haunted his legacy. Although recent research has largely discredited this theory[6] and the British Home Office has insisted that it has now released all its known Casement documentation, it is clear that the argument is anything but finished. It is not the role of this book to contribute more material to the mass of literature already available on the Black Diaries' controversy,[7] but it is clear that the difficulties with Casement's legacy run deeper than a simple debate about textual authenticity. Indeed, it can be argued that Casement is probably the most complex figure in twentieth-century Anglo-Irish history.

Born in 1864 in Dublin but with Ulster-Scots and Manx ancestry, he served with distinction as a British consul in Portuguese East Africa (now Mozambique), Angola, Congo Free State and Brazil. During this period he gained international recognition for revealing the brutal exploitation of native labourers by white colonists in both the Congo and the Putamayo River Basin, and was knighted for his efforts in July 1911. He was obliged to retire on the grounds of ill-health in 1912 and settled in Ireland. Although by this stage Casement's sympathies for Irish nationalism were already well developed – he was a Gaelic Leaguer, a close friend of Francis Joseph Bigger and had played a major role in the 1904 Feis in the Glens (as described in Chapter 4) – from the period of his retirement from the Consular Service onwards he became increasingly more militant in his political perspective, helping to organise the newly formed Irish Volunteers in 1913 and going to New York in 1914 to seek American aid on their behalf. With the outbreak of war, Casement travelled to Berlin[8] with the hope of persuading the Germans to support nationalist insurgency in Ireland and of recruiting Irish prisoners of war for a nationalist Irish Brigade. He was frustrated in both desires. By 1916 the German command had made it clear that they could not spare a force of men anything close to that which Casement desired and with his own attempts at converting prisoners of war largely a failure, he realised that the planned rising scheduled for later in the year would be a military disaster. Returning to Ireland by German submarine with the hope of persuading the Rising's leaders to abandon their plans and to rendezvous with the *Aud*, a boat carrying largely antiquated German weapons for the use of the Volunteers, he was captured on landing in Kerry on 21 April.[9] Meanwhile the *Aud*, awaiting instruction off the coast of Ireland, was identified by a British patrol boat and forced to make its way to Queenstown harbour, where the ship's skipper scuttled the vessel. The whole adventure had been an absolute failure and, indeed, as British naval intelligence had been intercepting Casement's communications from Germany for an extended period prior to his capture, it was also an inevitability. From this point on events moved quickly: Casement, ill, exhausted and in despair, was found guilty of treason and sentenced to death. On 30 June he was degraded from his knighthood and on 3 August he was executed at Pentonville Prison.

To the point of his execution and beyond, then, Casement remained recognisably both a British agent with residual loyalties to that state and a committed activist for militant Irish nationalism. Similarly, and inevitably, he was *mis*recognised within both these positions: as a traitor whose treachery was, at best, debatable and as an Irish patriot whose activities appeared to misunderstand the aims and motivations of Irish nationalism during that same period. These contradictions are identifiable in the mass of literature produced by the Casement affair, a corpus of texts which has established and now repeats its own recurring pattern despite the alignments forced by the continuing debate as to the integrity of the Black Diaries. Even if the considerable silences, ellipses and contradictions implicit within Casement's day-to-day experience are ignored, the slippages inherent in his political ideology have generated a biographical practice unusual in its desire, in the words of the dedication to Brian Inglis's *Roger Casement*, to 'help people to understand the problem'.[10] The blandness of this formula (whether understood in terms of Casement as 'problem', Ireland as 'problem' or Anglo-Ireland as 'problem') is increased through repetition, although it is often seasoned with a psychoanalytic approach that imputes coherent motives to what are assumed to be his often untenable activities.[11] It is not the ambivalences of Casement's activities or sexual orientation that has provoked this ongoing speculation – Anglo-Irish history is littered with similarly ambiguous figures whose legacies are now readily explicable – but rather the manner in which both the British and Irish states have proved unable to acknowledge the troubling role Casement has played in the subversion of their respective national narratives. Casement complicates a reading of the Easter Rising as foundational moment, just as his disavowal of Britain disturbs a perception of the British state as self-reforming in its capacity to analyse and ultimately discard its adherence to the colonial project through enlightened administration.

It was, coincidentally, precisely these kinds of issues that greatly occupied Casement himself. With his consular role, Casement's ability to move between the poles of colonialism – from the centre of imperial power where processed goods are consumed to the primary sites of raw materials and exploitation – granted him a keen awareness of the dialectic nature of the process and a concomitant belief that a comparative political philosophy was a necessity for an Irish revolutionary movement. It is for this reason that in his published writings on Ireland and elsewhere there is a reliance on the power of analogy to affirm an ethical position, a tendency that led inevitably to a form of postcolonial analysis in his writings. For instance, the logic of the parallels he drew between Ireland's status and the atrocities he witnessed in the Belgian Congo became the method by which he familiarised himself with the increasingly complex terms of the Ulster crisis in the period of his re-engagement with Irish politics. A letter to the *Ulster Guardian* reprinted in *The Crime Against Europe*[12] and signed 'Ruari Macasmund', is illustrative of Casement's compulsion:

> It recalls an incident of my earlier days in Africa. A French sailing ship was being piloted, in the eighties, into the harbour of Sierra Leone. The pilot, naturally, was as black as your hat, being a pure-bred African negro, inordinately proud of his British or Anglo-Saxon descent. The captain and he fell to verbal loggerheads over some trivial point of navigation, and after a sharp exchange of nautical civilities the pilot won the day with:
>
> 'Ah! well, neva mind, sah, we beat you at Waterloo!'
>
> It is this racial pride that has given birth to the Ulster Scots.

While a glib analogy, this satirical sense of 'racial pride' is one that recognises the inevitably hybridised foundation upon which any singular identity is built. In addition, although less controversially, Casement believed his own status as an 'Irish native' drove his humanitarianism, for 'the more we love our land and wish to help our people the more keenly we feel we cannot turn a deaf ear to suffering and injustice in any part of the world'.[13] Such a parallel led Casement, in 'The elsewhere empire', to develop the theory of the 'non-imperial instinct',[14] a condition that impels a moral empathy and one shared by Ireland, India and, indeed, most conquered nations. As he observed, 'it was only because I was an Irishman that I could understand fully I think their whole scheme of wrongdoing at work in the Congo'.[15] In light of the atrocities he witnessed in Africa, Casement's adherence to such a binarism is understandable – it was part of his mobilisation of rage – and yet he chose not (or was unable) to recognise its consequent dangers. It is this element of Casement's work that James Joyce identified in 'The cyclops' chapter of *Ulysses*:

> – Well, says J.J., if they're any worse than those Belgians in the Congo Free State they must be bad. Did you read that report by a man what's this his name is?
> – Casement, says the citizen. He's an Irishman.
> – Yes, that's the man, says J.J. Raping the women and girls and flogging the natives on the belly to squeeze all the red rubber they can out of them.[16]

In a book obsessed with an exploration of the efficacies and limits of analogy, the cyclopean citizen works through an exhaustive litany of colonial outrage which culminates in the inevitable violence he visits on Leopold Bloom, a figure who, unlike Casement, is denied the appellation of Irishman. Through this it can be argued that Joyce is not simply dismissing the parallels that can be traced across the global colonial system,[17] nor is he aligning Casement too closely with the brutalities of the drunken exchange, but rather he is warning of the dangerous teleologies that such analogies generate, that the seeming duality of a comparative method is in actuality monolinear in its momentum.

As with so many aspects of Casement's life, this interest in analogy, with its emblematic overtones, is one that has been used by biographers and commentators to extrapolate the contradictions of his life and beliefs. As early descriptions of Casement stressed his embodiment of a moral condition that he simultaneously lacked the ability to recognise, so there is an irony in the fact that, during and following his trial for treason, he was perceived to be a misplaced individual quite remote from the ideals of the Irish nationalism that he espoused so fervently. As a result, he has always fitted uncomfortably into the restrictive tropes of the classic martyr. To put this another way, as a British civil servant exposing human rights abuses, Casement was understood as embodying moral integrity, while as an Irish revolutionary he was perceived as a muddled fanatic espousing an ideological position remote from his own instinctive life.

Importantly, this is not necessarily an interpretation dependent upon the subsequent shift of opinion generated by the revelations of the Black Diaries (which, if anything, tend to confirm a perception of Casement as a figure dedicated to gratifying immediate instincts) but rather it is one that corresponds to a template dividing Casement's life into two distinct programmes: instinctive, unexamined genius followed by a painful reflection on its loss and a failure to recapture its power. This can be understood in Casement's own terms as a distinction between 'the real man' and the 'shadow',[18] while, more tellingly, it corresponds closely to the dominant interpretative paradigm through which the lives of Oscar Wilde and (before that) Charles Stewart Parnell have been read. Here, coincidental material dominates. Wilde and Casement were each brought to their own peculiar fates in British courtrooms partly because of their sexual obsession with profligate, parasitic younger men (respectively Lord Alfred Douglas and Adler Christensen). For Roger Sawyer, Christensen, the Norwegian 'travelling companion' who accompanied Casement on his ill-fated expedition to Germany, 'comes out of the whole sorry business more tarnished than anyone else. He was happy to betray his master solely for money',[19] while René MacColl achieves the feat of being both more blunt and yet more insidious in his accusations: 'Christensen was a plump twenty-four year old who had expensive tastes and used make-up',[20] he notes. Such scapegoating neatly dovetails the tropes of inexorable fate, the secret flaw and the instinctual, unexamined, life, while aligning Casement to a pattern of moral behaviour that had been employed and refined in the reception of Wilde's earlier disgrace.

As this analogy gains momentum so its tragic potential is underlined. Most notably, in the fall of both Casement and Wilde, a perception exists that a clear moment arises in which the possibility of escape is revealed and yet not taken. As has become well known, for Wilde this arises at the Cadogan Hotel immediately prior to his arrest on a charge of committing indecent acts. The opportunity to take a train to Dover and a boat to France is discussed but Wilde, according to Richard Ellmann, 'seemed disinclined to take it ... a half-packed suitcase lay on the bed, emblem of contradictory impulses. He was tired of action.'[21] Just as Wilde's refusal to save himself at this moment is also a demonstration of commitment, or at least a recognition of his inevitable fate within the British justice system, so Casement is presented with a similarly emblematic moment and makes the same choice, as the final entry in his German diary makes clear:

> The last days are all a nightmare, and I have only a confused memory of them, and some periods are quite blank in my mind, only a sense of horror

> and repugnance to life. But I daresay the clouds will break and brighter skies dawn, at least for old Ireland.
>
> I go tonight with Monteith and one man only of the 'boys', and I am quite sure it is the most desperate piece of folly ever committed; but I go gladly ... if those poor lads at home are to be in the fire, then my place is with them.[22]

As this indicates, Casement perceived his return to Ireland and his part in what he termed, according to papers released by MI5, a 'wholly futile scheme'[23] as an inevitability. Although his fate was effectively sealed through this action, at the same time, and with the plan of converting Irish prisoners of war a failure, no other option presented itself (even though he might have better served Irish republicanism by maintaining its presence in Germany). As Frank Hall, a senior MI5 officer who interrogated Casement, summarised Casement's predicament, 'he had been "let down" by the Germans and placed in the position of either refusing their offer, and so being branded by his friends in Ireland and America as a coward and a traitor ... or of going ahead'.[24] In a manner similar to Wilde's earlier prevarication, this moment signals the point at which freewill is subsumed by fate as the inexorable force of tragedy narrative takes over. A different perspective on this is provided by F. E. Smith, who, in his *Famous Trials of History*, reveals himself to be preoccupied with the notion of Casement as an inveterate gambler prepared to risk all in the hope that he might win. In these terms the state was justified in calling in its debts: 'Casement, blinded by hatred of this country, as malignant in quality as it was sudden in origin, had played a desperate hazard in our hour of need. He had lost, and his life was forfeit.'[25]

It is in these ways that both Casement's life and his theories of political emancipation have been understood in terms of an implicit 'flaw'. Best encapsulated by Sawyer's biography, *Casement: The Flawed Hero*,[26] invariably this takes two forms: firstly, the flaw is a manifestation of, to use the recurring description in the biographies, 'womanliness'; secondly, it is seen to exhibit itself as a form of childishness, mindlessness or, less pejoratively, innocence. Such accusations gain resonance when glimpsed through the frame of subsequent events. Paul Hyland, in his *The Black Heart: A Voyage to Central Africa*,[27] notes that the Congolese, as well as naming Casement 'Monofuma' ('son of a king'), also termed him 'Swami' ('woman's god'): an appellation the book, through its reluctance to consider the contexts of such a title, deems to be self-evident and, by inference, transcultural. Similarly, although of greater significance to Casement's ultimate fate, Sir Ernley Blackwell, the Home Office legal advisor to the Cabinet, in a memorandum to the Cabinet of 17 July 1916, detailed the case for execution rather than imprisonment by stressing Casement's sanity at the time he perpetrated his treachery. The question of Casement's homosexuality was of central importance to the establishment of such a case, as Blackwell had to account for it without, in turn, allowing an inference of insanity to be drawn:

> Casement's diary and his ledger entries covering many pages of closely typed matter, show that he has for years been addicted to the grossest sodomitical practices. Of later years he seems to have completed the full cycle of sexual degeneracy, and from a pervert, has become an invert – a 'woman' or pathic who derives his satisfaction from attracting men and inducing them to use him.[28]

Blackwell's model – the progression from perversion to inversion, described by Medb Ruane as 'the last taboo'[29] and much in vogue during this period – suggests that sexual identity, if disorientated from its original course, will inevitably circle back upon itself, finding desirable that which it originally once was. However, as the ultimate object of desire (the masculine) is simultaneously out of reach, unable to connect back to its own idealised self-image, so the condition of 'woman' that Casement achieves is one perceived to be perpetually in a state of desire for its other, a state which allows only the possibility of being 'used' – an inference which for Blackwell perhaps also suggests the way Casement, an honoured civil servant, was 'used' by Irish nationalism. As suggested above, it was around this pseudo-objective theorising that the British Cabinet's delicate case for execution was built, in that it allowed such degeneracy to be understood as both extraordinary and yet not the product of an insane or disordered mind. In these terms the relationship of perversion to what is termed 'closely typed matter' similarly indicates that a parallel can be traced between the vagaries of textual eccentricity (a charge that has been constantly associated with Casement) and what would subsequently become deviant behaviour.

While this example may tell us more about the psycho-sexual instincts of Blackwell and the contemporary fashion for sub-Freudian analysis than about Casement's actual crime, it is worth noting that similar equations of sexual degeneracy have subsequently been charted in order to explicate Casement's motivations. Even by 1976, B. L. Reid, in his *Lives of Roger Casement*, could state that Blackwell's bizarre diagnosis of Casement's temperament was 'clinically if cruelly accurate'.[30] The biographer Brian Inglis, unable to encounter Casement's 'womanliness' in any other way, accounts for it by citing Proust's description of the Baron de Charlus in *Remembrance of Things Past*, who 'belonged to that race of beings, less paradoxical than they appear, whose ideal is manly simply because their temperament is feminine',[31] a comparison which closely adheres to the parameters of Blackwell's analysis in its restatement of masculinity as the ultimate, yet unreachable, goal. Questions of temperament similarly obsess MacColl, who accepts without question Casement's inherent femininity but is perplexed as to its lack of signifying traces: 'Although Casement was a clandestine pervert, he certainly looked anything but degenerate, and there was nothing effeminate about his manner or speech',[32] he reports. MacColl's response here is symptomatic of a perception of Casement that has remained constant since the discovery of the diaries and which makes itself evident in both condemnations and vindications of Casement's life. At once the cause of both perplexity and outrage, it is Casement's refusal to signify, the fact that there is little material corroboration of his inner life in the manner of, say, Oscar Wilde, that renders him an invisible presence for biographical enquiry. If this suggests that Casement is, himself, something of an unstable text, it similarly indicates why the notion of the self-evident 'flaw' – a condition which can be alluded to with confidence and yet which remains tantalisingly beyond analysis – has become the staple term of reference and one which can encompass issues of gender and national affiliation. For Alfred Noyes, Casement was 'an impulsive Irishman' (a figure contrasted with 'any fair-minded Englishman') whose plan for national liberation was no more than 'the impossible scheme of a quixotic dreamer',[33] while for Ruane the issue is of more dramatic importance: 'the pleasurable forgoing of power implied by the act of being penetrated cracked open a faultline which reached from British manhood to the global powermongering of colonialism'.[34] Less sensationally, although of greater relevance to Casement's own destruction, for F. E. Smith, the attorney-general at the time and thus the figure in charge of Casement's prosecution, it was the attempt to persuade Irish prisoners of war to change allegiance in itself that was deemed 'unmanly'.[35]

Whether childlike or womanly, the ultimate result of such constructions is to portray Casement as mindless, or at least irrational, and, in turn, to depict his achievements as the result of sheer essentialist force: a reading that enables Casement's naivety to be allied to what were considered his supernatural powers (as I will discuss). After Casement's execution, Joseph Conrad, Casement's colleague and sometime friend in the Congo, summarised this conjunction neatly:

> already in Africa I judged that he was a man, properly speaking, of no mind at all. I don't mean stupid. I mean that he was all emotion. By emotional force ... he made his way, and sheer temperament – a truly

> tragic personality; all but the greatness of which he had not a trace. Only vanity.[36]

More poignantly, James McCarroll's memoir describes Casement himself, exhausted by the obsessive courtroom interrogation of his character, ultimately making sense of his experience in similar terms:

> It is a strange strange fate, and now I stand face to face with death I feel just as if they were going to kill a boy – and my hands so free from blood and my heart always so compassionate and pitiful that I cannot comprehend how anyone wants to hang me.[37]

It is for the failure to take such naivety into account, rather than for reasons of justice, that Casement's execution was perceived by W. B. Yeats as evil, the concept he invoked when appealing to prime minister Herbert Asquith on Casement's behalf in 1916.

As a creature of 'sheer temperament', it was Casement's ability to beguile by force of personality that dominates many contemporary accounts of him. The young Conrad was similarly impressed and his often-quoted first impressions of Casement remain powerful:

> I can assure you that he is a limpid personality. There is a touch of the conquistador in him too; for I have seen him start off into an unspeakable wilderness swinging a crookhandled stick for all weapon, with two bull-dogs, Paddy (white) and Biddy (Brindle) at his heels and a Loanda boy carrying a bundle for all company. A few months afterwards it so happened that I saw him come out again, a little leaner, a little browner, with his sticks, dogs, and Loanda boy, and quietly serene as though he had been for a stroll in the park.... I always thought some particle of La Casas' soul had found refuge in his indomitable body.... He could tell you things! Things I have tried to forget, things I never did know.[38]

Casement was similarly impressed by Conrad[39] but subsequent to this encouraging first beginning, and after a brief visit by Casement to Conrad's Pent Farm in 1904, their friendship cooled and, indeed, Conrad, the naturalised patriot, was unable to understand or forgive Casement's pro-German views and his ultimate repudiation of Britain and the honours it had conferred upon him. The germ of Conrad's ultimate denunciation of Casement, quoted above, that he had 'no mind at all.... Only vanity', is identifiable in this image of the mesmeric Casement striding into the interior; there is a similarity here, and ultimately a shared fate, between Casement and Kurtz, the mesmeric *Übermensch* of *Heart of Darkness*. Just as Casement would disappear into the jungle for months at a time so Kurtz would 'go off on another ivory hunt; disappear for weeks; forget himself amongst these people – forget himself'.[40] While Casement could 'tell you things! Things I have tried to forget, things I never did know', the Russian sailor says of Kurtz: 'You don't talk with that man – you listen to him',[41] 'this man has enlarged my mind!',[42] 'He made me see things – things'.[43]

An interview with Conrad in the *New York Evening Post* from 1923, intriguingly entitled 'Conrad and Casement: hut mates in Africa',[44] strengthens this parallel:

> In connection with *Heart of Darkness*, Conrad told me of an incident which happened in Africa while he, like Marlow, was waiting for rivets that did not come. For three months he shared a hut with Roger Casement, who was at that time recruiting labor for the Belgian ivory trade in the Congo. His first impression of Casement he told me so vividly that it stands out with the clearness and blackness of a silhouette caught unexpectedly in a lonely place, casting a hint of ill omen.
>
> Conrad was running his boat down the sluggish river when a tall, gaunt figure rose against the perpendicular face of a dark bluff. Crouching behind him, in an attitude suggesting a perverted sort of worship, was his servant and at his heels were two black bulldogs. The sinister picture did not fade, for Casement remained always mysterious, and, after months of the close companionship necessitated by a hut in the wilderness, Conrad knew him no better.
>
> Perhaps it is this vision of Casement that influenced Conrad in his conception of 'Kurtz.' Conrad waited years for the closing scene in this story and at last the phrase used by Kurtz 'my intended' came to him like a torch in the darkness.

As twenty years had passed between this account and Conrad's first impression of Casement quoted above, it is unsurprising that Conrad chooses to emphasise how little of Casement he actually knew, not least because of the inference that may have been drawn from the fact that they shared a hut together for three months and the subsequent revelations about Casement alluded to by the article's reference to 'perverted' worship. However, this account is still far removed from Conrad's record in his diary of their first meeting: an event 'which I should consider a great pleasure under any circumstances and now it becomes a positive piece of luck. Thinks, speaks well, most intelligent and very sympathetic.'[45] Even accounting for Conrad's own paranoia about the ways in which sexual and national identity could be misconceived, if nothing else such a comparison demonstrates the ease with which Casement's personal charm was subsequently reread as sinister manipulation.

Such parallels between Casement and Kurtz, and the fear that Casement would recognise that Conrad's perspective on the Congo in *Heart of Darkness* was greatly exaggerated, suggest why Conrad in a letter to Casement referred to the novel as 'an awful fudge',[46] and yet they also prompt their own morbid coincidences. Just as Conrad ultimately denounces Casement for his 'vanity', so Kurtz is described as 'contemptibly childish. He desired to have kings meet him at railway-stations on his return from some ghastly Nowhere, where he intended to accomplish great things',[47] a condemnation echoed by Casement's own sense that 'I *very near* came to doing some big things ... on the Congo and elsewhere'.[48] In this way both Kurtz and Casement were figures lost in the savage interior, indicting the violence of colonialism just as they embodied, through their implication in the machinery of exploitation, its worst excesses. If this seems excessive it is worth noting that Kurtz, too, would have been the paradigm of the perfect colonial administrator, an *agent exceptionnel*[49] like Casement, but for his own flaw, his own hamartia.

It is important to recognise that such constructions gain most resonance when considered alongside the supernatural powers that Casement was also perceived as exercising. Again, as a creature of 'sheer temperament', it was Casement's ability to beguile by force of personality that dominates many contemporary accounts of him. E. D. Morel, writing four years before Casement's trial and execution, described him thus:

> There is in the whole carriage and play of the man a something which would stamp him as distinctive and apart in any assembly; a something which speaks of pure metal and a soul almost primitive both in simplicity and strength, set in the frame of an athlete and seen through the outward trappings of a grave courtesy and perfect ease of manner. I have never known such personal magnetism emanate from any man. It is felt by all. Alike by the cultured statesman and cynical diplomatist of the West, and by the naked savage. It is not the physical gifts which are the primary cause, rather the mental unuttered conviction that is instantly formed that this man is the soul of honour, and has imbibed from his solitary communion with Nature an unerring faculty of distinguishing truth from falsehood.[50]

This combination of primitivism with aspects of supernaturalism is not coincidental; indeed, the latter is a function of the former and as a result Casement's character is read as an embodiment of an almost savage simplicity. In many ways, and despite the sophistication of recent historical enquiry into Casement's life, traces of this have remained potent. One of the key issues implicit in the debate about the status of the diaries (and in light of the 'physical gifts' referred to by Morel) is Casement's remarkable sexual stamina that their testimony demands. For Angus Mitchell, such an inference is conclusive: 'The diaries speak of him having five sexual partners in one night. I can tell you the climate there is such that to have one partner is heroic – five would be downright impossible.'[51] Similarly, Blackwell's memorandum to the Cabinet of 17 July 1916 records 'the impression that Casement's own account of the frequency of his performances was incredible and of itself suggested that he was labouring under hallucination'. Because there was until recently a paucity of evidence on Casement's sex life to corroborate the Black Diaries, this became a crucial factor in establishing their veracity, for, if they were not genuine, then Casement appeared to have been a man without any sex life at all. As with other aspects of his life, an unlikely 'all or nothing' scenario emerged.

That said, the sense of Casement we gain through the diaries as an embodiment of sexual charisma is an interpretation that is strikingly similar to other contemporary accounts of his more general character. As I have described in Chapter 4, Cathal O'Byrne describes Casement as the centre of attention at a ceilidh held in his honour at Bigger's Ardrigh home[52] and it is clear that all the habitués of Ardrigh were, to varying degrees, inspired, galvanised and, perhaps, a little daunted by Casement's regular visits. He appeared to have the ability to transfix his listeners with the force of his arguments (even if later, and with the spell broken, such arguments often appeared fantastical) and the devotion he regularly inspired led some to believe his powers occupied the realm of the uncanny. In 1916 Canon T. S. Lindsay, of Dublin's Christchurch Cathedral, described Casement as both a 'crack-brained fanatic' and the possessor of 'some strange psychic power which fascinated and almost paralysed the minds of those he sought to influence',[53] while more positively Gertrude Bannister (later Parry), Casement's much-loved cousin, believed his mystical talents, even at the time of his trial, when his powers were considered largely to have been spent, enabled him to exchange thoughts across the crowded courtroom with Eva Gore-Booth – and this despite the fact that they had never met previously.[54]

As these examples suggest, despite Casement's obvious charisma, his charms were often received with some ambivalence. Indeed, while there is no doubt as to his ability to inspire individuals to an ever-greater commitment to extreme republican politics, in retrospect many were not grateful to have been so motivated. Nowhere was this more apparent than at Ardrigh itself, the house that was in many ways to become his spiritual home. Casement first visited Ardrigh in 1904 and the connection would endure until his death. Under Bigger's influence, Casement played a role in the organisation of the Glens Feis of that year but it was in political rather than cultural terms that Ardrigh would be of most significance in his development. Regular contact with the Irish Republican Brotherhood (IRB) organisers Denis McCullough and Bulmer Hobson enabled Casement to bring a degree of political coherence to his Anglophobic instincts, and the two would remain faithful to him during his later trials. Others clearly harboured doubts. Shane Leslie was always of the opinion that Casement's 'work for the natives had unhinged his mind',[55] and, despite his own commitment to nationalist orthodoxy, maintained a belief that the Black Diaries were genuine, as 'John Quinn had recognised the handwriting'.[56] The response of Bigger himself to Casement's arrest was more complex. While at one level he was clearly one of those responsible for lighting the fire of modern militant republicanism in the North, at the same time his own involvement in the events that would lead up to 1916 was usually tangential and typified by an extreme wariness. Casement's arrest threatened to shatter this carefully constructed disguise and as such left Bigger in a desperately apprehensive state. This was not merely because of the degree to which a Casement trial might reveal the extent of his own connection with those who organised and led the Easter Rising, but also because the now feverish rumours about Casement's private life were clearly capable of confirming what many believed to be true about Bigger's own sexuality. For this reason Bigger's support for Casement in 1916 was decidedly half-hearted. By comparison, it is interesting to observe that if O'Byrne had similar fears for his own reputation – as he surely must have done – these did not prevent him from providing emotional support for Casement through the exchange of letters and gifts during the period of his imprisonment. This was typical of his kindliness and O'Byrne would always refer to Casement as 'that gallant gentleman and unforgettably most gracious friend'.[57]

Bigger was able – albeit in a small way – to minimise some of the potential damage. Casement had left many of his private papers at Ardrigh for safekeeping and in a telegram to the German embassy in Washington on 6 November 1914 (and one intercepted by British naval intelligence) had requested that a message be communicated telling 'Bigger, solicitor, Belfast to conceal everything belonging to me'.[58] The exact timetable of Bigger's actions in response to this request is uncertain but, as Jeffrey Dudgeon has proved in impressive detail,[59] that he did eventually destroy the papers is beyond doubt. The contents of the papers will always remain unknown, but Dudgeon also provides a convincing argument that, because they relate to the period prior to Casement's direct involvement with Germany, he would have had little reason to desire their concealment had they been anything but sexual in content. This is confirmed by Bigger's nephew, Joseph W. Bigger, who in 1937 disclosed that in 1915 his uncle had burnt material belonging to Casement that proved he was both actively plotting against the British and engaging in homosexual activity.[60] Surprisingly, perhaps – especially considering that by this stage Christensen was also implicating Bigger in the conspiracy – the security forces never searched Ardrigh and Bigger managed to ride out the worst of the scandal, although the discreet distance he maintained between himself and Casement following the latter's arrest was a perceived betrayal that Casement's niece, Gertrude Parry, would never forget. Indeed, when the crisis finally broke it was five women who would prove to be Casement's bravest allies: Parry, Alice Milligan (to whom, during the trial, Casement slipped a message saying simply 'Write a poem about *this*, Alice!'), Alice Stopford Green, Ada McNeill and Eva Gore-Booth.

Casement's final days while waiting for execution have been well documented and, as with other aspects of his life, have attained emblematic status. Most notable of his activities during this period was his decision to convert to Catholicism, although in fact, as Casement had been baptised into the Catholic church as a child at the urging of his mother (another feature of his life he shared with Wilde), he had only to be 'reconciled' to its teachings. Despite this, Casement's path to Catholicism was complicated by the archbishop, Cardinal Bourne, who requested that Casement sign a recantation of his political beliefs before being accepted into the Church. This was eventually overcome by treating Casement as being in *articulo mortis* (i.e. facing imminent death) and so able to receive the sacraments without further question.[61] Casement's decision had been greatly encouraged by his Belfast associates, particularly O'Byrne and Bridget Matthews, Bigger's housekeeper at Ardrigh and 'a pure Gael and deeply religious'.[62] O'Byrne had what can only be described as a lifelong obsession with conversion from the errors of Protestantism and along with Matthews he bombarded Casement with religious icons while he awaited execution. O'Byrne's subsequent accounts of this period[63] acknowledge the success of this encouragement and in one ('Roger Casement's last will') he reproduces with pride 'the last letter written by him from his cell', an epistle to Matthews:

> Your letter came to me yesterday in this prison cell and it was like a glimpse of the garden, with the wall-flowers and the Japanese cherry, to get your message.
>
> First, I want to tell you that your crucifix, the medals and the scapular came to me three weeks ago, but the letter only yesterday. They are always with me, and, please God, will be as long as I am here.
>
> Remember me to so many, and thank those friends who pray for me – and don't pay attention to the lies, they are compliments really, and we need not mind compliments, you and I, Biddy dear.

> Do you remember the cradle song I liked so much? Get Cathal to sing it for me, and give him my love and thanks from my heart, also to Colm [O'Lochlainn], if he is near you, and Dinnny [McCullough] and Seaghan Dhu [Rooney], whenever they come back to you and the old room again. I dreamt last night I was lying before the fire in it, and the boys were there telling stories, and you standing at the door....

The night that Casement recalls here is the same evening that O'Byrne describes in his article 'Roger Casement's ceilidhe', as discussed in Chapter 4. Casement had not always been as sentimental about Bigger's efforts, writing once to Alice Stopford Green that 'those gatherings are amusing but one does not want too many of them',[64] but in this instance the memory of Ardrigh comes to embody that period of innocence before the ideal of 'Irish Ireland' became inextricably linked to revolutionary violence. O'Byrne himself would find comfort in the same memories in the years after partition.

Alongside things given by Matthews, O'Byrne had sent Casement a statue of 'Our Lady' blessed by a 'dear old learned priest'. Bannister's memoir corroborates the impression that O'Byrne, Matthews and the days he spent at Ardrigh were much in Casement's thoughts during this final period.[65] She records that one of the few possessions he managed to conceal from the wardens was 'a long letter from C___ (a man who knew him and who was constantly at Mr Francis Joseph Bigger's Ardrigh Belfast)', while, in turn, Casement left O'Byrne a copy of Rupert Brooke's *1914 and Other Poems*[66] with the second verse of O'Byrne's poem 'O friend of my heart' inscribed on the front endpaper, an indication that Casement must have memorised it. There is nothing surprising about the fact that Rupert Brooke's poetry was the subject of the exchange. Despite its pro-British sentiments, *1914 and Other Poems* was a publishing phenomenon as much for the posthumous cult of Brooke's personality as the poems themselves and the tragic nature of his early death would have appealed to the romantic, slightly maudlin, characteristic that O'Byrne and Casement shared. Moreover, Brooke's poetry can appear oddly Irish in its relationship to 'the nation', in that the poet figure it evokes encapsulates its spirit, makes it manifest and then re-presents that spirit back to the nation itself. Certainly, it would not have been hard for Casement to have transferred the emotion of Brooke's most famous poem 'The soldier' ('If I should die, think only this of me:/That there's some corner of a foreign field/That is forever England') to his own predicament. The inscription itself – memorably if bizarrely described by B. L. Reid in a garbled account of its provenance as a 'homosexual poem'[67] – had appeared in the collection *The Lane of the Thrushes: Some Ulster Love*

Songs, which O'Byrne had co-written with Cahir Healy in 1905, and describes a passionate if obscure relationship:

> O Friend of my Heart!
> 'Tis a debt I pay in this telling
> for hours of delight,
> To lay my wreath of bays at
> Your feet I would climb afar
> to your height.
> I would walk the flints with
> a terrible joy, if at the
> Journey's end
> I would greet you, O Friend![68]

In an often angry denunciation of Reid's analysis, Séamus O'Neill, one time professor of history at Carysfort College, denies that Casement could have been the subject of O'Byrne's paean and proposes Bigger as a more likely candidate, on the grounds that Bigger was 'a Maecenas to struggling artists and his praise would have meant much to O'Byrne'.[69] Certainly, there is no evidence to contradict this view and even O'Byrne's own account of the exchange does not propose Casement as the poem's subject. That said, when taking into account the manner in which Casement configured his own desires, the masochism of the poem's concluding image seems entirely appropriate to the way in which he lived his life. Either way, this small volume was, so O'Byrne claims, 'the only thing he had with him in his cell the night before he died'.[70]

As Casement reconciled himself to his end he was forbidden to see anybody alone save for the Catholic chaplain Father McCarroll, Father Carey and Canon Reid. Thirty-four years later McCarroll produced a short memoir of Casement's last days for private circulation[71] which reproduced many of Casement's final statements, including an indication that Catholicism had become the central, and ultimately resolved, issue in his life: 'if I die as I think is fated tomorrow morning, I shall die with my sins forgiven and God's pardon on my soul and I shall die with many good and brave men'. So impressed was McCarroll with Casement's piety that his ultimate judgement of his character was simply: 'He was a saint. We should be praying *to* him rather than *for* him.'[72] Despite this powerful assertion, the suspicion remains that Casement's final days have been so resolutely placed within the paradigm of the conversion narrative by Catholic proselytisers that few traces of more earthly agonies remain. An important antidote to such eulogising is Gertrude Bannister's remarkable memoir of her final memories of Casement;[73] this is a harrowing testimony of his arrest and trial, and one of the most powerful hidden documents of twentieth-century Anglo-Irish politics. Its agonising account of her movements after seeing Casement for the last time serves as a corrective to those writings which manifest an impatient desire to celebrate Casement's elevation to the status of martyr:

> I said 'Stop [to the warder], I can't go yet' – I was shaking so I could scarcely stand and the sobs were rending me. 'You can't wait' he said 'you must go'. 'I can't go like this', I said, 'into the public street. So ask the policeman outside to get me a taxi'. 'No' he said 'pull yourself together, go on now' and he opened the gate and pushed me out and locked it with a clang behind me. I wanted to shriek and beat on it with my hands, my lips kept saying 'let him out, let him out'. I staggered down the road, crying out loud and people gazed at me – I got home somehow. Now writing it down, I cry and cry and want to scream out but what's the good – I can't see now to write any more today – he was inside waiting for death, such a death – I was outside and I wanted to die.

As the memoir dies away at this point so the handwriting becomes increasingly wild and the grammar and punctuation more erratic. Such a confused and desperate sense of the effect of state power on an individual (who within a few days of writing this account was to lose her livelihood as a teacher as a result of her support for Casement) serves perhaps as an appropriate text of closure for a man whose own life was concluded in the tangled nets of spurious legal procedure and nationalist hysteria.

Casement was hanged on the morning of 3 August after receiving what was to be his first and last holy communion. The appeal against the sentence had been slightly half-hearted and he had expected its dismissal. Indeed, it can be argued that Casement had been preparing himself for death for the previous two years. In this context, his final cry of 'for God and Kathleen ni Houlihan' provided a neat summary of the pre-occupations that had eventually taken over his life. One hour before the execution a crowd had gathered on Caledonian Road outside Pentonville Prison. It consisted mostly of women, children and munitions workers, but the only sign they would gain that the sentence had been carried out was the striking of the prison's minute bell. Nevertheless, on hearing the hour struck a small group within the crowd raised a cheer – a moment that inspired Milligan, who had remained in what she called 'gay, blood-guilty London' after the trial, to write one of her most powerful poems:

> How from England's beauty
> Can I my heart withhold?
> *By thinking of her crowds that cheered*
> *When a death bell tolled.*[74]

Back in Belfast the *Irish News* also responded forcefully to Casement's death and, despite noting that 'the Irish people as a whole do not accept him as an addition to their martyrology', recognised with some prescience that 'the slanders with which those who clamoured for his death supported their demand' were little more than 'the emanations of a brutal "war" spirit which threatens more and more, as time goes on, to debase the standard of whatever civilisation is left'. As the editorial continued:

> A glimpse at this process of decay was afforded by the conduct of some who, when the solemn death bell was tolled at Pentonville, raised cheers. While these thoughtless persons, who, for the sake of humanity, we are glad to learn from one newsagency were mainly women and children, were hailing the announcement of the departure of a soul from this world with notes of jubilation, it is gladdening to record that the devout Irish people who were present 'fell to their knees and with bowed heads remained a few minutes silently praying for the repose' of the dead. It is a striking contrast which relieves the tragedy of some of its horror.[75]

The *Irish News* had been no friend to Casement and his schemes[76] and, as such, its anger at the English 'popular lust for blood' indicates something of the resentment which the execution of the last of the 1916 leaders provoked in nationalist Ireland. Indeed, one correspondent to the paper proposed that the cheering crowds outside Pentonville represented nothing less than 'downright unchristian brutality' and argued that 'we shall have to look beyond Belgium and France to find a parallel'.[77] Casement's death completed the process of alienation of nationalist Ireland that had begun with the execution of his co-conspirators four months earlier and the dream of Home Rule was, to all useful purposes, now finished.

In 1934 de Valera, when asked to respond to a proposal for a film about Casement by Universal Studios in Hollywood, expressed the belief that 'a further period of time must elapse before the full extent of Casement's sacrifice can be understood'.[78] While enticingly ambiguous in itself, de Valera's caution is salutary if only because the web of motivations structuring Casement's activities remains almost as tangled now as it did then. This, however, has not prevented the fascination of the Casement case from prompting considerable literary and biographical speculation. Aside from the many accounts of Casement's life that this chapter has referred to, there have been plays,[79] a novel,[80] four transcripts of the diaries, a transformation of his final speech from the dock into ballad form ('the ideal recitation for volunteers')[81] and a considerable amount of poetry. Of the last, Dora Sigerson Shorter's elegy for Casement, 'The choice',[82] written soon after his death but not published until 1919, is typical of the immediate desire of Irish nationalist poets to understand Casement's role within the wider pattern of martyrdom established by the events of 1916. The poem concludes:

> Ah! Irish Casement, in the roar of war
> That stung his blood and whipped his manhood's fire.
> What did he hear upon red shaken earth,
> Where little nations struggle and expire?
> Some banshee cry upon the hot wind thrills!
>
> And Roger Casement – he who freed the slave,
> Made sad babes smile and tortured women hope,
> Flung all aside, King's honours and great years,
> To take for finis here a hempen rope,
> And banshee cries upon far Irish hills.

Despite the confident momentum established by the poem at this point it is worth noting that its pointed reference to 'Irish Casement' suggests that Casement's loyalties were perceived as more problematic than perhaps was desirable for the subject of such a verse.[83] However, this apart, the poem conforms to Casement's own expressed belief that it was his knowledge of colonial violence as he witnessed it in the Congo and the Putamayo that deepened his interest in the affairs of Ireland and in this way his humanitarianism functions in the poem in place of what can be considered explicable nationalist fervour. Certainly, for the poem's author the episode was deeply traumatic. Sigerson Shorter never recovered from the shock of the 1916 executions and began to suffer from serious mental illness soon after Casement's death. She committed suicide in 1918, leaving distraught the close friends she had made through her involvement in the national movement.[84]

Yeats's poetic response to the Casement affair was similarly ambivalent and one which occurred fully twenty years after Casement's execution. Such a lapse in time is unsurprising if Yeats's similarly delayed response to the Rising in 'Easter 1916' is taken into account and, as with that text, Yeats's Casement poems, 'Roger Casement' and 'The ghost of Roger Casement',[85] encounter the historical moment with a confident public declamatory mode troubled by a more insidious sense of unease. Yeats had been enraged by the evidence against Casement's accusers detailed in *The Forged Casement Diaries* by W. J. Maloney[86] and wrote as follows to Ethel Mannin in November 1936:

> Casement was not a very able man but he was gallant and unselfish and had surely his right to leave what he would have considered an unsullied name. I long to break my rule against politics and call these men criminals, but I must not. Perhaps a verse may come to me, now or a year hence.

Predictably perhaps, the first of the poems, a ballad to the tune of 'The Glen of Aherlow', was written within a few weeks and appeared in de Valera's *Irish Press* on 2 February 1937. Yeats had fervently hoped that the poem would be 'sung by Irish undergraduates at Oxford'[87] and the final stanzas embody the insistent rhythm of the emotional imperative that typifies Yeats's later ballads such as 'Come gather round me, Parnellites' and 'Colonel Martin':

Come Tom and Dick, come all the troop
That cried it far and wide,
Come from the forger and his desk,
Desert the perjurer's side;

Come speak your bit in public
That some amends be made
To this most gallant gentleman
That is in quicklime laid

That such a form is also a mask is almost a truism and, indeed, the passionate advocacy of Casement's cause in this poem disguised the ambivalent feelings Yeats, in reality, had for his actions and his private suspicions that the diaries were, in fact, genuine. It is for this reason that 'Roger Casement' bleeds the Casement case of any specificity and instead locates in his fall a template which is, as the poem insists, 'nothing new'. The penultimate stanza had originally called Alfred Noyes to task for direct complicity in smearing Casement ('Come Alfred Noyes, come all the troop'), an accusation which, bearing in mind the monumental nature of the poetic legacy Yeats was finalising in the last years of his life, forced a hasty retraction from Noyes and the alteration of the line to the less satisfactory 'Come Tom and Dick, come all the troop'. As this suggests, the poem gains its momentum from a simple suspicion of British motives, a suspicion articulated by Maud Gonne in a letter to Yeats at the time of Casement's arrest when she notes that 'the disgraceful trick of trying to dishonor Roger Casement is already beginning'.[88] For Yeats, Casement fell far short of the example set by Parnell but in his public humiliation by the British the pattern of Parnell's suffering could be reapplied.

'The ghost of Roger Casement', Yeats's second and final poem on the Casement affair, is a more complex exercise and was written at the start of 1937. In many ways the image of Casement it establishes, that of an angry, vengeful ghost demanding justice, is one that has remained current,[89] as subsequent accounts have circled around its insistent cries for reparation:

Draw round, beloved and bitter men,
Draw round and raise a shout;
The ghost of Roger Casement
Is beating on the door.

While the history and form of Yeats's Casement poems suggest their interventionist credentials, it is more difficult to understand what kind of intervention Yeats intended. For Malcolm Brown, 'the unspoken burden of his song is: *Wir fahren gegen Engelland!* (We are marching against England!)' in that Casement's 'function in the poem is to signify that if he could come back to Wilhelmstrasse in 1938 he would find Unity of Being there, not the cynical decadence that greeted him in 1916'.[90] In these terms, Yeats's second poem ventriloquises the ways in which outright Nazi sympathisers such as the Irish novelist Francis Stuart would interpret Casement's legacy during the 1930s and 1940s.[91] That said, just as the spectre that is summoned in 'The ghost of Roger Casement' is an unsatisfied, aimless figure, so Yeats himself is at this point far from the poet of, to use Declan Kiberd's terms, 'public, textual duty (to name and praise the warrior dead)'.[92] While in 'Easter 1916', even taking into account the poem's prevarication that Kiberd analyses, the heroes of the Rising ultimately can be named and recognised as part of a necessary historical process, Casement is left as an embodiment of rageful excess, a figure (both literally and rhetorically) that gestures to a future of injustice and the ongoing entanglement, both emotionally and politically, of Anglo-Irish relationships. Perhaps for this reason it is appropriate that in 1956 'The ghost of Roger Casement' gained the unusual privilege of being quoted in the House of Commons during a debate on the Casement diaries by Montgomery Hyde,[93] MP for Belfast North and a keen advocate for an independent enquiry.

Hyde was not the only 'beloved and bitter' man to have rallied to Yeats's call. For T. E. Lawrence, Casement had 'the appeal of a broken archangel',[94] while the poet Richard Murphy in his 'Casement's funeral'[95] notes how the 'death-cell flame' 'purged for martyrdom the diarist's flesh', the inference being that the earthy desires of the diarist and the figure of martyr cannot coexist within the politically austere climate of the new Irish state. Perhaps for this reason Northern Irish poets have had less difficulty in mobilising the complexity and contradiction of Casement's legacy. For example, in Louis MacNeice's *Autumn Journal*, Casement, along with Maud Gonne, is cited as an example of 'how a single purpose can be founded on /A jumble of opposites'[96] and thus become a vengeful figure of childhood dread who may 'land at the pier/ With a sword and a horde of rebels'. It is Casement as this 'jumble of opposites' that Paul Muldoon invokes in his remarkable 'A clear signal', published on St Patrick's Day in 1992, in the *New York Times*.[97] Like Yeats's Casement poems, the poem is an interventionist text, although as the title suggests, one with a more discernible function. It rounds fiercely on the sentimental nationalism of Irish-America and its historical complicity with a repressive Ireland typified by the abortion laws in place in the Republic and from this point broadens the scope of its attack to encompass the refusal of the AOH to sanction St Patrick's Day parades by lesbian and gay Irish groups:

> I feel almost churlish in taking this occasion
> to appeal to our Irish-American cousins
>
> never again to be seen to rain
> on their own parade, not to be heard to cry '*Aryan*
>
> *Go Bragh*.' As for the 'Hibs' standing in the way
> of Irish Lesbian and Gays,
>
> would they have stopped Casement when he tried to land
> a boatland of guns on Banna Strand?
>
> The Ghost of Roger Casement would now call 'enough'
> to the claymore and the Kalashnikov.

Muldoon, of course, cannot be as confident of Casement's instincts as 'A clear signal' proposes, but the Casement that the poem constructs – a liberal humanist involved in violence only for specific and transitory reasons – resurrects the humanitarian Casement of the Putamayo and also clears a space for what might become codifications of Casement as, to quote Éibhear Walshe, 'a distinct ... gay presence'[98] within Irish nationalism. As this suggests, the question of whether Casement was indeed homosexual, regardless of the veracity or otherwise of the Black Diaries, is one that has been quietly put aside by most authorities in the debate. Indeed, it is Casement as a gay liberal pluralist which is celebrated in Michael Carson's novel *The Knight of the Flaming Heart*. In this Yeats's ghost of Casement re-emerges but, rather than operating as an instrument of retribution, he magically prevents terrorist atrocities and continues his work with the oppressed. As the ghost comments: 'I learnt to accept the mixture in myself. The living was all.'[99]

Even taking into account literary criticism's tendency to celebrate what can be termed the 'unstable text', it is difficult to envisage a more fraught instance of such instability than Casement's Black Diaries: volumes which, even now, lack the material foundations upon which a literary critical practice can be built. Indeed, textual instability dogged Casement's life, culminating, with grotesque irony, in the laborious courtroom interpretation of a medieval Norman-French treason statute from 1351 that may have contained a crucial comma or may merely have been folded in such a way as to have cracked the parchment. As Casement himself noted with morbid humour, 'God, deliver me, I say, from such antiquaries as these to hang a man's life upon a comma, and throttle him with a semi-colon'.[100] While this parody of scholarly procedure mimics other dubious texts within Anglo-Irish cultural politics,[101] this inability to find closure through textual analysis suggests some of the many loose threads implicit in the Casement affair and indicates the continuing heterogeneity of his legacy. Lucy McDiarmid, in a perceptive essay on this subject,[102] identifies the 'indeterminacy' of this achievement and constructs his life as 'between accents, nationalities, allegiances, and genders, hybrid and subversive'.[103] The recognition of such 'indeterminacy' is not new, but McDiarmid's argument is important because of its awareness that such indeterminacy is not merely an unwelcome conundrum – a problem to be 'solved' – but also in actuality defines and embodies the totality of the Casement case in Ireland and elsewhere. In these terms Casement's legacy is one not so much bedevilled by rumours and controversies but rather one which has had little existence beyond such unofficial, almost carnivalesque, moments. For this reason, as she observes, 'Ireland has lived vicariously through Roger Casement, using the manifold and extraordinary facts of his life to explore without risk topics otherwise unapproachable'.[104] It is perhaps for this reason that McDiarmid resists the temptation often prevalent in other analyses of Casement to codify the numerous contradictions implicit in his activities and to find in them some latent order. Instead, in her reading, Casement is allowed to remain ambivalent, perceived almost as a collection of discourses,[105] and it is in this way that his disruptive power remains. Any attempt to rehabilitate Casement, to read him within the legitimising discourses of the state, provokes, it seems, a further dissident form of his legacy. As McDiarmid notes:

> Beneath the knighted Protestant consul-traitor lay of course the classic martyr, the Catholic Irish-speaking gun-running rebel; such was the Casement of Yeats's poems, the hero of the 1937 *Irish Press* controversy. But Casement Martyr was obviously as official, as much a figment of state ideology, as Traitor Casement, and beneath the perfect martyr another rebel Casement had been evolving, a rebel against the dominant pieties of the high de Valeran period. So long as the 'state' involved was Great Britain, an Irish Casement was a folk hero. But once the Irish state had him, another folk-Casement emerged.[106]

Such sensitivity is necessary if only to interrupt the interpretative circularity within which the Black Dairies have become trapped: they are read firstly as ethical documents indicting colonialism, then in turn are judged ethically in relation to Casement's own homosexual practices, and are then contextualised in relation to the British government's mobilisation of the scandal they record. Just as Casement, like Conrad in his response to colonial outrages in the Congo, was trapped within a polyphony of conflicting ideological responses – liberal outrage, radicalism, humanist despair, racism and romantic nationalism – so the strategies of the diaries, both black and white, public and private, embody these contradictions and suggest their own inevitable teleology. For this reason, the diaries have become metonymic: as their status is uncertain so the status of Casement remains debated. In these terms the dominance of 'the flaw' in assessing the nature of his achievement indicates little more than a continuing tendency to understand Irish nationalism as just a form of irrepressible juvenilia. What more, then, can be said about a figure whose situation remains provisional and whose legacy (whatever that may prove to be) is yet to be inherited? As the premature foreclosure of Casement within aesthetic models of Irish history has led to the creation of a Wilde-like figure marginally capable of disrupting the binarisms of Anglo-Irish cultural politics, perhaps it is time to assert a different, equally conditional, analogy. Until we know better, we might do worse than to return to Conrad's troubled, half-realised vision of Casement as a vengeful Kurtz, a figure keenly aware of the contradictions of European nationalism but one who, with a savage despair, mobilised that contradiction within his own life as the only weapon available.

NOTES

1 Letter to Richard Morten, 28 July 1916, National Library of Ireland, MS 4902.
2 Oswell Blakeston, *Thank You Now: An Exploration of Ulster* (London: Anthony Bond, 1960), p. 148.
3 Seamus Deane, *et al.*, eds, *The Field Day Anthology of Irish Writing, Vol. 3* (Derry: Field Day, 1991), p. 1338.
4 Dermot Keogh, *Twentieth-Century Ireland: Nation and State* (Dublin: Gill and Macmillan, 1994), p. 288.
5 Tim Pat Coogan, *De Valera: Long Fellow, Tall Shadow* (London: Arrow Books, 1995), p. 683.
6 With a desire finally to resolve the question, W. J. McCormack, then of Goldsmith's College, London, instigated a full-scale forensic examination of the Black Diaries with the financial support of a number of institutions in both Britain and Ireland. In March 2002 he reported of its findings:

> The unequivocal and confident conclusion which the Giles Laboratory has reached is that each of the five documents known as the Black Diaries is exclusively the work of Roger Casement's hand, without any reason to suspect either forgery or interpolation by another hand. (*British Association of Irish Studies Newsletter*, no. 31, July 2002, pp. 5–9)

7 Two recent works of Casement scholarship can be highly recommended: W. J. McCormack, *Roger Casement in Death or Haunting the Free State* (Dublin: University College Dublin Press, 2002) and Jeffrey Dudgeon's *Roger Casement: The Black Diaries* (Belfast: Belfast Press, 2002).

8 The understandable tendency to see Casement's pro-German sympathies as strategic should be resisted. As his text *The Crime Against Europe* indicates, Casement was an enthusiastic supporter of the German cause: 'Counting by heads, the Germans, Austro-Hungarians and Turks are fighting in the proportion of one against six; counting by hearts, they are something more than equal'. See Herbert O. Mackey, ed., *The Crime Against Europe: Writings and Poems of Roger Casement* (Dublin: C. J. Fallon, 1958), p. 121.

9 For an engrossing eye witness account of this episode see Captain Robert Monteith, *Casement's Last Adventure* (Dublin: Michael Moynihan, 1953).

10 Brian Inglis, *Roger Casement* (London: Hodder and Stoughton, 1973).

11 The most energetic and engaging reading of Casement in these terms is David Rudkin, 'The chameleon and the kilt: the complexities of Roger Casement', *Encounter*, 41 (August 1973), pp. 70–7, which mobilises the Freudian concept of 'emancipated anality' as a way of reading against Inglis's models of interpretation.

12 Letter, *Ulster Guardian*, 14 May 1913, in Mackey, *The Crime Against Europe*, p. 91.

13 Alfred Noyes, *The Accusing Ghost or Justice for Casement* (London: Gollancz, 1957), p. 42.

14 Mackey, *The Crime Against Europe*, p. 84.

15 Dudgeon, *Roger Casement*, p. 176.

16 James Joyce, *Ulysses* (London: Penguin, 2000, first published 1922), p. 435.

17 It is worth noting in relation to this argument that the major analogy which underwrites much of the conversation in the bar is that of Sinn Féin's Hungarian policy – an idea, it is mooted, that Bloom himself suggested to Arthur Griffith.

18 Letter to Richard Morten, 28 July 1916.

19 Roger Sawyer, *Roger Casement's Diaries, 1910: The Black and the White* (London: Pimlico, 1997), p. 23.

20 René MacColl, *Roger Casement: A New Judgement* (London: Hamish Hamilton, 1956), p. 62.

21 Richard Ellmann, *Oscar Wilde* (London: Penguin, 1997, first published 1988), pp. 428–9. The tone of fatalistic weariness imputed to Wilde here underplays the extent to which waiting for the inevitable arrest was also a form of action, an argument that Ellmann subsequently develops.

22 Inglis, *Roger Casement*, p. 311.

23 Richard Norton-Taylor, 'Irish hero knew uprising would fail', *Guardian*, 15 June 1998, p. 3.
24 Norton-Taylor, 'Irish hero knew uprising would fail'.
25 F. E. Smith, *Famous Trials of History* (London: Hutchinson, 1920), p. 255.
26 Roger Sawyer, *Casement: The Flawed Hero* (London: Routledge and Kegan Paul, 1984).
27 Paul Hyland, *The Black Heart: A Voyage to Central Africa* (London: Gollancz, 1988), p. 73.
28 Noyes, *The Accusing Ghost or Justice for Casement*, pp. 17–18.
29 Medb Ruane, 'Who owns Casement?', *Irish Times*, 14 October 1997, p. 17.
30 B. L. Reid, *Lives of Roger Casement* (New Haven: Yale University Press, 1976), p. 465.
31 Inglis, *Roger Casement*, p. 381. It is of interest to note that Ellmann, *Oscar Wilde*, p. 261, also has recourse to Proust in explicating Wilde's 'invert' tendencies: '"For the invert," says Proust in *Sodome et Gomorrhe*, "vice begins ... when he takes his pleasure with women"'.
32 MacColl, *Roger Casement*, p. 301.
33 Noyes, *The Accusing Ghost or Justice for Casement*, p. 79.
34 Ruane, 'Who owns Casement?'
35 Smith, *Famous Trials of History*, p. 251.
36 Hyland, *The Black Heart*, p. 266.
37 James McCarroll, *Passages Taken from the Manuscript Written by Roger Casement in the Condemned Cell at Pentonville Prison* (private circulation). A short memoir by Father James McCarroll. Preface by Herbert O. Mackey, 18 January 1950.
38 Joseph Conrad, letter to R. B. Cunninghame Graham, 26 December 1903. Most biographies extensively misquote this letter. A reliable transcript can be found in Noyes, *The Accusing Ghost or Justice for Casement*, pp. 39–40.
39 In a letter to E. D. Morel, 23 October 1903, from Loanda, Casement noted: 'Conrad is a charming man – subtle, kind and sympathetic and he will, I hope move his pen when I see him at home'. Dudgeon, *Roger Casement*, p. 138.
40 Joseph Conrad, *Heart of Darkness* (London: Penguin, 1987, first published 1902), p. 95.
41 Conrad, *Heart of Darkness*, p. 91.
42 Conrad, *Heart of Darkness*, p. 92.
43 Conrad, *Heart of Darkness*, p. 94.
44 'Conrad and Casement: hut mates in Africa', *New York Evening Post*, 11 May 1923, p. 15. I am extremely grateful to Sandra Dodson of Trinity College, Oxford, for drawing my attention to this article.
45 July 1890. See Zdzislaw Najder, 'Conrad's Casement letters', *Polish Perspectives*, 17.12 (1974), pp. 25–30.
46 Letter from Conrad to Casement, 1 December 1903. See Najder, 'Conrad's Casement letters'.
47 Conrad, *Heart of Darkness*, p. 110.
48 Letter to Richard Morten, 28 July 1916. See Najder, 'Conrad's Casement letters'.

49 See Inglis, *Roger Casement*, p. 32: 'When his year's contract expired, he [Casement] decided not to renew it, and returned home. His employers expressed their opinion of him by describing him, in their testimonial, as an *agent exceptionnel*'.
50 E. D. Morel, *Daily News*, 20 July 1912. See MacColl, *Roger Casement*, pp. 300–1.
51 Mitchell quoted by Nigel Jones, 'The killing of Roger Casement', *Guardian*, 28 February 1998, p. 6.
52 Cathal O'Byrne, 'Roger Casement's ceilidhe', in *Capuchin Annual* (Dublin: Capuchin Franciscan Fathers, 1946–47), pp. 312–14.
53 Dudgeon, *Roger Casement*, p. 504.
54 Gertrude Bannister, 'Events in Easter 1916', National Library of Ireland, MS 7946. Bannister also notes that Gore-Booth's own mysticism was a much celebrated fact at this time.
55 Shane Leslie, *The Film of Memory* (London: Michael Joseph, 1938), p. 385.
56 Shane Leslie, *Long Shadows* (London: John Murray, 1966), p. 188.
57 Cathal O'Byrne, *As I Roved Out* (Belfast: Blackstaff Press, 1982, first published 1946), p. 171.
58 Tim Coates, ed., *The Irish Uprising 1914–21: Papers from the British Parliamentary Archive* (London: The Stationary Office, 2000), p. 37.
59 Dudgeon, *Roger Casement*, pp. 553–8.
60 Dudgeon, *Roger Casement*, pp. 553–4. See also McCormack, *Roger Casement in Death or Haunting the Free State*, pp. 77–9.
61 See Denis Gwynn, 'Roger Casement's last weeks', *Studies*, 54 (spring 1965), p. 71.
62 John S. Crone and F. C. Bigger, eds, *In Remembrance: Articles and Sketches by Francis Joseph Bigger* (Dublin: Talbot Press, 1927), p. xii.
63 Cathal O'Byrne, 'Roger Casement's last will', *Irish Monthly*, 65 (October 1937), pp. 668–72; Cathal O'Byrne, 'Roger Casement's ceilidhe'.
64 Dudgeon, *Roger Casement*, p. 190.
65 Bannister, 'Events in Easter 1916'.
66 Verse by Roger Casement dedicated to Cathal O'Byrne on front endpaper of a copy of Rupert Brooke's *1914 and Other Poems*, with a letter by G. Una Parry to O'Byrne concerning the return of the book, 5 May 1917, National Library of Ireland, MS 14,220.
67 Reid, *The Lives of Roger Casement*, p. 487.
68 Cathal O'Byrne, 'O, friend of my heart', in *The Lane of the Thrushes: Some Ulster Love Songs* (Dublin: Sealy, Bryers and Walker, 1905), p. 7. Casement's memory is precise, although his transcription alters the line breaks.
69 Séamus O'Neill, 'Note: Roger Casement, Cathal O'Byrne and Professor Reid', *Studies*, 68 (spring/summer 1979), pp. 117–21.
70 Cathal O'Byrne, 'Roger Casement's last will', *Irish Monthly*, 65 (October 1937), pp. 668–72.
71 McCarroll, *Passages Taken from the Manuscript Written by Roger Casement.*
72 Noyes, *The Accusing Ghost or Justice for Casement*, p. 158.

73 Bannister, 'Events in Easter 1916'.
74 Brighid Mhic Sheáin, *Glimpses of Erin. Alice Milligan: Poet, Protestant, Patriot* (Belfast: Fortnight Educational Trust Supplement, 1994), p. 25.
75 'Casement's fate', *Irish News*, 4 August 1916, p. 3.
76 See 'Casement case: impressions of a remarkable trial', *Irish News*, 1 July 1916, p. 6: 'We could wish that Sir RC had not cast this blot on the Irish name which the valour and loyalty of our Irish fellow-subjects have illumined afresh on so many of the hardest-fought fields in the present war'.
77 M. McD, letter, *Irish News*, 4 August 1916, p. 5.
78 Sawyer, *Roger Casement's Diaries*, p. 12.
79 Of which David Rudkin's *Cries from Casement as His Bones Are Brought to Dublin* (London: British Broadcasting Corporation, 1974) is probably the most well known.
80 Michael Carson, *The Knight of the Flaming Heart* (London: Doubleday, 1995).
81 Anonymous, 'Sir Roger Casement's last speech from the dock done into verse: the ideal recitation for volunteers' (handbill) (Dublin: Independent Newspapers, 1916).
82 Dora Sigerson Shorter, 'The choice', in *Sixteen Dead Men and Other Poems of Easter Week* (New York: M. Kennerley, 1919). I am grateful to Colin Graham for bringing this poem to my attention.
83 In 'Roger Casement's last will' and 'Roger Casement's ceilidhe', O'Byrne is similarly insistent on this point of Casement's Irishness. Joyce's *Ulysses* pokes fun at such doubts through the figure of the citizen and his immediate response to the mention of Casement – 'He's an Irishman' (see discussion above).
84 See Clement Shorter, *In Memoriam Dora Sigerson 1918–1923* (London: privately published, 1923), a pamphlet produced by her widower consisting of poems by Eva Gore-Booth, Alice Furlong, W. N. Ewer, William Kean Seymour and Katherine Tynan. In it, Gore-Booth writes of Sigerson Shorter that she 'died of the grief that tore my heart'.
85 *Collected Poems of W. B. Yeats* (London: Macmillan, 1982), pp. 351–2, 352–3.
86 W. J. Maloney, *The Forged Casement Diaries* (Dublin: Talbot Press, 1936).
87 W. B. Yeats, letter to Dorothy Wellesley, 28 November 1936.
88 Letter from Maud Gonne to W. B. Yeats, May 1916. See Anna MacBride White and A. Norman Jeffares, eds, *The Gonne–Yeats Letters 1893–1938* (London: Pimlico, 1993), p. 373.
89 In this context see also Alice Milligan's poem 'The men on the hill', in *Poems*, ed. H. Mangan (Dublin: Gill, 1954), pp. 186–7. The note to the poem provides the following information:

> The Cairn at Tor-na-Mona, County Antrim, in memory of Séan O'Neill was inaugurated by Francis J. Bigger and other helpers. An annual celebration was held here and the praises of the great Ulsterman spoken by some distinguished Irishmen. The late William Bulfin delivered the address one year and Eoin MacNeill another. Roger Casement took a great interest in the celebration,

> and he himself was the speaker at the gathering held in June, 1914. The anniversary was allowed to lapse then for three years; but in June last [1918] as some children were gathered round the Cairn on a fair Sunday afternoon, one suddenly exclaimed: 'See! Who are all those men coming to the Hill?' The Glensmen had resumed the hill-assembly in memory not only of Séan but of him who had last spoken the praises of Séan.

The poem itself includes the stanza:

> The faces of men are stern,
> Some eyes are dim.
> But it is not for aught that is said
> Of Shane and his gory head –
> The grief of the men of the Glens,
> Is not for him.

90 Malcolm Brown, *The Politics of Irish Literature: From Thomas Davis to W. B. Yeats* (London: Allen and Unwin, 1972), p. 322.

91 In 1940 the Irish writer Francis Stuart (who had just accepted a permanent post at the University of Berlin) wrote:

> Casement's name is now immortal in the history of Ireland – raised high over the repugnant slander of English forgers. And the German victory, on which he placed so much, is at the moment I am writing these words almost complete.
>
> Perhaps one day, no longer lying far away, Irish and German soldiers will stand together before Casement's unmarked grave in the Pentonville Prison in order to honour the great patriot who has done so much to further friendship between the two nations.

See Samuel Levenson, *Maud Gonne* (London: Cassell, 1977), p. 389.

92 Declan Kiberd, *Inventing Ireland: The Literature of the Modern Nation* (London: Jonathan Cape, 1995), p. 213.

93 *Hansard*, 3 May 1956, p. 52.

94 Letter from T. E. Lawrence to Charlotte Payne-Townshend, December 1934. See Angus Mitchell, ed., *The Amazon Journal of Roger Casement* (London: Anaconda, 1997), p. 19.

95 Originally part of Murphy's *The Battle of Aughrim* (1968). See Peter Fallon and Derek Mahon, eds, *The Penguin Book of Contemporary Irish Poetry* (London: Penguin, 1990), p. 69.

96 Louis MacNiece, *Selected Poems*, ed. Michael Longley (London: Faber, 1988), p. 61.

97 Paul Muldoon, 'A clear signal', *New York Times*, Tuesday, 17 March, 1992, p.3. See also Muldoon's *Kerry Slides* (Oldcastle: Gallery Press, 1988, p. 38):

> Why would a British Knight
> plot to overthrow
> those who had violated human rights
> in Mayo and the Putomayo?

98 Éibhear Walshe, ed., *Sex, Nation and Dissent in Irish Writing* (Cork: Cork University Press, 1997), p. 3.

99 Carson, *The Knight of the Flaming Heart*, p. 112. See also Carson's 'A homosexual hero for our times', *Guardian*, 3 March 1998, p. 15.

100 Letter to Richard Morten, 28 July 1916.

101 For instance, the 'Parnellism and crime' forgeries of 1887, or the card left by Queensbury for Wilde at the Albemarle Club, which precipitated Wilde's destruction and which said either 'Oscar Wilde, ponce and somdomite' or 'To Oscar Wilde posing somdomite'. On the latter, see Ellmann, *Oscar Wilde*, p. 412.

102 Lucy McDiarmid, 'The posthumous life of Roger Casement', in *Gender and Sexuality in Modern Ireland*, eds Anthony Bradley and Maryann Gialanella Valiulis (Amherst: University of Massachusetts Press, 1997), pp. 127–58.

103 'The posthumous life of Roger Casement', p. 127.

104 'The posthumous life of Roger Casement', p. 153.

105 Perhaps the most powerfully realised perception of Casement in these terms is Rudkin's *Cries from Casement as His Bones Are Brought to Dublin*. This play, along with Rudkin's accompanying essay, 'The chameleon and the kilt', constitutes one of the more astute analyses of the various modes through which the postcolonial state attempts to render dissident material as signifying tradition.

106 'The posthumous life of Roger Casement', p. 144.

CHAPTER SEVEN

Exile, return and the life of a *shanachie*

> An incident which happened in the City Centre last evening caused a good many eyes to gaze skywards. A toy balloon, which broke away from a vendor, soared rapidly upwards, and, propelled by a good breeze, soon vanished from view.
>
> 'Gleanings of general Irish news', *Irish News*, 14 December 1926

ON 21 August 1920[1] Cathal O'Byrne arrived at New York's Ellis Island immigration centre on board the *Aquitania*, from Southampton. According to his immigration record, he travelled second class, was in possession of $200 (would-be immigrants to the United States had to have at least $50) and intended to stay with a 'Mr M. Cook' of Vernon Avenue, Brooklyn. O'Byrne claimed to be forty years old, and is described as being five feet eight and a half and in good health, with a 'fresh' complexion, dark hair and blue eyes. Unlike most of his fellow passengers eager to escape the shattered conditions of post-war Europe, O'Byrne did not express a desire to settle permanently in America and proposed instead only a two-year residency. This may have been little more than trepidation on his part because, on a subsequent journey through the often labyrinthine procedures of Ellis Island's immigration process, following a visit back to Ireland in 1923, he recorded a wish for permanent citizenship. Certainly, the enthusiasm for America, and specifically Chicago, he would discover during this period would remain with him for the rest of his life.

The reasons why O'Byrne left for the US at this stage of his life are unclear. Approaching middle age and with a successful career in Ireland, starting over again as a freelance writer and singer in a country where he was unknown and without many friends represented a considerable challenge. With the contacts and status he gained from his background in the

Irish Republican Army (IRA) he could, like his friend Denis McCullough and many other Northern republicans, have escaped the new and politically uncongenial Northern Irish state and made a life in Dublin. What is more certain, however, is that the first six months of his stay in America were dedicated to raising funds – via the charitable Irish White Cross Society – for victims of the troubles back in Ireland and especially those who suffered in the Belfast pogroms. According to John Hewitt,[2] O'Byrne achieved this by means of a lecture tour during which he spoke on the subjects of Irish folk music and Irish songs that appear in the plays of Shakespeare.[3] The success of the venture was startling and an indication of the popularity of his fine tenor voice is provided by the publication in 1921 by the American Irish Folk Song Publishing Corporation of 'Kittie's toys', a ballad by O'Byrne's old friend from 1916, Dora Sigerson Shorter, sung, as the cover puts it, 'with enormous success by Cathal O'Byrne, the famous Irish folk singer'. It features a photograph of O'Byrne with a waxed moustache and dressed in his usual tartan costume, and exudes an air of distinct, if now faded, glamour. Such recognition allowed O'Byrne greatly to increase the amount of capital he could raise among the Irish-American community. Hewitt notes that Amcomri Street in the Beechmount area of Belfast was rebuilt as a result of funds O'Byrne collected,[4] while J. J. Campbell, in his introduction to the third edition of *As I Roved Out*,[5] records that O'Byrne 'was an outstanding success and amassed a modest fortune. During the terrible days of "the Troubles" in Ireland he raised $100,000 to help victims of the pogroms in his native Belfast.' Although other accounts place the figure at £20,000,[6] it was clearly a vast sum by any measure and indicative of O'Byrne's practical compassion for those he had left behind in Ireland. Alongside this, it was also an early indication of the instinct towards self-reliance that the Northern Catholic community would increasingly adopt as a strategy of survival in the years following partition.

What other few details are known about O'Byrne's stay in America tend to derive from his own sparse and (one suspects) highly selective accounts. His entry for the bibliography *Ireland in Fiction*[7] informs us that he 'toured America twice, drawing very large audiences in New York, Philadelphia, Buffalo' while in 1948 he published a fuller record of his impressions of California in the *Capuchin Annual*.[8] Although the motivation for the article derives from a subsequent visit to America, as with much of O'Byrne's later writing, it is dominated by the recollection of earlier times and, more specifically, an exchange of letters with another of his talismanic figures, the actor Rudolph Valentino. While resident in Chicago, O'Byrne had witnessed the demolition of the old market on

South Water Street in 1925, part of the extensive redevelopment of the city during this period. In observing the spectacle, O'Byrne's attention was taken by an Italian construction worker with 'white teeth' and 'dark eyes' labouring in the sun. This fleeting encounter immediately inspired him to write 'Italia', one of his more extraordinary poems:

> I saw a dago delve in the mud of South Water Street,
> A 'wop' with great bare chest and tired, dreamful eyes,
> Smiling he looked at me, and in an instant fleet
> Around and over me leaned the clear and lustrous skies.
>
> Of shadowy old Verona, by the green Adige water,
> Where 'neath the fading gleam of a lily moon
> Sad Giulietta, stern Capulet's one fair daughter,
> Heard in the tender dawn the lark sing all too soon.
>
> Back came the misty memories of earlier, happier ages –
> Swift in a flash of white teeth, the laughter of dusky eyes,
> As one will open haphazard some long dead poet's pages
> And find one's rarest dream writ fair, in glad surprise.
>
> Over broad landlocked water, azure and amber shaded,
> The Ave Maria ringing slow died out with the dying day,
> And kissed by a warm sweet breeze, with the sea tang heavily laded,
> Napoli lay in glad content in the arms of her amorous bay....

The technique deployed here is typical of much of O'Byrne's writing in that it locates a moment in the fallen present in order to trigger a more profound reflection on an imagined past. Although he had yet to visit the country, O'Byrne's fascination with Italy was lifelong and was usually figured in his writing as the imagined other to Protestant, heterosexual, northern Europe – an opposition that was already firmly embedded in both literary and popular culture.[9] 'Italia', then, is a meditation on the condition of exile, a poem alive to the perpetual tensions that existed between immigrant communities in America and, most importantly, a coded statement of desire. As the glimpse of the 'great bare chest and tired, dreamful eyes' of the 'wop' is transformed into a vision of a 'flash of white teeth, the laughter of dusky eyes' so there is suggested a covert invitation that is ultimately realised in the poem's vision of Naples as engaged in an act of eternal sexual congress. In turn, the fact that Naples was the foremost gay colony in Italy during this period – it was the place where Oscar Wilde and Lord Alfred Douglas had resumed their intimacy in 1897 and where Casement had conducted an affair in 1900 – bears its own obvious encryption.[10] As such, the poem displaces desire from the dangerous present to a safe aesthetic and temporal distance, where its troublesome energies could be more securely contained. Rarely again would O'Byrne's writing be as daring.

Valentino was one reader who was certainly well able to decode these not so subtle inferences. 'Italia' was published in a local newspaper and according to O'Byrne's own account:

> called forth letters of appreciation from many of Chicago's educated Italians, one of whom, a dear friend of my own, asked permission to send a copy of my poem to a schoolboy friend, Rudolf Valentino.
>
> The great movie star replied at once, thanking his friend for the exquisite pleasure he had given him, and expressing in his letter great surprise that an Irishman who had never seen Italy could describe its cities and their characteristics so minutely and correctly.
>
> My friend then suggested that I should write thanking Valentino for his eulogy of my verses. This I did, and the kind letter that lies before me was the result.
>
> It is written from the Ambassador Hotel, Park Avenue, New York City, and in it, amongst many other gracious things, the great actor said he would surely look me up when passing through Chicago on his way west, and that he was looking forward with particular pleasure to meeting an Irish poet whom he could call a friend.[11]

The meeting was destined never to take place but Valentino certainly had reason to be grateful for any friendly words during this period. In July 1926, while passing through Chicago on a publicity tour for his film *The Son of the Sheik*, an editorial in the *Chicago Tribune* had cited Valentino as one of the reasons for what it saw as the ongoing 'effeminization of the American male'. Incensed by this accusation and mindful of the damage it would cause to his reputation, Valentino wrote an open letter challenging the author of the piece to a boxing match. He received no response, and while Valentino declared himself vindicated as a result, it was clear that the persistent rumours about his sexuality were not going to disperse so easily. At this point Valentino returned to New York, attempted to reinforce his masculine credentials by taking part in a highly publicised one-round boxing match on the roof of his hotel, and on 26 August died as a result of a post-surgical infection after an operation on an acute perforated gastric ulcer. The letter that Valentino wrote to O'Byrne from the Ambassador Hotel was one of his last pieces of correspondence.

As the defamatory comments that had triggered Valentino's reckless actions had appeared in O'Byrne's home newspaper, it is almost inconceivable that he was not aware of the controversy. As such, his recollection of this exchange of letters in the ultra-conservative and Catholic

Church-sponsored *Capuchin Annual* some twenty-two years later stands as a covert defence of Valentino's reputation in a manner comparable to his defence of Roger Casement in the same publication in the previous year.[12] Certainly, the similarities between the two cases are striking: both Casement and Valentino died far from their homelands, both were filled with nostalgic longings for the places they had left, both were followed to their graves by accusations of sexual impropriety and both found themselves in correspondence with O'Byrne immediately beforehand. It cannot be doubted that, if nothing else, O'Byrne was a loyal defender of the reputations of the dead.

After his early period of touring, O'Byrne eventually settled at 1426 West Jackson Boulevard in Chicago, a place he believed was 'destined to become the greatest American city',[13] but nurtured hopes of returning to Ireland and opening a bookshop in Dublin with the capital he had amassed from his concerts. However, fate was to treat him harshly. In September 1928, eight years after he had departed, he returned to Ireland, but was to lose his savings in the Wall Street Crash of October 1929. Forced by economic necessity to remain in Belfast, he moved to 43 Cavendish Street, off the Falls Road, with his sister, and settled into a life of respectable semi-poverty. One of his final acts before leaving Chicago had been to reprint – at his own expense – his collection of poems from 1917, *The Grey Feet of the Wind*.[14] The name he gave to the fictional publishing company responsible for its production, Ard-Ree Press, suggests that he was nostalgic for the cherished days he had spent at Ardrigh with his mentor, F. J. Bigger. That path, however, was also now closed. Bigger had died two years previously and while the house's new owner, O'Byrne's one time intimate Joe Devlin, briefly attempted to maintain something of Ardrigh's former vibrancy, in truth the cultural vigour of the Northern Revival had long since expired.

The return of O'Byrne to the city that had done so much to shape him was, at least in part, an admission of failure, but it was considered a significant enough event to warrant a short announcement in the *Irish News*,[15] the paper whose fortunes had, in many ways, been inextricably bound to his own. The tone of the piece was indicative of the difficult position that O'Byrne now found himself in. While it stressed the success of his concert tours in America and noted the plans he had for future literary work, its predominant perception of O'Byrne was as a figure from a previous, and now almost forgotten, era. He was remembered as the singer 'who was the first to popularise our folksongs', 'a familiar figure at the country Feisanna in his kilts', while 'his funny stories, featuring the Belfast accent, were long a laughable feature of our concerts'.

Understood in these terms, O'Byrne's return was welcomed, and yet it was a welcome based on a nostalgic recognition that, during the period of his absence, the cultural and political landscape of the North had been irretrievably transformed. If the Northern Revival in the years leading up to 1916 had, to a significant extent, understood itself as the cultural wing of the Home Rule movement, so the subsequent collapse of that political aspiration had, in turn, led to an immediate and startling disintegration of its fundamentally optimistic and frequently progressive instincts. By the time of O'Byrne's return in 1928, the residues of this cultural energy were typified by nothing more ambitious than a tendency to recycle nostalgic images of loss and betrayal. Alongside this retrogression, partition had damaged the cultural life of the minority Catholic community in the North in other profound ways. The border further isolated the North from the cultural life of the rest of the island, while the mutual suspicion on which the internal politics of Northern Ireland was based inhibited the possibility of any significant cross-religious cultural exchange between the two communities. Protestant involvement in the Irish nationalist movement in the North – for so long such a distinctive feature of the Northern Revival – ceased to be a meaningful possibility as the examples of such radicals as Bigger, Bulmer Hobson and Alice Milligan became legacies that were simply too dangerous to inherit.

These factors go some way towards explaining why cultural activity among the Catholic minority in the North in this period was often typified by a disabling insularity. Moreover, what activity there was appeared to lack inspiration, leadership and direction. By 1928 nearly all the major figures of the Northern Revival had died, emigrated or, as in the case of Milligan, simply run out of energy. Given the increasingly segregated nature of Northern Irish society, it is therefore unsurprising that the Catholic Church began to play a much more important role in the cultural and social life of the minority community, a change reflected to a striking degree in the pages of the *Irish News*, which reported on the growth of the Saint Vincent de Paul Society and the rise of such institutions as the Apostolic Work Society, the Legion of Mary and the Catholic Young Men's Society with unfettered enthusiasm. It was this often extraordinary level of dedication that did much to create the distinctive character of Northern Catholicism. As Oliver Rafferty has perceptively noted:

> the energies, which in a more normal environment would have been channelled into society at large, were turned inwards and gave to the practice of Catholicism in the north an intensity rarely displayed elsewhere in the country.[16]

Maurice Hayes' description of the degree of observance the Church demanded during his childhood in the 1930s and 1940s well illustrates this dedication:

> There were novenas for this and that which meant nine evenings on the trot, and nine Fridays, which involved mass and communion every Friday for nine weeks in succession ... November Devotions and May Devotions and Lenten Devotions and Advent and Saint Patrick's Day and Corpus Christi and Sundays and Holy Days of Obligation and almost anything else anybody could think of, and the Men's Confraternity once a month and the Women's sodality and Perpetual Novena every Friday night so that there seemed to be few days in the year in which we did not go to church.[17]

For many Northern Catholics, then, it was through the Church that life gained meaning. Because the state institutions of Northern Ireland were generally perceived as being essentially sectarian, so the Church became a form of internal government in exile, and the only organisation to which many in the North could give any form of loyalty. Again, the intensity of this identification was often remarkable. Unlike for their fellow co-religionists in the South, as Marianne Elliott has observed, for a Northern Catholic to criticise the Church was implicitly to 'play the Protestant card'.[18] In this way every utterance about both self and society was predicated on an irreducible external threat.

As it was with religion, so it was with politics. While the desire for a united Ireland remained the fundamental aspiration, the terms of this desire were now perceived not as a political possibility but rather as an imaginative enclave remote from the realities of an increasingly permanent-looking border – a perception that the shelving of the Boundary Commission report in 1925 had done nothing to allay. Moreover, it is important to recognise the extent to which Catholic Northerners were finding in the South a displaced sense of home, but this was a misrecognition that was both inevitable and yet dangerous. Elliott again:

> Because so many nationalists believed (or, rather, wanted to believe) the political rhetoric in the south claiming an overwhelming desire to unite the six Ulster counties with the republic, they began culturally to think of it as home. Of course it was not and never had been. But above all they wanted to belong to a state and their rejection of and by the Northern one caused the identification with the southern state to become a necessary crutch. This was the essence of romantic nationalism – a psychological need. However, their experience was often one of rejection. Northern Catholics were treated as troublesome and embarrassing by the South, at best lumped together with all the other 'black northerners', at worst treated as far more problematic than the Unionists (the latter tendency predominant after the onset of the Troubles).[19]

It was in this unique and confused atmosphere that O'Byrne announced his return. And yet uncertain and depressing as circumstances appeared to be for the Catholic minority, they provided a set of conditions that, in many ways, O'Byrne was uniquely able to recognise and cultivate. As a one-time energetic enthusiast for the ideals of the Northern Revival and a veteran of the IRA, his reputation within the tightly woven community of Catholic Belfast was secure, while his increasingly devout religious beliefs enabled his writing to harmonise with what was a more general shift away from secular expressions of identity and community. Just as this tendency was accompanied by an increasing interest in – or even obsession with – nostalgic visions of the pre-partition Ireland that had been lost, so O'Byrne's own seemingly inexhaustible fund of stories, myths, fables and folklore about that period gained an enthusiastic readership. It was this knowledge that would eventually find its ultimate expression in his masterwork, *As I Roved Out*, in 1946.

In all ways, then, the time was right for O'Byrne to reinvent himself. While he would remain an occasional singer and performer in Belfast's theatres (and was thus well placed to witness the lingering death of the city's once vigorous music hall and vaudeville traditions), such activity was to become secondary to his new role as a storyteller, hoarder of the community's secrets and guardian of its myths of origin. As a result, O'Byrne was to become nothing less than 'the *shanachie* of Belfast, and its red-brick Gaeltacht',[20] as an anonymous appreciation of O'Byrne in the *Irish Times* from 1955 memorably described him. One can argue that this transformation was driven by the changed material conditions of the North at this time – O'Byrne had recognised an opportunity and was well able to exploit it, and yet in his reinvention was symbolised a more profound cultural reorientation, the implications of which are still being felt in Ireland today. As O'Byrne's work moves from the contemplation of a future possibility in the early years of the century to a painful recognition of historical loss in the years following partition, so the transient became intransigent, history became myth, and memory hardened into nostalgia, a process similar to what David Harvey has described as the inevitable movement of social recollection from history to poetry, and from time to space.[21] In this way, the themes of O'Byrne's writing from this point until his death in 1957 articulated a more widely held series of preoccupations within the Northern Catholic community. It would not be until the late 1960s that the monotony of this lament would be disturbed, and then only in circumstances which O'Byrne himself would have been unable to imagine.

This progression, crucial as it proved to be, was not, however, seamless. While O'Byrne had recognised the manner in which the cultural possibilities of life in Belfast had narrowed, there was also a reluctance to abandon all that the Northern Revival had attempted and achieved. Bigger was dead but his example continued to cast a long shadow. It was with this optimism that, in May 1930, O'Byrne attempted to reinvigorate something of the old Revival energies by founding a theatre company that cleaved to some of the early vitality of the Ulster Literary Theatre (ULT). The Cathal O'Byrne Comedy Company was a venture that allowed O'Byrne to produce a number of his own plays while also performing the leading roles. As a means of maximising personal profit, such an arrangement was near flawless. In gathering his new company O'Byrne turned to many of those who had worked with him in the period before his emigration. Carl Hardebeck, O'Byrne's old music teacher and a figure with an immaculate Revival pedigree of his own,[22] had returned to Belfast in 1923 after a spell as the master of the School of Music in Cork and provided the accompaniment to his songs. Mary Crothers and Bride O'Gormon, two ULT actors from the halcyon days of the 1909 Grand Opera House productions, played a variety of parts, while the *Irish News* was again relied upon for favourable publicity. Announcing the Company's short season at St Paul's Hall in Belfast, the paper previewed the event as a 'performance of outstanding interest',[23] and reported on its first night in glowing terms:

> In spite of summerlike conditions without, quite a large audience had the pleasure of seeing the first dramatic effort of the Cathal O'Byrne Comedy Company, recently formed, in St. Paul's Hall, Belfast, on Sunday night. The company appeared in two comedies by Mr. Cathal O'Byrne. One of these – 'The Returned Swank' – has never previously been staged, while the other, 'The Burthen,' is a very old favourite with playgoers in Belfast, Derry and elsewhere.
>
> Their talented author himself only returned from America a few months ago. During his stay there he was not unmindful of his fellow-countrymen at home, for during his first six months in America Mr. O'Byrne made more money for the Irish White Cross Relief Fund than any other living Irish singer.
>
> During the interlude between the comedies we had the old Cathal O'Byrne once more in a wealth of folk songs and stories, all of which were a delightful treat. In these songs, which are racy of the soil, Mr. O'Byrne struck a vivid note in the heart of his listeners which will not be readily forgotten.[24]

Despite this praise, the plays[25] cannot be regarded as anything other than slight affairs. *The Returned Swank*, described by the *Irish News* as 'something more than a laughable sketch',[26] was a modern morality drama in which Julia Merrigan, the young heroine returned to her home in County Antrim after emigration to America, provides her gossipy and malicious neighbours with what the *Irish Book Lover* called 'a lesson in Christian charity'.[27] In doing so she makes a husband of the local garage keeper and achieves as much happiness as this outcome can afford. The degree to which this plot was derived from O'Byrne's own experience is unknown but it is legitimate to note that his own return from America had been the subject of much speculation. *The Burthen* was the more popular of the two plays, but this was, perhaps, as much to do with the familiarity of its comic preoccupations than any unique merit. Summarised by the *Irish News* as 'the heroic attempt of a lady to rid her husband of his burden of laziness',[28] O'Byrne recycles many of the key elements of previous ULT successes, with his most obvious debt being to Rutherford Mayne's play of 1908, *The Drone*. Damned with heavily qualified praise by the drama critic of the *Irish News* as 'the best one act Northern comedy yet written', the energy of the play derives less from the formulaic nature of its exchanges than its attempts to capture the rhythms of vernacular Ulster speech – a skill that O'Byrne had honed many years previously in his 'Mrs Twigglety' columns for *Ireland's Saturday Night*. The final word on both plays is probably best left to the *Irish Book Lover*, which in a short review could say little else about them other than to emphasise the convenient fact that they 'would be very suitable to the needs of rural societies looking for vehicles lending themselves to natural acting and presenting no difficulty of production'.[29]

The 1930 premiere of the Cathal O'Byrne Comedy Company was not the first time that O'Byrne had combined acting with producing. As I discussed in Chapter 3, in 1913, the high-water mark of the ULT's popularity and the moment at which Gerald MacNamara's *Thompson in Tír-na-nÓg* was about to begin its protracted dominance of Ulster stages, O'Byrne had gained considerable success with his own organisation, the Celtic Players. One perhaps need do no more than note the change of emphasis in the names of these respective companies to recognise something of the manner in which the preoccupations of the Revival had given way to a new set of cultural and political realities. Not only was the age of Celticism over but, in the North at least, theatre was no longer perceived as an appropriate vehicle for cultural and political agitation. Indeed, with the contraction of theatre space in Belfast during the 1930s, the rise in the popularity of cinema, the increasingly intractable sectarian divisions of the city and the catastrophic effects of the Depression on the local economy, even the frivolous 'Irish' entertainments of the kind offered by O'Byrne's Comedy Company would appear an increasingly implausible venture. Belfast was retreating back into its constituent elements and was becoming – once again – a factionalised and bitter city, suspicious in its politics and intolerant in its social relationships.

O'Byrne's response to these harsh conditions was, in many ways, indicative of a more general trend among the educated middle-class, especially lower-middle-class Northern Irish Catholic population. While the extent of this class's engagement with Northern Ireland's public realm had always been limited, the gradual process of its withdrawal from the mechanics of the state gained momentum during the 1930s until a condition of almost total internal separation pertained. Given the implicitly sectarian nature of Northern Irish public institutions, there was an inevitability about this rupture, but what is more surprising was the limited extent of Catholic agitation against the material reality of this injustice. Indeed, middle-class Catholic withdrawal from Northern Irish civic life can be better understood as a more general rejection of the political realm as a whole, and was underwritten (and to some extent legitimised) by a concomitant and marked increase in devotion to the Church. For many Irish nationalists on both sides of the border there was a powerful logic to this transition, for if the process of secular politics had led only to the disaster of partition, the ideal of an Irish *Catholic* nation subtending political boundaries and united through faith remained potent. It was, then, via the Church that the two Irelands maintained something approaching a unified identity and as a result what can now be understood as moments of political possibility within Northern Ireland itself – such as the cross-community outdoor relief riots of October 1932 – were regarded with a caution bordering on suspicion. Not for nothing could Eamon de Valera triumphantly proclaim in his 1935 St Patrick's Day radio broadcast:

> Since the coming of St Patrick, fifteen hundred years ago, Ireland has been a Christian and a Catholic nation. All the ruthless attempts made through the centuries to force her from this allegiance have not shaken her faith. She remains a Catholic nation.[30]

This turn towards the religious life found its supreme expression in the fervour generated by the Eucharistic Congress held in Dublin in June 1932, an event described by the *Irish News* as 'the greatest day in Ireland's history'[31] and by Joseph Connolly, a one-time Ardrigh intimate of O'Byrne, as 'the greatest manifestation of religious joy and devotion that has ever been known in the country'.[32] Among the estimated one million pilgrims who welcomed the papal legate, Cardinal Lorenzo Lauri, were such prominent Northerners as Joe Devlin, Cahir Healy and

T. J. Campbell, while O'Byrne himself sang at a concert organised to celebrate the event at Dublin's Mansion House (at which, according to Séamus O'Neill, he 'was the most popular artiste of the evening'[33]). So significant would O'Byrne deem the Congress that he published three devotional poems in celebration of the event in a special commemorative edition of the *Capuchin Annual* in 1933.[34] For a country still negotiating the violent legacy of the Civil War and one embarked upon an experimental programme of cultural and economic isolationism, the resonances of the Congress were both complex and significant. This was because, while the consciously all-Ireland nature of the celebrations indicated that the issue of partition remained a painful if not fully acknowledged compromise, the extraordinary devotion provoked by the visit suggested that a conception of Irish identity based on faith might be able to succeed where the Revival's often determinedly culturalist approach had failed. As Connolly observed:

> Evening after evening, as the different groups made their way to the Phoenix Park, men one night, women another, and children having their own special occasion, there was the quiet atmosphere that accompanies prayerful devotion. Ireland was on its knees not as former rulers would have wished to have it to a foreign monarch but in prayerful devotion to the only king that it would ever acknowledge.[35]

It was through the expression of this collective emotion that the Congress seamlessly integrated religious unity and national feeling: a synthesis neatly symbolised by the welcome afforded to the papal ship as a squadron of the Air Force of the Free State Army flew overhead in crucifix formation. However else this symbol could be read, the conjunction it insisted upon perfectly encapsulated the deepest fears of Northern Unionists, and indeed the Congress as a whole reverberated through Northern Ireland in largely predictable ways. For Catholics the celebrations were unconfined: a crowd of 80,000 listened to a live relay of the Phoenix Park high mass in Belfast's Corrigan Park (an event organised by the ever faithful *Irish News*) and devotional shrines were placed in the streets of West Belfast. Loyalists, in turn, responded to the excitement by erecting Orange arches in protest and by attacking the special trains and buses organised to transport the thousands of pilgrims across the border. 'Ireland's honour and the North's shame', the *Irish News* thundered.[36]

Perhaps the real significance of the 1932 Eucharistic Congress was, however, the manner in which it marked the final triumph of the ascendant Catholic bourgeoisie in the Irish Free State. It was this class who had transformed the country's institutions through a determined programme of state building and as a result these institutions bore overwhelmingly the imprint of its moral and religious preoccupations. Many Northerners such as Connolly and Denis McCullough were happy to take part in this process in the years following partition, but even those who had remained in the North such as O'Byrne were able to benefit from the class's increased economic mobility. For if the market for O'Byrne's work remained limited in an increasingly factionalised North, in the South there was a constituency ideally suited to his talents: a voracious readership anxious for cultural and religious reassurance and one easily scared by the merest hint of creative innovation. Accordingly it was to this energetic, if fundamentally conservative, readership that O'Byrne would direct most of his writing during the 1930s, his most productive period. As this suggests, his writings at this time were overwhelmingly religious in focus but usually combined this necessary piety with a sentimental nationalism and a concern with the niceties of bourgeois morality appropriate to his assumed readership. It was an unpromising mix, and even that element in O'Byrne's imagination drawn to the bizarre, the uncanny and the misplaced could scarcely redeem some of its worst didacticism.

O'Byrne was considerably aided in this work by his continuing association with Colm O Lochlainn, proprietor of the Sign of the Three Candles press in Dublin, and an old friend from Ardrigh and the War of Independence. O Lochlainn's company was one of the most vigorous presses in Ireland and, alongside devotional material, published many titles on Irish folklore, music and history.[37] Karl Uhlemann, a Dubliner of German extraction, was the junior lithographic artist at the press and his immediately recognisable designs were to become a striking feature of many of O'Byrne's books. It was with the Sign of the Three Candles press that, in 1930, O'Byrne published *Pilgrim in Italy*, an account of his travels across that country which had as its centrepiece a description of O'Byrne's audience with Pope Pius XI in Rome. The image of Pius XI as a masculine and energetic figure capable of reforming the Church was already well developed – great emphasis was placed on both his scholarly prowess and his skills as a mountaineer[38] – but even in that context O'Byrne's description of him is both hyperbolic and slightly unsettling:

> He is tall. Taller than we had expected. He walks briskly and erectly, with the carriage of a mountaineer. His white soutane fitting perfectly, shows the strong, powerful torso, well-knit, and sinewy as that battered marble one, so beloved of Michael Angelo, away yonder in the long, bright, lovely gallery where it sits, a thing of beauty unsurpassed, amid the crowds of bloated porphyry Caesars.

> He has the noble, frank face and the changeful kind eyes of his country people, eyes that are deep and dark as the velvet heart of a sunflower. While he speaks he keeps smiling, that wonderful Italian smile that has in it so much mirth, so much tenderness, so much pathos. Surely, we say to ourselves, as we watch it play about his mouth and eyes, surely the tenderness unsurpassed of the sunny smile of Italy is the loveliest thing left in all the width and weariness of the world.[39]

Although it is not unusual to find sexual desire sublimated into adoration for the Virgin Mary in Catholic Irish literature, it is certainly less common to find the Pope fulfilling the same function. As a piece of devotional writing the passage describes a moment of religious ecstasy, but as Pius XI becomes both the embodiment of faith indivisible and the Italian homoerotic masculine ideal we have found O'Byrne fixated on while in Chicago, one might also argue that it speaks of nothing less than desire in its most intensely abstracted form: a swirl of multiple displacements and repressions which speaks of both longing and denial. It is for this reason that O'Byrne's descriptions of the Italian masculine character are as much a condemnation of what he sees as an inherent natural cruelty as they are a celebration of that character's gentleness and sexual allure.[40]

O'Byrne's next publication, *The Gaelic Source of the Brontë Genius* from 1933,[41] was little more than a pamphlet and yet it articulated preoccupations that would become increasingly important to him during the rest of his writing life. Consisting of two essays, 'The Gaelic source of the Brontë genius' and 'Charlotte Brontë goes to confession' (the first published in America and the second in England), the text argues for the Irish ancestry of the Brontë family as a crucial factor in their subsequent achievement and casts doubt on the importance of what it terms their 'ultra-Protestant'[42] background. Such appropriations were, in themselves, not new and have been repeated since,[43] but what gives *The Gaelic Source of the Brontë Genius* its particular energy is its assertion of the significance of the *shanachie* tradition to the Brontë family, deriving from Hugh Prunty of Ballynaskeagh, the novelists' grandfather and 'an Irish *shanachie*, or story-teller'.[44] Here, as elsewhere in his writing, O'Byrne reveals himself to be fascinated by the possibilities of the *shanachie* tradition, the connections it has to other forms, such as the novel, and the possibility of extending its scope to encounter and assimilate material and contexts previously considered unfamiliar – an interest to be fully realised only in *As I Roved Out*. Central to this desire is a conception of Gaelic culture as one naturally capable of transformation into diverse forms and contexts. As he comments:

> The 'natural inheritance' of the Brontë family was a knowledge – imbibed by their father beside a kiln fire in an Irish cottage, and later imparted to them at Haworth – of the vast store of old authentic Gaelic tradition, its wealth of folk-lore, romance, legend and poetry.[45]

To illustrate this thesis, the essay juxtaposes a translated fragment of a third-century Gaelic poem ascribed to Finn MacCool with a passage from *Wuthering Heights* and attempts to demonstrate that the cadences of the latter's descriptive passages contain an echo of the earlier text. While the implications of this are left undeveloped, O'Byrne is astute in his assertion that Catherine Linton's fasting in order to punish her husband in *Wuthering Heights* is strongly reminiscent of the Gaelic tradition of 'fasting on', as dramatised in W. B. Yeats's play *The King's Threshold*, from 1904.[46] While elsewhere in the essay much of the argument is derivative of Elizabeth Gaskell's *Life of Charlotte Brontë* (and, in turn, takes many liberties with Celtic history[47]), 'The Gaelic source of the Brontë genius' argues its position forcefully and ultimately proposes a positive model of cultural interaction that is capable of bringing the past and the present into some form of imaginative dialectic. It is in this awareness that the text's significance for O'Byrne's future work resides.

'Charlotte Brontë goes to confession' is a shorter piece. It is based upon a letter Charlotte wrote to her sister Emily from Brussels in September 1843. In this Charlotte describes how (despite, as O'Byrne puts it, her 'stupid anti-Catholic attitude'[48]) she was tempted to confession in the Cathedral of Saint Gudule out of a combination of boredom and loneliness. After confession, Charlotte resists the priest's further attempts to counsel her away from her heresies and, as the essay's gloomy final sentence asserts, 'Charlotte Brontë remained a Protestant'. While Charlotte's original letter emphasises the light-hearted nature of the expedition, O'Byrne chooses a different emphasis:

> Charlotte Brontë set her feet for an instant on the Road that would have led her Home – home to the Church of her fathers. But it was only for an instant. Her promise to see the priest again she never kept, and so –
> The choice went by for ever
> 'Twixt that darkness and that light.[49]

This sectarian-tinged moment of missed opportunity constitutes for O'Byrne a defining point in Charlotte's life and can be contrasted with his interpretation of Henry Joy McCracken's death in *As I Roved Out*: 'in his last hour on earth ... [he] quite naturally ... wanted to go to confession'[50] – a process repeated throughout the volume as the leaders of the United Irishmen are gradually revealed to possess essentially Catholic longings. Here, as in most of his work during the 1930s, O'Byrne's view of Protestantism is entirely negative and any positive achievement attained by a Protestant is usually ascribed to some obscured Catholicism in his or her ancestry. This is the case with Charlotte, who suffers in the comparison with the saintly Emily, about whom the text comments with some satisfaction: 'there was a Catholic drop in her for all that'.[51]

Two years after the publication of *The Gaelic Source of the Brontë Genius* O'Byrne continued these explicitly religious themes with *From Far Green Hills,*[52] a collection of stories derived from the New Testament that he had first published in a variety of American Catholic newspapers and magazines. According to the effusive 'Foreword by another hand', by this stage of his career O'Byrne's 'reputation as a storyteller [was] well-established both in this country and in America', some of his work being 'publicly adjudged as the "best of its year"'.[53] The rationale behind *From Far Green Hills* is outlined with similar enthusiasm:

> Simon the Cyrenian, the Roman soldier who lanced the Master's side, the bride of Cana, Mary Magdelene [*sic*], the Samaritan woman at the well of Jacob, Pilate's wife, and others, are among the men and women who make but a brief appearance, each, in the Gospel narrative; and having performed their respective parts in relation to the Saviour, they are suffered to sink again into obscurity. Yet their significance in the divine ordinance is very great, and many a devout reader has doubtless wished that something more were known of their antecedents and of what happened to them in the sequel.
>
> And here Cathal O'Byrne steps in and by a happy exercise of his imaginative powers he provides us with what – if it please us – we may accept as a possible answer.... Our author's solutions are something more than mere conjectures. They possess at least the rare merit of ARTISTIC TRUTH and dramatic fitness, for every one of these stories is worked out so naturally, so harmoniously with the circumstances of place and time, that the total effect is almost as convincing to the heart as it is certainly enchanting to the fancy.[54]

While this makes great claims for the strength of O'Byrne's narrative powers, the tension it unwittingly suggests between 'artistic truth' and the sanctity of the Gospel narrative is one that troubles *From Far Green Hills* throughout. The result is a disjointed collection unafraid of letting the demands of the scriptural source material get in the way of its authorial initiative. As such the text risks heresy in effect if not in intention. It is, however, through this often bizarre synthesis that the book is able to explore themes that concern O'Byrne elsewhere in his writings: characters speak in Ulster vernacular English – an adaptation, perhaps, of Christ's own vernacular Aramaic – while the epiphanies of religious salvation presented here will be transformed in *As I Roved Out* into historical revelation. Underwriting this formal process is the constant urge to indict the guilty, whether that be the planters who have destroyed Ulster's Gaelic inheritance as *As I Roved Out* insists, or, in the case of *From Far Green Hills*, the Jews responsible for the murder of Christ. As this latter preoccupation suggests, *From Far Green Hills* is a work of reckless and often vicious anti-Semitism, a tendency most visible in its account of the crucifixion, 'The Cyrenian's day', based on the story of Simon from Matthew 27:32 and Mark 15:21. Moving beyond the account of the events contained in the Gospels, O'Byrne's story has Simon and a Roman soldier united in horror at the 'brutal and ruthless cruelty' of 'the Jew-dogs of Jerusalem'.[55] When Simon carries Christ's cross he is beaten down by the 'cruel and merciless' 'Jewish rabble'[56] and flees the city in disgust and terror. In suggesting that the Jews bore responsibility for the execution of Jesus, rather than all mankind, and that in some way the crucifixion could have been averted had others acted more forthrightly, O'Byrne's heresy was of a type common among right-wing Catholic groups in both Ireland and America during the 1930s, a relaxed anti-Semitism that was tacitly accepted within much of Irish society and which the Revival had often explicitly encouraged.[57] There are no other instances of such anti-Semitism in O'Byrne's writing and, unlike many of his other works, O'Byrne subsequently rarely mentioned *From Far Green Hills*. Indeed, one is left with the suspicion that by this stage of his career he was instead more preoccupied with the historical reconstitution of Belfast and its betrayals – a story which he would also recreate in the form of a Gospel narrative.

As these publications indicate, while the Irish publishing industry remained relatively weak (and was always vulnerable to the crushing force of Catholic moral opprobrium liable to bear down upon the most seemingly innocuous books), religious publishing had become a flourishing area of the economy in both the North and the South. One of the clearest symptoms of this was the dramatic rise of the Catholic Truth Society of Ireland, an organisation formed in Belfast in 1898 by Bishop Henry, which had as its aim the diffusion 'by means of cheap publications sound Catholic literature in popular form so as to give instruction and edification in a manner most likely to interest and attract the general reader'.[58] The Society was to become an increasingly vociferous and influential voice in Irish life. It consistently asserted an aggressively pro-Catholic stance on issues of constitutional legislation and public policy, and was a firm believer in the value of state censorship as a means of protecting Ireland's natural virtue. This unequivocal position was deeply attractive to many and at the Society's congress held in Belfast in 1934 some 120,000 communicants attended the pontifical mass. It was, though, through its publications that the Society had the most vivid success. Alongside Irish-language prayer books and other devotional works, by 1938 the Society had published nearly 1500 pamphlets asserting the centrality of Catholic teaching for both social and individual life. Indeed, it is no exaggeration to suggest that through this series the Society attempted to provide an entire ideological world view for the willing Irish Catholic reader, an 'antidote against the poison of dangerous or immoral writings', as the initiative proclaimed itself.[59]

Perceived in this way, the ambition of the series was as extensive in its scale as it was limited in its content. As the publisher's publicity on the back cover of the pamphlets stated:

> The first concern of the Veritas Company Limited in the handling of books is SAFETY. Those, therefore, who have control of Convent, School, or Parochial Library can depend upon our lists when making their purchases. Nothing we supply will offend the innocent but our range is wide and liberal.

Such aspirations were easily satirised and it is appropriate that when Flann O'Brien, perhaps the writer best able to crack the intricate codes through which Ireland's Catholic middle class constituted itself in this period, wished to find an image for all that was most stultifying and intellectually timid in Irish life in his 1964 novel *The Dalkey Archive*, it was to the Catholic Truth Society pamphlet series that he turned.[60] That said, one person's recognition of philosophical and spiritual paralysis can be another person's publishing opportunity and, given the particular preoccupations of the Society, it is not surprising that between 1934 and 1942 O'Byrne was one of its most prolific authors, producing a large number of pamphlets on such varied subjects as the social life of middle-class Dublin housewives, the Irish woman present at the birth of Christ, the Gaelic lullaby that the Virgin Mary would sing while nursing her infant, various legends and lore of St Patrick, and a history of the Lough Derg pilgrimage.[61] It is likely that some of this material was not rooted in sound historical research, but given the earnest tedium of many of the Society's political and theological pamphlets, the occasional lunacy of O'Byrne's religious imagination must have been welcomed by many devout subscribers.[62]

Had circumstances been different, it is possible to imagine that O'Byrne could have produced this kind of hack work indefinitely. The Ireland that he spoke to was one still in a deep post-revolutionary slumber, and by shifting the ideal of Irish nationhood from the political to the religious realm his writing simply refused to acknowledge the compromises of a partition that in many ways had come to dominate so many other aspects of his life. Such a vision, however, had undeniable limits. For while Northern Catholics could express an Irish identity through religious affiliation, the territorial imperative could only be repressed through an act of often exhausting collective will. Indeed, as the likelihood of a united Ireland receded into improbability, the community's signature discourse was more liable to be an overwhelming sense of betrayal and loss, an emotion painfully articulated by an anonymous poem, entitled 'A Belfastman at the GPO., Dublin', published in the 1942 *Capuchin Annual*, a special edition commemorating the twenty-fifth anniversary of the Easter Rising:[63]

> There is no word can tell
> My loneliness.
> Our dead too fought and fell.
>
> Now you have your peace
> And liberty,
> Pray god for our release.
>
> My joy exults to-day.
> My loneliness
> There is no word can say.

If the South was capable of hearing such desperate entreaties, there is little evidence to suggest it was going to act upon them. Besieged within the siege, the lonely passion of Northern Catholicism was set to endure.

In the face of this neglect there are, then, signs of a marked shift back to the local and the regional in the cultural preoccupations of the Northern Catholic community during the late 1930s. If this tendency was, in part, made inevitable by the South's own increasing isolationism, the manner in which World War Two was to cast the border into even starker relief was further to reinforce its necessity. Alongside this, Northern Ireland's own cultural realm was beginning to show signs of rejuvenation and, while this activity could hardly be compared with the scale of the Northern Revival thirty years previously, it did at least have something of the same ecumenical spirit.[64] This activity was most evident in the coterie of writers gathered upstairs at Campbell's Café opposite Belfast's City Hall, the production of 'little magazines' such as *Lagan* and *Rann*, the re-emergence of local theatre and theatrical companies, and the appearance of poets such as John Hewitt and W. R. Rodgers.[65] Encouraged by the foundation in 1943 of the Council for the Encouragement of Music and the Arts (renamed the Arts Council of Northern Ireland in 1962) these promising signs needed careful husbandry in order to survive Northern Ireland's still volatile public sphere, but by the 1950s the *City of Belfast Tourist Handbook* could claim – albeit in a slightly tentative manner – that 'the writers of Eire have been well written-up, but the fact that there is a "Belfast School" which can be best described as realistic but not depressing, is not so widely known'.[66]

O'Byrne, of course, was of a previous generation to these writers and publishers and, in a more profound sense, articulated a political, artistic and cultural vision that remained ill-adapted to the changed conditions of the North. For all that, however, it is in his weekly series of articles about Belfast and its surroundings published in the *Irish News* from the late 1930s onwards that we can identify an early sign of this renewed appetite for the history and folklore of Ulster itself. Certainly, by the time he collected these articles to form his major work, *As I Roved Out*, he was at the most productive stage of his literary career, as a breathless account of his accomplishments in the gossip column of the *Irish Bookman* indicate:

> The other day I met Cathal O'Byrne, who has provided such grand entertainment, with voice and pen, to so many Irish, both at home and overseas. Casually I enquired if he was doing any writing, and discovered he had no less than four books on the stocks! One, a book of short stories, *Ashes on the Hearth* will be published by Colm O Lochlainn; another will be published by *The Irish News*; another will appear in New York (Kenedy) and will be called, if I remember aright, *Voice of the Irish*: it will be a book of legends about Saint Patrick; the fourth is a book of folk-tales for which Cathal had access to the library of the Folklore Commission: the tales are told in Cathal's own inimitable style. And he is probably writing another book![67]

As with the mysteriously abandoned *Collected Poems*, *Voice of the Irish* and the collection of folktales were never to reach press, but *As I Roved Out* was published in September 1946 and, according to the Foreword of the 1957 edition, 'sold out almost at once'. There were a further three reprints in the years that followed, and O'Byrne developed a profitable sideline selling the book directly from his home on Cavendish Street for 10*s* 6*d* (or 11*s* for an autographed copy).[68] Perhaps partly because of this method of distribution *As I Roved Out* soon gained the status of something of a *samizdat* text – a work of popular history decried by professional historians but one that has continued to fulfil an affective need through its provision of a foundational myth for Belfast Irish nationalism. Indeed, for Joe Graham, editor of the Falls Road community magazine *Rushlight*, the book is no less than the 'Bible of Belfast'. As this suggests, *As I Roved Out*'s influence has been great and most subsequent accounts of Belfast and its history tend, at some point or another, to have recourse to the wealth of detail it contains – even if it is only to question some of its more fantastical claims. The structure of the book is simple: it consists of 128 short pieces on Belfast and its surrounding area (these had previously appeared as a series in the *Irish News*). To describe the pieces themselves is a more complex task: strictly considered, they are not essays, recollections or stories but share instead interlocking aspects from all these forms. From this diversity a kind of order emerges. Beginning with many stories and myths about the United Irishmen and their relationship to old Belfast, the collection then moves on to consider the city in the nineteenth century, before culminating with accounts of areas, particularly graveyards, outside Belfast. The momentum of the collection begins to decrease the further from Belfast it roves and the second edition (from 1957) omitted those articles not pertaining to the city and removed passages that were considered excessively sectarian. Frank Benner, a close friend of O'Byrne in his final years and one-time chairman of the Lyric Players Theatre,[69] was granted the copyright to the book for £25 on the condition that he would endeavour to keep it in print, and a subsequent edition was published in England in 1970.

Of the more recent editions of the work, Blackstaff published the best in 1982. This restored the text to its original length and added a slightly uneasy, although affectionate, Foreword by Hewitt. Although Hewitt's perception that *As I Roved Out*'s are 'the only pages to which we can conveniently turn for a readable account of the past of our own city'[70] can be justified on the grounds of the text's frequent republication, there were a number of significant precursors to the book. For instance, Richard Hayward, a ULT colleague of O'Byrne from the days of the Revival and a liberal Protestant writer of a type increasingly rare in Ireland during this period, had gained some success with *In Praise of Ulster* in 1938,[71] a work that corrected and revised some of the enthusiastic excesses of historical detail found in the writings of more forthrightly nationalist figures such as Bigger. Coming from a very different tradition but with interests and sympathies markedly similar to O'Byrne's, Aodh De Blácam's *The Black North*,[72] from 1938, had sought to illuminate Ulster's long tradition of nationalist agitation for presumably uncomprehending readers from the South, but perhaps the most significant antecedent was H. A. MacCartan's *The Glamour of Belfast*,[73] from 1921, a book that, in its cyclical structure, appears to have provided O'Byrne with a template for his own preoccupations. What distinguishes *As I Roved Out* from these previous titles is, however, not so much a matter of content (after all, to a lesser or greater extent, all these works assert a prelapsarian narrative of the North based around the fall of the United Irishmen) but rather what can be better understood as O'Byrne's *orientation* towards the past: the sense in which the book asserts itself as the only thing standing in the way of an overwhelming collective amnesia. In this, O'Byrne's approach is that of the preservationist, the guardian of minute details and broken cultural fragments. As Thomas Fox noted in a perceptive review of the first edition:

> For in [*As I Roved Out*] a thousand of the things passed over inevitably by the ordinary historian are carefully preserved: the habits, and customs, and oddities, and eccentricities, the very atmosphere of the lives of men and women dead for years. In the bumpy streets of Belfast and all over the Ulster countryside Cathal O'Byrne discovers and revives stories that would otherwise have been forgotten – to the great loss of all who love good stories.[74]

Not all reviewers have been so kind and significant criticism of *As I Roved Out* has tended to focus on its habit of too frequently repeating and revisiting its own anecdotes. As Hewitt remarks, this can become at times 'a monotonous litany'[75] and, indeed, at few points are we spared the reminder that Thomas Russell was 'the man from God knows where' or that Thomas McCabe was 'an Irish slave'. It is, however, only when employing critical criteria appropriate to the homogeneous single volume that such repetition appears tedious. The original *Irish News* articles deliberately deployed this reiteration to create a community of readers adept at piecing together the various wider significances of that week's narrative through O'Byrne's seemingly casual deployment of keywords, cultural touchstones and rhetorical asides. In this way, and in a manner that reveals O'Byrne's debt to the *shanachie*, the technique is mnemonic in its function for both teller and listener. This cyclical aspect of the book creates other resonances for readers of the single volume; as a recent enthusiastic reviewer has suggested, the book provides us with 'the 1940's equivalent of surfing the Net',[76] as the reader leaps from strand to connective strand. Certainly, it was because of this technique that the work steps beyond the predictability of much of O'Byrne's previous writings, for while many of his earlier works also appear to occupy a site of residual values, the hypnotic swirl of myth and memory created by repetition in *As I Roved Out* now appears as a precursor to a more distinctly modern perception of the possibilities inherent to folk memory and the urban landscape. The book's unyielding focus on memory and reverie as a means of recreating that which has been destroyed (regardless of whether this is the physical fabric of the old city or the ideals of the United Irishmen) forces the reader to submit to the claustrophobic weave of the text, to sense that the narrative it contains does not begin in 1798 but can be entered at any point. As Fox asserts, the whole point of the book is that one 'can begin anywhere and read in any direction',[77] and it is in this that the simultaneity of the text is located. A typical piece from the book, 'Tradition and the Falls Road', articulates O'Byrne's sense of this movement:

> The little stone of truth rolling through the many ages of the world has gathered and grown grey with the thick mosses of romance and superstition. But tradition must always have that little stone of truth for its kernel, and perhaps he who rejects all is likelier to be wrong than even foolish folk like myself who love to believe all, and who tread the new paths thinking of the ancient stories.[78]

This is a sentimental perception, of course, and yet it is one that also suggests the structural principle of the volume. When O'Byrne roves around Belfast it is not that he sees the old proclaim itself in the presence of the new, but rather that he places the present under a perpetual erasure. For this reason *As I Roved Out* takes on the appearance of a closed – almost secret – text available only to its select community of readers. In turn, the Belfast society it recreates is one dominated by shibboleths and passwords; it is literally haunted by its betrayals and amidst it all is the sometimes unsettling figure of O'Byrne himself peering through windows and asking seemingly endless questions. There was inevitably some mystery about how O'Byrne gained the astonishing depth of information about Belfast the book demonstrates. Denis Ireland – perhaps mischievously – posits the idea that he had many friends who were bread servers 'and for getting and hearing things it's hard to beat bread servers',[79] while, more prosaically, an anonymous obituary notice observed that:

> [O'Byrne] would read anything he could lay his hands upon in the Linenhall or Public Libraries specialising in the history of the streets of the city, noting the changing names and the traders or people connected with them from time to time.[80]

Alternatively, the dedication to the work itself cites Bigger, whose 'erudition, generously shared, made the writing of it possible'. Clearly, without Bigger there could have been no *As I Roved Out* and O'Byrne's recollection of sitting astride one of the old cannons that guarded the entrance to Ardrigh and listening 'enthralled while the great man talked – as only he could – of the old times, the people, and the old places that are now no more' suggests the profound nature of the debt.[81]

If there is an overall theme to *As I Roved Out*, then it lies with its preoccupation with the betrayal of the ideals of the United Irishmen and the subsequent slide of Belfast into Orangeism. This defeat, however, also functions as a mere precursor to the more serious, if largely unmentioned, rupture of partition and in its repetitive elegies *As I Roved Out* is a text severely bruised by the immediate effects of this sundering. As a result, *As I Roved Out* is unable to see modern Belfast as a loved or even familiar location; instead, it deliberately and insistently transforms the reader into a stranger, who must examine the few traces of what has remained from before the catastrophe with the hope of allowing an imaginative reconstruction. It is because of this fundamental refusal that the book retains its capacity to surprise. Here the city is no organic developing whole but a site of rupture and fragmentation, a place written over by successive, and often incompatible, eras of power, which suffers from, 'to use the jargon of the moment, an incurable "inferiority complex"'.[82] While for O'Byrne this explains what he refers to as the 'crass manners and bigotry of Belfast',[83] it also leads to increasingly extreme renunciations: it is Protestantism, or, as O'Byrne has it, 'religion, so called',[84] that is deemed responsible for the persecution of witches in County Antrim, while even reference to the skills of a pioneering shipbuilder must be qualified by the knowledge that 'there were ships built in this Northern land, ships that sailed away to Iceland, Iona, Narroway, the Lowlands of Holland, and to far away Rome itself, centuries before this Planter from Ayrshire was ever heard of'.[85] With this, O'Byrne is adamant that 'the only thing of any cultural value we Irish in the North have to thank the Planters for'[86] is a slim collection of folk songs and, indeed, any Protestant whom O'Byrne finds admirable (whether that be McCracken or a personal friend) is inevitably found to have possessed secret Catholic longings (the symptom of which is usually that upon their death 'a Rosary was discovered wound tightly around his wrist'[87]).

The Belfast that emerges through a reading of *As I Roved Out* is, then, a place of both considerable sentimentality and unremitting bitterness. The humour of the book is usually grim, its comparative technique only ever indicates an ironic absence in the present, and its sense of loss is irredeemable. Despite this, however, the book can occasionally forget itself and yearn for what Ciaran Carson has described in his review of the 1982 Blackstaff edition as 'a republic of the imagination, all ease, contentment, and, if possible, Irish-speaking'.[88] It is through this that what Carson identifies as the book's 'essential gentleness, its passion, self-involvement, and occasional sentimentality' become manifest and as such the work's implicit theme becomes – almost despite itself – the search for how one might reconnect the modern city to its ruptured past. It is not the least powerful element of the book that it undertakes this task despite full knowledge of its impossibility, and its most powerful moments derive from the repeated assertions of this awareness:

> During our visit to the Lagan Village we left the main thoroughfare and got lost in a maze of streets – streets that ended in blind alley-ways and culs-de-sac, or led us to the entrances of great yards, through the open gateways of which we caught a glimpse of green fields that sloped away to the edge of the Lagan water, with the seagulls wheeling and screaming under the grey sky, and the great masses of the gas-tanks on the farther side looming dark and ugly beyond.[89]

That *As I Roved Out* is greatly superior to O'Byrne's other work is largely inarguable. For Carson it is nothing less than a 'great book'[90] and, certainly, it can be considered as one of the most significant obscured texts of twentieth-century Irish literature, a work that is as unexpected as it is original. Described in these terms, and taking into account its sometimes extraordinary breadth of historical vision, it is unsurprising that O'Byrne would not achieve such heights again, but despite the fact that he was now an old man he was still able to produce one last noteworthy work. In 1948, at the age of seventy-two, O'Byrne returned to his friend Colm O Lochlainn's Sign of the Three Candles press for *The Ashes on the Hearth*, a collection of fourteen stories. These pieces had originally appeared as articles in the *Irish Monthly* and the *Irish Rosary* and in its assertion of an ideal of a Catholic nation extending across state boundaries the volume as a whole had a greater structural coherency than *As I Roved Out*. There were, however, similarities. *As I Roved Out*, as the title suggests, was constructed around the idea of the wandering *flâneur*, who comes to the point of recollection through the stimuli of the environment. Each story (in fact 'reverie' might be a more apt description) in *The Ashes on the Hearth* similarly begins at a point in the present and succeeds in an imaginative recreation of various historical characters through the reconstitution of that which had been destroyed, or, to express it more appropriately, the contemplation of the ashes leads to the memory of the previous night's fire. Just as O'Byrne in *As I Roved Out* could gaze out across a ruined landscape of gas holders and urban waste and see the fields and the farmers who had lived there prior to industrialisation, so in *The Ashes on the Hearth* the narrator visits modern Stratford-upon-Avon by train and finds himself in conversation with John Dowland, the sixteenth-century lutenist and some time friend of Shakespeare. As this example suggests, *The Ashes on the Hearth* roams more widely than *As I Roved Out* and has a cast of characters that includes Joan of Arc,

James Clarence Mangan, the Belfast betrayer of the United Irishmen, Belle Martin (who also features in *As I Roved Out*), Shakespeare, Thomas Moore and Dante. This technique, however, was by no means original. O'Byrne's imaginative constructions were, for instance, similar to the reveries of Charlotte Moberly and Eleanor Jourdain in their recreation of Marie Antoinette in *An Adventure*,[91] from 1911, and other women writers of this period were also discovering the powers of reverie as a means of forcing a creative and often covertly political intervention. If such a manoeuvre was deeply implicated in the gendered positions available to female writers of the period, for O'Byrne the resurrection of a despised or forgotten history of which he is the sole arbiter was intended to re-emphasise the continuity of Irish nationalism as an unbroken narrative and its inseparable union with the Catholic Church.

Both the efficacies and weaknesses of this approach are well illustrated by the first story in the collection, 'A true ghost story', which strikes the sectarian note present across the collection as a whole.[92] It begins in the contemporary Dublin of the 1940s, 'the evening of a grey September day, a day of lowering clouds and sullen skies'. The narrator appears to be wandering aimlessly until he comes to Marlborough Street, the original site of 'The Bowling Green' where 'one hundred and eighty odd years ago the city belles and beaux played and promenaded in the vain idle thoughtless and foolish fashion of the Dublin of their day'. Although this is not yet revealed to us, this attack on the youth of the Anglo-Irish ascendancy is more specifically, as the story will frame it, an attack on the moral bankruptcy and the heresies shielded, or indeed encouraged, by their Protestantism. Taking a seat in front of Tyrone House, the narrator is disturbed by a 'little old man' who asks if the narrator wishes to hear a ghost story. Leading him into the house and up to the bedroom of Lady Beresford, he tells the story of the ghost of Lord Tyrone. Lady Beresford and Tyrone were childhood friends 'educated in the principles of Deism' and on reaching maturity they promised to each other that 'whichever died first would, if permitted, appear to the one left alive and make known what religion was most acceptable to the Supreme Being'. Some time later Lady Beresford is at breakfast with her husband when he notices that she is wearing a black ribbon on her wrist. Forbidding him to ever enquire as to the reason for this, she then tells him that she has knowledge of Tyrone's death on the previous Tuesday. Recounting the events to a friend of the family, the foundation of her knowledge is revealed:

> One night, her ladyship explained, she woke in this very room to find Lord Tyrone standing by her bedside. Terrified she screamed out 'For heaven's sake, Lord Tyrone, by what means and for what purpose do you come

> here at this time of night?' 'Have you forgotten our promise?' he asked. 'I died last Tuesday night, and am now permitted to appear to you to assure you that the revealed religion is the true and only one by which you can be saved. More I am not permitted to say, but if, after this warning, you persist in your infidelity, you will be miserable indeed'.

Demanding proof, Lady Beresford insists that Tyrone clasps her wrist. On contact with the spirit her mortal flesh withers and shrinks: an act which explains her subsequent concealment of the scars by the black ribbon. Finishing his story the old man vanishes in the great hall before he can be thanked and the narrator is left to continue his wanderings, like the wedding guest in the *Ancient Mariner*, a sadder – and presumably wiser – man.

The conclusion of 'A true ghost story' tends to beg more questions than it answers and is symptomatic of other irregularities found across the collection as whole. In attacking the principles of deism, faith by the testimony of reason alone is disproved by revelation, but the melodramatic encounter here described is far from that normally considered as defining the principles of revealed religion made known by supernatural agency. To express this differently, in disproving a heresy O'Byrne commits another of more importance and one is left confused as to why the deist Lady Beresford and Tyrone would consort in a plan which entirely refutes the principles by which they have been educated. In this way the doubt that leads to Lady Beresford's mutilation mirrors the doubt of the narrator and the demand for proof of which 'A true ghost story' is, in itself, symptomatic. These contradictions are summarised by the title of the story, which places the revelation of (spiritual) truth within the remit of the superstitious conception of the ghost story.

The Ashes on the Hearth as a whole continues this theme of explicit moral education (a tendency appropriate to the journals of first publication) but lacks the innovation and sheer energy of *As I Roved Out*. In professing the ability to see that which is concealed to others, the revelations of the collection acquire a hectoring quality which inadvertently manages to express doubt while insisting dogmatically on the veracity of the vision described. This is only an issue in that the collection strives to achieve a status beyond that of mere recollection. In revisiting the scenes of past wrongs (the martyrdom of Joan of Arc, the betrayal of the United Irishmen, the execution of Robert Emmet) it is part of O'Byrne's purpose to account for the fallen (usually Protestant and British) present and to stress the coincidental, almost arbitrary nature of its occurrence, a historical perspective which also informs his interpretation of the crucifixion in *From Far Green Hills*. As with all of O'Byrne's work, *The*

Ashes on the Hearth balances itself between an awareness of irretrievable loss and the desire to revisit time and again the moment of missed opportunity. As such restlessness indicates, O'Byrne's last writings would bring no ultimate reconciliation or peaceful acceptance. His rage against the iniquity of history and the helplessness of its victims remained with him to the end.

O'Byrne's final years were spent in quiet, pious and increasingly impoverished retirement on Cavendish Street. Hewitt records that he was a peripheral if still active member of Belfast's literary scene during the 1940s and describes meeting him at the house of the eccentric artist John Langtry Lynas in April 1949. His notes of the meeting describe O'Byrne as 'about my height, slighter than I, with a flushed face and scant blackish hair. He wore an enormous ring on the little finger of his left hand.'[93] He maintained his friendships with the old generation of Northern republicans scattered by partition and was a frequent visitor to the families of Denis McCullough and Joseph Connolly in Dublin – visits which are still remembered with great affection by the children of those two veterans. Also of significance was the weekend visit to O'Byrne's house of an old and fragile Maud Gonne McBride in April 1948, forty-six years after she had interceded on behalf of the ULT in its row with W. B. Yeats over the company's desire to produce his *Cathleen ni Houlihan*. If O'Byrne had reason to feel bitterness at the straitened circumstances attendant on his old age he did not reveal it. As Darach Connolly, son of Joseph, recalled many years later:

> his manner was unfailingly courteous (even courtly!), gracious, deferential (even to us children) but never servile or unctuous, always self-possessed but never self-conceited. I can remember that as I grew from teens to twenties, even then I had a sense of admiration and sympathy for a man who had so much talent and so much kindness in him and yet had reaped so very little in material rewards.[94]

In the jumble of documents relating to O'Byrne in the Public Record Office of Northern Ireland is a record of his stay in Nazareth House on the Ormeau Road from 1954 until his death, three years later.[95] There he was nursed by the sisters through a long and debilitating illness and the sparse account of this period by one of their number contrasts pathetically with the exuberance of O'Byrne's own prose. The unwitting sense of an exhaustion, of a language running out of energy, that it creates provides its own coda:

> Cathal come to Nazareth House on March 2nd 1954. The person who asked to get him in was J. Clifford who then lived at O'Hanlon Park,

> Dundalk. The Sister who cared for him is Sr. Claudia who now lives in Nazareth House Sligo. The friend who came to visit him was Martin Morrison who then lived in Church St. (also his girlfriend Cissy). The Dominican Convent did one of his plays around 1960, it was called 'The Cherry Bough'.

It is in this way that O'Byrne's life was finally enclosed by silence. He had suffered a stroke one month prior to his death and, as an anonymous appreciation of his life in the *Irish News* put it, 'there was a pathos in Cathal's silence that was almost ironical. Cathal of the cheerful greeting! Cathal of the gay song and story and the ringing laughter!'[96] He died on 1 August 1957 and was buried at Milltown cemetery. He left behind him four nieces and two nephews as his only family. In St Paul's Church, where a requiem mass was celebrated by the Bishop of Down and Connor, crowds gathered outside, unable to gain entrance to the packed building, while 'for some distance along the Falls Road, hundreds of admirers of the deceased were lined on either side. Blinds were drawn in many houses along the route.'[97] His gravestone records: 'In thankful remembrance of Cathal O'Byrne, singer poet and writer who brought Joy into the lives of others'. It is worth noting that, of his achievements, 'singer' is given highest prominence.

Why, then, is O'Byrne's writing now so little regarded? If one were to compile a list of the cultural values that are inimical to modern sensibilities in Northern Ireland then O'Byrne's writings would be seen to fulfil many of them. But this is not simply a distaste for his sentimentality – for which there remains a ready market – but rather the lack of authenticity that this perspective appears to betray. Certainly, the stern onward march of identity politics that currently constitutes what passes for a political process in the North is ill at ease with such discomforting moments of self-parody. For although O'Byrne may not have intended it, to immerse oneself in the endless circularity of *As I Roved Out* is not only to become aware of the manner in which identity is inescapably parasitic on that which it opposes, but also to recognise the extent to which such positions are maintained only through a process of constant reiteration and rehearsal. It is in this way that O'Byrne's celebration of the Belfast urban life and language bears witness to an arch sense of camp. As the extraordinary phenomenon of Mrs Twigglety demonstrates, in this O'Byrne recognised and exploited a slightly self-congratulatory vernacular tweeness that has remained current within Northern culture ever since. This tendency is cast into sharper relief if considered alongside his all-pervasive nationalist beliefs, for it is through the very self-consciousness of national identity – the necessary utterance of that which should be simultaneously obvious – that camp ultimately intrudes. Either way, such is the durability of camp that it is appropriate that one of the few places where one can encounter O'Byrne's work in the recent past is the appearance of his 'Lullaby' on the 1998 album *Voice of a Angel* by the Welsh child singer Charlotte Church. This poem was set to music by Hamilton Harty in 1908 and until this time had an obscure, almost forgotten, existence. Clearly, nothing disappears quite without trace.

Camp is about surface, not depth, about dwelling without roots and, indeed, for all O'Byrne's concentration on Belfast in *As I Roved Out*, his writing might be said to haunt rather than inhabit the city in which he lived. This is not least because it is a place that, in its modern manifestation, he loathed with an unwavering consistency. As his work repeatedly asserts, Belfast 'is one of the ugliest cities in the world',[98] a place where there is no 'beginning or end to the bigotry'.[99] Despite this he was incapable of fixing his gaze on anything other than the fallen urban present – his writings on rural life, for instance, are never able to escape stylised tropes of nostalgia – and so most of his later writing is locked perpetually into embittered and residual habits of thought. In this way O'Byrne's work demonstrates well the uncompromising refusals of cultural pluralism that underpin this particular strain of Celtic eulogy – a strain that owes more to his Hibernianism than republicanism – and as such it expresses a peculiarly intense sense of betrayal, a betrayal from which no redeeming feature could be found and no future possibility countenanced. It can be argued that it is from this perception of loss that the jackdaw-like retention of facts and stories displayed in much of his work is given ideological momentum just as it also illustrates the pessimism of his overall vision. To put it another way, as historical process is rendered as betrayal, so folk memory and anecdote are galvanised.

For this reason one can propose that O'Byrne's work, even in its whimsicalities, is an entirely totalitarian venture. Constantly setting itself up against history as institutional discourse, it seeks a communal past hospitable to folk memory but one that is simultaneously predicated on a future Irish all-island state. In this way his writing offers us no imaginative culs-de-sac: encountering what appears to him to be the absolute defeat of the nationalist ideal in the North, repetition and commemoration become the only possible responses. This extended process of mourning, one can argue, embodies the fate of the Catholic minority in the North after partition, a cultural stance made inevitable by the collapse of confidence in the ideal of institutional advancement and with it the end of a belief that formally organised groups, movements and societies can press claims for political representation through copying the structures of Northern Protestant civic society. In place of this confidence there arose a mode of collective memory, an idea of community maintained and defined by what is now only spectrally present. It is this discourse that O'Byrne's obsessive dwelling on the past articulates. To put this differently, in his fragmented, obsessive reveries we can glimpse what Conor Cruise O'Brien once identified as 'the tragedy of a people in a place: the Catholics in Northern Ireland'.[100]

NOTES

1 In *As I Roved Out* (Belfast: Blackstaff Press, 1982, first published 1946), p. 282, O'Byrne dates his arrival in New York to 1921. While it is curious that he should misremember an event that was so significant to his life history, this vagueness is, in actuality, entirely typical of his work.

2 John Hewitt, Foreword, in O'Byrne, *As I Roved Out*.

3 This lecture series eventually formed the basis of O'Byrne's ingenious (if historically dubious) essay 'Shakespeare's debt to Ireland', *Irish News*, 2 May 1934, p. 8.

4 This seems likely, if only because Amcomri is a compression of 'American Committee for Relief in Ireland'. The family of Tom Williams, an IRA volunteer executed in Crumlin Road Goal in 1942, was one of the many who found a home in Amcomri Street after they had been burnt out of their previous house in the Shore Road area in 1922. In total, the American Committee for Relief in Ireland raised over $5 million during this period. For more information see F. M. Carroll, 'The American Committee for Relief in Ireland, 1920–2', *Irish Historical Studies*, 23.89 (May 1982), pp. 30–49.

5 J. J. Campbell, Foreword, in O'Byrne, *As I Roved Out* (Wakefield: SR Publishers, 1970).

6 Eamon Phoenix, 'Homecoming for a poet and a storyteller', *Irish News*, 8 September 2000, p. 8 (introduction to a reprint of an article from 8 September 1928).

7 Stephen J. Brown and Desmond Clarke, eds, *Ireland in Fiction: A Guide to Irish Novels, Tales, Romances and Folklore, Vol. 2* (Cork: Royal Carbery Books, 1985), entries 1135 and 1136.

8 Cathal O'Byrne, 'Sunny days in Hollywood California', in *Capuchin Annual* (Dublin: Capuchin Franciscan Fathers, 1948), pp. 268–71.

9 See Robert Aldrich, *The Seduction of the Mediterranean: Writing, Art and Homosexual Fantasy* (London: Routledge, 1993).

10 I am grateful to Howard Booth of the University of Manchester for drawing my attention to the cultural and sexual contexts implicit to the representation of Italy in much writing of this period.

11 O'Byrne, 'Sunny days in Hollywood California', p. 270.

12 Cathal O'Byrne, 'Roger Casement's ceilidhe', in *Capuchin Annual* (Dublin: Capuchin Franciscan Fathers, 1946–47), pp. 312–14.

13 Phoenix, 'Homecoming for a poet and a storyteller'.
14 Cathal O'Byrne, *The Grey Feet of the Wind* (Chicago: Ard-Ree Press, 1928).
15 Phoenix, 'Homecoming for a poet and a storyteller'.
16 Oliver Rafferty, 'Catholicism in the North of Ireland since 1891', in *A Century of Northern Life: The Irish News and 100 Years of Ulster History 1890s–1990s*, ed. Eamon Phoenix (Belfast: Ulster Historical Foundation, 1995), p. 160.
17 Marianne Elliott, *The Catholics of Ulster: A History* (London: Penguin, 2000), p. 469.
18 Elliott, *The Catholics of Ulster*, p. 468.
19 Elliott, *The Catholics of Ulster*, p. 399.
20 'Portrait gallery: Cathal O'Byrne', *Irish Times*, 23 July 1955, p. 12. The author of this piece was probably Denis Ireland.
21 'And if it is true that time is always memorialized not as flow but as memories of experienced places and spaces, then history must indeed give way to poetry, time to space, as the fundamental material of social expression.' David Harvey, *The Condition of Postmodernity* (London: Blackwell, 1990), p. 218.
22 See Cathal O'Byrne, 'An appreciation of Carl Gilbert Hardebeck', in *Capuchin Annual* (Dublin: Capuchin Franciscan Fathers, 1943), pp. 235–6.
23 'Performance of Cathal O'Byrne's comedies in St Paul's Hall', *Irish News*, 23 May 1930, p. 8.
24 'Comedies in St Paul's Hall', *Irish News*, 26 May 1930, p. 8.
25 Cathal O'Byrne, *The Burthen: A One-Act Comedy* (Dublin: James Duffy, 1948) and *The Returned Swank* (unpublished).
26 'Comedies in St Paul's Hall'.
27 J.J.H., 'Review of two one-act comedies by Cathal O'Byrne', *Irish Book Lover*, 21.1 (January/February 1933), p. 23.
28 'Comedies in St Paul's Hall'.
29 J.J.H., 'Review of two one-act comedies by Cathal O'Byrne'.
30 Terence Brown, *Ireland: A Social and Cultural History 1922–85* (London: Fontana, 1990), p. 151.
31 'Ireland's honour and the North's shame', *Irish News*, 27 June 1932, p. 4.
32 J. Anthony Gaughan, ed., *Memoirs of Senator Joseph Connolly (1885–1961): A Founder of Modern Ireland* (Dublin: Irish Academic Press, 1996), p. 287.
33 Séamus O'Neill, 'Note: Roger Casement, Cathal O'Byrne and Professor Reid', *Studies*, 68 (spring/summer, 1979), p. 119.
34 Cathal O'Byrne, 'The red cock's cry', 'To one who is monsignor' and 'The one thing needful', in *Capuchin Annual* (Dublin: Capuchin Franciscan Fathers, 1933), pp. 73, 147, 273.
35 Gaughan, *Memoirs of Senator Joseph Connolly*, p. 288.
36 *Irish News*, 27 June 1932, p. 4.
37 For more information on O Lochlainn and the Sign of the Three Candles press see Chalmers Trench, 'The Three Candles Press in the "thirties"', and Dermot McGuinne, 'Colm O Lochlainn and the Sign of the Three Candles: the early decades', *Long Room*, 41 (1996), pp. 35–42, pp. 43–51.

38 In an Irish context, see, for instance, Rev. C. C. Martindale, *Pope Pius XI*, unnumbered Catholic Truth Society of Ireland pamphlet (Dublin: Veritas, 1937).
39 Cathal O'Byrne, *Pilgrim in Italy* (Dublin: At the Sign of the Three Candles, 1930), pp. 31–3.
40 Elsewhere in *Pilgrim in Italy* O'Byrne defined the Italian character thus: 'The Italian keeps the smile that God gave in his eyes, but in his heart the Devil's arrow rankles still. Some call this barbed shaft Cruelty, some ignorance; maybe its poison is from both; but be that how it may, as the old legend says, it is the duty of all Italians to pluck hard at the Arrow of Hell, so that the Smile of God alone shall remain with their children's children' (p. 125).
41 Cathal O'Byrne, *The Gaelic Source of the Brontë Genius* (Edinburgh: Sands, 1933)
42 O'Byrne, *The Gaelic Source of the Brontë Genius*, p. 38.
43 Anthologies such as John Cooke's *Dublin Book of Irish Verse 1728–1909* (Dublin: Hodges, Figgis, 1924) include Emily Brontë's poetry as a matter of course. More recently, one might also place Terry Eagleton's *Heathcliff and the Great Hunger: Studies in Irish Culture* (London: Verso, 1995) within this tradition.
44 O'Byrne, *The Gaelic Source of the Brontë Genius*, p. 13.
45 O'Byrne, *The Gaelic Source of the Brontë Genius*, p. 28–9.
46 See *Collected Plays of W. B. Yeats* (Dublin: Gill and Macmillan, 1982), pp. 105–44.
47 See *Irish Book Lover*, 22.2 (March/April 1934), p. 46–7, for an unsigned critical review of this aspect of the work.
48 O'Byrne, *The Gaelic Source of the Brontë Genius*, p. 39.
49 O'Byrne, *The Gaelic Source of the Brontë Genius*, p. 44–5.
50 O'Byrne, *As I Roved Out*, p. 128.
51 O'Byrne, *The Gaelic Source of the Brontë Genius*, p. 39.
52 Cathal O'Byrne, *From Far Green Hills* (Dublin: Browne and Nolan, 1935). Interestingly and (one would have to say) unexpectedly the work was reprinted in the United States in 2003 as *From Green Hills of Galilee* by the R. A. Kessinger publishing house.
53 O'Byrne, *From Far Green Hills*, p. 9.
54 O'Byrne, *From Far Green Hills*, pp. 9–10.
55 O'Byrne, *From Far Green Hills*, p. 109.
56 O'Byrne, *From Far Green Hills*, p. 118.
57 Ethna Carbery's *In the Irish Past* (Cork: Mercier Press, 1978, first published 1904) is a collection of stories from the turn of the century that similarly attempts an imaginative reconstruction of the crucifixion. More ambitiously, Carbery assumes the presence there of Conal Cearnach, the champion of the Red Branch Knights. This is a belief that she claims was widely held by the peasantry of the Glens of Antrim. At the point of Christ's death the story has Conal exclaim 'My grief, oh! my bitter grief, that the Red Branch Knights were afar, else a sure and fierce revenge would overtake these Jews, aye, their city should be levelled and their name effaced had the chivalry of Uladh been here this day' (p. 12). In this atmosphere, and as an antidote text to the brutality of *In the Irish Past* and *From Far Green Hills*,

it is worth acknowledging the significance of the remarkable clause in de Valera's 1937 Constitution recognising the rights of the Jewish community and faith in Ireland.

58 See the online Catholic encyclopaedia at http://www.newadvent.org/cathen/15077a.htm.

59 Online Catholic encyclopaedia. Consider, for instance, such works as Rev. J. J. Conway, *Bolshevism: Considered in its Economics, Civics and Religious Attitude* (Dublin: Veritas, 1934), or Mary De R. Swanton, *Feeding Your Family* (Dublin: Veritas, 1936) (both pamphlets unnumbered in the Catholic Trust Society of Ireland series).

60 Flann O'Brien, *The Dalkey Archive* (London: Grafton, 1986, first published 1964), p. 175. The novel describes the middle-aged James Joyce living quietly in the town of Skerries, bitterly regretting the immorality of his earlier novels, and quietly composing unsigned pamphlets for the Society on the subjects of marriage and of the dangers of alcohol.

61 Cathal O'Byrne, *Mrs Farrell's Fancies* (Catholic Truth Society of Ireland pamphlet no. 879), *The Green Willow: An Irish Tale Told in the Gaelic Fashion* (no. 1225) , *Our Lady's Brooch* (no. 1444), *The Legend of the Cave of Lough Derg* (no. 1638) (Dublin: Veritas, 1934–42). O'Byrne's 'The cross of peace', another article intended for the Catholic Truth Society, was instead published in *The Tree* (Belfast: no publisher indicated, 1936), a charity publication in aid of the Ulster Society for the Prevention of Cruelty to Animals. Other contributors in what was a heterogeneous volume included Alice Milligan, Thomas Carnduff, the leading Belfast Rabbi J. Shechter, George Bernard Shaw, St John Ervine and E. J. Alexander.

62 An annual subscription to the Catholic Truth Society of Ireland cost one guinea. Subscribers received a copy of every publication issued during the year and a copy of its magazine *Catholic Truth Quarterly*.

63 'A Belfast man at the GPO., Dublin, East Sunday, 1941', in *Capuchin Annual* (Dublin: Capuchin Franciscan Fathers, 1942), p. 197.

64 That said, the key codification of this movement, Robert Greacen, ed., *Northern Harvest: An Anthology of Ulster Writing* (Belfast: Derek MacCord, 1944), expresses an unmistakable cultural unionism in its desire to 'win a sympathetic audience in Great Britain' (editor's introduction, no page number).

65 For more on this Revival see Patricia Craig, 'The liberal imagination in Northern Irish prose' and Tom Clyde, '*Uladh*, *Lagan* and *Rann*: the "little magazine" comes to Ulster', both in Eve Patten, ed., *Returning to Ourselves: Second Volume of Papers from the John Hewitt Summer School* (Belfast: Lagan Press, 1995), pp. 130–44 and pp. 145–53.

66 Anonymous, *The City of Belfast Tourist Handbook* (Belfast: Belfast City Council, 1958), p. 20.

67 Anonymous, 'Bookman's gossip', *Irish Bookman*, 1.2 (September 1946), p. 73.

68 *Irish Bookman*, 1.10 (June 1947), p. 87.

69 For a detailed account of Benner's controversial period as chairman of the Theatre see Conor O'Malley, *A Poet's Theatre* (Dublin: Elo Press, 1988), pp. 78–9.

70 Hewitt, Foreword.
71 Richard Hayward, *In Praise of Ulster* (London: Arthur Baker, 1938).
72 Aodh De Blácam, *The Black North. An Account of the Six Counties of Unrecovered Ireland: Their People, Their Treasures, and Their History* (Dublin: M. H. Gill, 1938). De Blácam was a Catholic convert from Ulster who wrote under the name 'Roddy the Rover' for the *Irish Press*.
73 H. A. MacCartan, *The Glamour of Belfast* (Dublin: Talbot Press, 1921). Hugh Augustine MacCartan was another whose life fitted the classic Northern Revival template. Born in 1885 in County Down, he was later to become a habitué of Ardrigh, the author of a slim volume of Celtic Twilight poetry, *The Little White Roads and Other Poems* (London: Heath Cranton, 1917) and, alongside *The Glamour of Belfast*, a peculiar collection of prose sketches, *Silhouettes: Some Character Studies from North and South* (Dublin: Talbot Press, 1921). Following partition he had a small role on the Boundary Commission and, like Bulmer Hobson and Joseph Connolly, joined the Irish civil service in Dublin. He died in 1943 and, like O'Byrne, is buried in Milltown cemetery.
74 Thomas Fox, review of *As I Roved Out*, *Irish Bookman*, 1.5 (December 1946), p. 85.
75 Hewitt, Foreword.
76 Anonymous review of *As I Roved Out* on Amazon (http://www.amazon.com).
77 Fox, review of *As I Roved Out*, p. 84.
78 O'Byrne, *As I Roved Out*, p. 91.
79 Denis Ireland, 'Prince of storytellers: Cathal O'Byrne', *Belfast Telegraph*, 26 May 1956, p. 5.
80 'Cathal O'Byrne: some reminiscences' by "C."', *Irish News*, 2 August 1957, p. 7.
81 O'Byrne, *As I Roved Out*, p. 287.
82 O'Byrne, *As I Roved Out*, p. 85.
83 O'Byrne, *As I Roved Out*, p. 376.
84 O'Byrne, *As I Roved Out*, p. 252.
85 O'Byrne, *As I Roved Out*, p. 185.
86 O'Byrne, *As I Roved Out*, p. 163.
87 O'Byrne, *As I Roved Out*, p. 171.
88 Ciaran Carson, 'Interesting times', *Honest Ulsterman*, 74 (winter 1983), p. 37.
89 O'Byrne, *As I Roved Out*, p. 162.
90 Carson, 'Interesting times', p. 37.
91 Charlotte Moberly and Eleanor Jourdain, *An Adventure* (London: Macmillan, 1911), published under the pseudonyms Elizabeth Morison and Frances Lamont. I am grateful to Anthea Trodd of Keele University for drawing my attention to this work.
92 O'Byrne's piece is an adaptation of a basic story well known in Ireland. See for instance 'X – the grip of the ghost', *Northern Whig*, 7 May 1909, p. 10. The writer of this version of the story is anonymous, but the style is strongly reminiscent of O'Byrne's.
93 Hewitt, Foreword.

94 Private correspondence, 5 November 2000.
95 Public Record Office of Northern Ireland, T/3306/D4.
96 JC, 'Cathal: an appreciation and a memory', *Irish News*, 6 August 1957, p. 6. 'JC' is probably Joseph Connolly.
97 *Irish News*, 6 August 1957, p. 6. Despite this remarkable display of public affection, it is, of course, of no surprise to note that his funeral went unrecorded in the *Belfast Newsletter*.
98 O'Byrne, *As I Roved Out*, p. 116.
99 O'Byrne, *As I Roved Out*, p. 325.
100 Conor Cruise O'Brien, 'A slow north-east wind', review of *North* by Seamus Heaney, *Listener*, 25 September 1975, pp. 23–4.

AFTERWORD

The legacy of the Northern Revival

> Indeed, long after the excursion was over, members were seen straggling about Connemara and the islands of the sea, quite unable to drag themselves away from the glories and mysteries of the west, ever seeking for that Hybrasil which lay in the lap of the setting sun.
>
> Francis Joseph Bigger, writing in the *Irish Naturalist*, 1895[1]

THE myth of Hy Brasil, the legendary Irish island paradise said to lie to the west of Ireland itself, appealed strongly to the Northern Revival's cultural imagination. Francis Joseph Bigger's report on the first excursion of the Irish Field Club Union to Galway in July 1895 mingled scientific enquiry and historical speculation in a manner that was entirely typical of his methods, and concluded – also typically – with an evocation of the west as a transcendent possibility. For the late-Victorian bourgeois mind, this was, after all, one of the rewards that science could bring. Through the application of scholarly scientific methods there lay a spiritual possibility that was neither strictly confined to the realm of the material nor entirely without substance. As I. T. Galwey glossed the phenomenon in his *Hybrasil and Other Verses* in 1872:

> the Islands of Hybrasil have, like Hesperus, been celebrated from ancient times as the abode of immortal bliss, and to these legends Irish saintly lore has given a deeper and more sacred character. They are still sometimes visible in the shadowy regions of Cloudland, from the Northern and Western coasts of Ireland, especially in fine spring weather.[2]

Galwey may have been overoptimistic: at the time most believed that the last reliable sighting of Hy Brasil had occurred in 1791, and that subsequent conditions in Ireland – whether meteorological or ideological – had inhibited its reappearance.

It is no surprise, then, that Bigger and his fellow naturalists were frustrated in their search. A few years later, however, in 1899, Dora Sigerson Shorter, the poet and eventual eulogist of Roger Casement, had better fortune, which she described in her self-explanatory 'I have been to Hy-Brasail':

> I have been to Hy-Brasail,
> And the Land of Youth have seen,
> Much laughter have I heard there,
> And birds amongst the green.[3]

Although once memorably described by no less than Douglas Hyde as 'the greatest mistress of the ballad, and the greatest story-teller in verse that Ireland has produced',[4] 'I have been to Hy-Brasail' is not one of Shorter's more compelling efforts. Domiciled in London, she was always preoccupied with the creation of Irish utopias – as her great friend Katherine Tynan remarked, 'her heart was always slipping away like a grey bird to Ireland'[5] – and, as such, her poetry does not always indicate precisely where the western seaboard might end and Hy Brasil begin. That said, 'I have been to Hy-Brasail' is a variant on this mode, in that it depends precisely on the boundaries that lie between the two locations for its efficacy. In its description of a fleeting vision of paradise followed by a harsh return to the physical world 'before my time was told', the actual subject of the work becomes not Hy Brasil itself but rather the unendurable nature of a relentless grief. Sadly, this emotion was one that Shorter would become all too familiar with as the shock induced by the execution of the leaders of 1916 – and Roger Casement especially – provoked an agonising descent into mental illness and eventual suicide. This, however, is to run ahead of the course of Irish martyrology. In fact, 'I have been to Hy-Brasail' is actually haunted by another of Shorter's Irish heroes, Charles Stewart Parnell, and thus takes its place in the extraordinary corpus of elegiac literature written in the wake of his death. Certainly, it is appropriate that Shorter would eventually be buried near Parnell in Glasnevin cemetery, as close to Hy Brasil as she could, perhaps, aspire. Fittingly, Casement's remains would join them there in 1965.

Three years after Shorter's vision, in 1902, Ethna Carbery would attempt a more ambitious evocation. Her poem 'I Breasil', included in her collection *The Four Winds of Eirinn*,[6] one of the foundational texts of the Northern Revival, describes Hy Brasil in terms that would ultimately find an echo in Yeats's creation of Byzantium, the land of eternal aesthetic perfection:

The sacred trees stand in rainbow dew,
Apple and ash and the twisted thorn,
Quicken and holly and dusky yew,
Ancient ere ever grey Time was born.

The oak spreads mighty beneath the sun
In a wonderful dazzle of moonlight green –
O would I might hasten from tasks undone,
And journey whither no grief hath been!

Were I past the mountains of opal flame,
I would seek a couch of the king-fern brown,
And when from its seed glad slumber came,
A flock of rare dreams would flutter down.

But I move without in an endless fret,
While somewhere beyond earth's brink, afar,
Forgotten of men, in a rose-rim set,
I-Breasil shines like a beckoning star.

In contrast to Shorter's often sentimental London-inscribed projections, Carbery's poetry on behalf of Ireland was deeply imbued with a family tradition of radical Belfast republicanism. For this reason it is appropriate that her search for Hy Brasil would be ultimately frustrated. In the poem the island remains strictly off limits, as, indeed, it had to be, for its function in the nationalist imagination lay finally in its very unobtainability. Not Tír-na-nÓg, Atlantis nor even the fifth province, Hy Brasil is most obviously the place of a promise deferred, 'looming, floating in the sapphire empyrean, that green Hy Brasil of my dreams and memories',[7] as the Young Irelander John Mitchell had put it in his *Jail Journal* of 1854. For this reason, Hy Brasil offers the vision of a once and future Ireland untainted but, paradoxically, this aspiration can exist only alongside the certain knowledge that it will never be achieved. Ireland is fallen, and as a cracked mirror image of Hy Brasil's perfection it is crazily distorted and endlessly refracted. Understood as such, contemplating Hy Brasil becomes a peculiar form of aesthetic and political masochism. Exquisite in its contemplation, its phantasmagoric essence brings only agony.

Such agony became the particular, albeit unfortunate, provenance of those Northern Revivalists left marooned by the partition of Ireland. For them, Hy Brasil now lay at two degrees of separation, as remote as the Brazil to which it purportedly gave its name. For individuals such as Bigger, the only logical response to this sundering was simply to call off the search. Although he would continue his archaeological and scientific work after 1920, it was no longer with the expectation that it would have any constitutive effect, or that it would lead to a glimpse of a future untainted Ireland. Even the more mundane boundary between Northern Ireland and the Free State was a line that Bigger felt unable to cross. For if the institutional sectarianism of Northern Ireland was an unhappy if predictable reality, for many irreconcilable republicans the state that lay to the south was a much more disturbing perversion of everything that Hy Brasil had once embodied. As with his friend and fellow Revivalist Alice Milligan, it is for this reason that the continuation of Bigger's work after partition appears to be little more than a reluctance to give up a well rehearsed series of habits and familiar practices of mind. As he was essentially late Victorian in his world view, it was simply too late for reinvention. Such stubbornness could not, however, prevent the overwhelming sense of bewilderment that typified Northern nationalism in the years immediately following partition. For Bigger and Milligan, as well as Catholics such as Cathal O'Byrne, the maelstrom of events in the first twenty years of the century indicated only that, in the North at least, the rules of cause and effect had become fundamentally distorted. As Shane Leslie, that eccentric although usually perceptive barometer of the shifting moods and enthusiasms of Ardrigh, noted in 1923:

> But there were never results in Ireland. There are sometimes explosions or disasters, and the country may take fire on the wings of an enthusiasm or a new secret society or a new agitation. But normal results, the mathematical or theoretical procession of effects from causes, are not to be expected.[8]

Certainly, the narrative of the Irish cultural Revival – a movement envisaged, mapped and executed so determinedly by energetic propagandists in both North and South – was never meant to conclude with so many compromises, betrayals and recriminations.

If anything, this state of confusion was to deepen as the years passed. At the time of O'Byrne's death in 1957, the ideals that had driven the Northern Revival half a century earlier appeared at best naive, and at worst wilfully and dangerously unaware of the realities of the depth of ethnic hatred that structured Ulster society. Indeed, the thirty-year period of violence that would begin in the late 1960s – and which flared initially from the tight-knit jumble of streets in West Belfast where O'Byrne had made his home – appeared only to confirm the essential accuracy of this diagnosis. Here, finally, was the antithesis of the Revival's restless experimentation with identity and culture. Political discourse in the North became little more than an often tortuous exchange of atrophied identity positions, communicated through an increasingly denuded language of justification, condemnation and counter-accusation. This is not to suggest that during this period social and political change in the North was not occurring – such stasis is a logical impossibility – but rather to observe that such change as there was remained deeply obscured and difficult to identify. Again, it is hard to imagine a more vivid contrast with the activities of the Northern Revival, which, at its best, had an almost instinctive understanding of identity as strategic, performative and, by its very definition, in flux. It was this spirit that inspired both the 1904 Feis in the Glens of Antrim and the combustible satires of the Ulster Literary Theatre (ULT) – perhaps the Northern Revival's two most noteworthy achievements.

John McGahern has recently remarked that 'Ireland has changed more in the last twenty years than it did in the preceding 200 years'[9] and, indeed, such is the speed of recent events that, in many ways, this period of ethnic violence increasingly feels like a sometimes bizarre anachronism. Certainly, it can be argued that, at the time of writing, the greatest threat to the border and the internal integrity of Northern Ireland no longer appears to be the tradition of armed republicanism – that potent legacy of Bulmer Hobson, Roger Casement and Denis McCullough, shaped and refined in the library at Ardrigh – but instead a force that many of those radicals ostensibly despised: aspirational free market capitalism, built upon an essentially secular vision of individual economic advancement. This ideology – with its suspicion of state intervention and impatience with ethno-national restrictions on the free flow of capital – has demonstrated more powerfully than any nationalist discourse of faith and territory the essential impossibility of the border. It is through its restless urgings that institutional and commercial links between North and South have been forged and will strengthen in the future. For this reason, it is no longer either possible or desirable to read the internal antagonisms of Ireland solely within the discourses of ethnicity, religion and culture. Instead, the extent to which Ireland's increasingly aggressive capitalist economy – primed essentially by a dynamic perception of Ireland's place in Europe, and interested in identity politics only insofar as such politics might further generate opportunities for economic growth – can maintain any degree of social and cultural cohesion will become one of the major issues for Irish political theory in the future. In turn, it is not fantastical to predict a concomitant reduction of interest in the border and the ideologies of partition that maintain it. The Northern Revival was frequently criticised for its naivety, but the idea of an enduring and monolithic state of partition also constitutes a form of peculiar cultural fantasy.

But, despite these speculations, there remains too much about the North's experience of the twentieth century that remains silenced, unspoken or simply ignored, and this is an ellipsis that damages not just the cultural memory of the island of Ireland but, indeed, that of the archipelago in its entirety. In this context, one of the greatest problems of public life for both communities in the North has been the constant emigration of their intellectual class to Dublin, Britain and the United States. To express this differently, the number of significant cultural, political and philosophical thinkers to have emerged from the North during the last century is impressive, bordering on remarkable; the number who have stayed is depressing, bordering on tragic. For unionism this has tended to manifest itself in a marked inability to articulate its history and aspirations. As there are so few cultural and philosophical articulations of unionist ideology, so it has become a political discourse increasingly typified by clichés of the taciturn and stubborn Ulster Protestant. For Northern nationalism the causes and effects are different again. Because great swathes of the nationalist intelligentsia in the North fled South after partition, so, in Austen Morgan's words, 'the topic of Belfast Republicanism remains microhistorical – big individuals in small organisations who leave for Dublin'.[10] It was for this reason that nationalist opposition to the Stormont regime was so curiously half-hearted, while it also allowed the Catholic Church a greatly increased (and not always positive) role in the social life of the community.

Cultural accounts of this period of intellectual famine remain vivid and constitute its most enduring memorial. Even now, Brian Moore's 1955 novel *The Lonely Passion of Judith Hearne*[11] retains its capacity to shock such is its unremittingly bleak depiction of the creative and emotional sterility of Belfast's Catholic middle class. As if to emphasise this condition, the fact that Moore had secured his own exile to Canada by the time of the book's composition bears an inevitable grim irony. Similarly, the Belfast Protestant John Boyd's autobiographical study *The Middle of My Journey*[12] speaks more often than not of a provincialism so emphatic that it can almost be seen as Belfast's defining characteristic. An account of Boyd's role in the BBC in Northern Ireland during the middle decades of the century, the work articulates the precarious nature of such public institutions and the extent to which they were vulnerable to the same exclusions and hierarchies that disfigured other elements of Belfast's public sphere. Even Boyd's descriptions of what passed for a cultural community in Belfast at this time – the minor poets and novelists gathered around Campbell's Café in the city centre – speak of an essentially unhappy coterie culture dominated by petty jealousies, alcoholism and figures such as Denis Ireland, who, by this stage, were rapidly slipping into their anecdotage.

Such observations are salutary because they again cast in sharp relief the startling if transitory nature of the Northern Revival's achievement. Between 1900 and 1920, the variety and vibrancy of the movement invigorated the discourses of economics, industry, science, art and culture to such a degree that, for almost the first time, a fledgling intelligentsia was able to contemplate a future rooted in the North itself. Moreover, the Revival also attracted figures from outside Belfast, such as George Birmingham, Patrick Pearse, Yeats and Maud Gonne, and in this way the intellectual life of Ulster was further enriched. It was as a result of these exchanges that ideologues in Belfast began to inform – and indeed shape – Irish nationalism's mode of appeal. Organisations such as George Roberts's Maunsel Press in Dublin, which had always been sympathetic to publishing Northern writers, played an important role in allowing these debates, but it is also necessary to recognise the significance of developing intimacies such as that between Bigger and Pearse. These dialogues were abruptly foreshortened by the events of 1916, of course, and as a result it became inevitable that Dublin and Belfast would resume their cultural and political antagonism. Alongside this sundering, the collapse of the Northern Revival immediately silenced many of the important and complex debates and arguments that had been developing within Belfast itself. Prior to this event, it is striking to note that movements such as the ULT were tentatively beginning to explore ways of appealing to the unionist community while still maintaining an ostensibly nationalist position. Such gestures were quickly to become too dangerous and, as such, constituted risks that the ULT was no longer prepared to take.

In these terms the biggest success of the Northern Revival would also become its biggest failure. Its ambition was to push at the limits of identity politics in the North to a degree that had never been attempted before and, one can argue, has not been contemplated since. This was articulated most powerfully in terms of an idea of nascent 'Northernness' – an elective affiliation that not only might have provided a means of talking across the divisions of Ulster society, but which could also have functioned as a way of disturbing the monolingual nature of Irish nationalist discourse. However, as the debate in the pages of *Uladh*, the ULT's journal, vividly illustrated, 'Northernness' proved to be too problematic as an organising concept, too fraught with potential misunderstandings and schisms. Early proponents of the idea, such as Bulmer Hobson and Joseph Campbell, were eventually to abandon it and instead threw in their lot with a concept of Irish nationalism shaped by Dublin. This was to no one's benefit, and certainly not to those who ultimately found themselves politically, economically, culturally and even emotionally stifled by the final flowering of that restricted ideal of Irish nationalism – the inglorious Irish Free State. In the North itself, a peculiar ideological migration has taken place that means that now the most vigorous discussion of Northernness as a political and cultural possibility occurs not among nationalists or republicans but at the fringes of loyalist political thought.

These factors, taken as a whole, explain something of why political culture in the North was silenced after partition, and yet too many studies of twentieth-century Irish culture have assumed that this voicelessness was characteristic of a province more generally inclined towards the taciturn. As a result, the role of the North in Irish political life prior to 1920 has remained too little considered. In this sense, at least, the distinctive voice of the Northern Revival has been gagged by subsequent events. Although there are signs that this is beginning to change, certainly those critical works that aspire to the status of the definitional or summative continue to fix their gaze away from Belfast,[13] uneasy perhaps not just with the fact that accounting for the North necessitates a geographical relocation but also because the predominant genres of the Northern Revival are often something other than the literary and the dramatic. Indeed, even when the Northern Revival has contributed to one of the Revival's central cultural genres, such as the ULT, that intervention has often appeared somehow discordant, somehow not properly *serious*. This was understandable when so much of the Revival's energy was directed towards creating a canon of national cultural achievement and yet, even now, the satires of the early ULT are still able to discomfort some of the more deeply embedded pieties of the Irish nationalist imagination.

But, then, if the example of O'Byrne can teach us anything, it is that there are other ways of telling a story, other ways of orientating yourself towards the past. Although academic interest in O'Byrne and his contemporaries has been scant, recently there has been a striking contrapuntal tendency emerging from Belfast itself. Arguably this has been at its most sophisticated in the reevaluation of O'Byrne's achievement by the Belfast poet Ciaran Carson, but in a more forthright manner the Falls Road community magazine *Rushlight* has energetically promoted O'Byrne as one of 'Ireland's perhaps greatest writers', no less, indeed, than 'the patron saint of Belfast storytellers'. Inspired by this enthusiasm, in 2002 Belfast's Cathedral Quarter Festival celebrated O'Byrne as 'one of Belfast's greatest writers' and a boat tour along the River Lagan featured a selection of readings from *As I Roved Out* – a work which has now run to five editions. In 2004, after much vigorous lobbying by Joe Graham, the indefatigable editor of *Rushlight*, the Ulster Historical Circle erected a plaque on O'Byrne's old house on Cavendish Street.

Sponsored, appropriately enough, by the *Irish News*, it was unveiled by the distinguished local historian Eamon Phoenix, who commented that 'Cathal was a gentle soul, a poet rather than a revolutionary – erudite, charming and imbued with a deep love of Ireland and its people'.[14] That the local Member of Parliament, Gerry Adams, was present at the ceremony was also fitting. The revelation in his speech that *As I Roved Out* was one of the first books he ever read enables an understanding of him as yet another Irish republican inspired, albeit indirectly, by the spontaneous energies of Bigger and Ardrigh.

Nationalist Belfast is, then, belatedly beginning to reconnect to its past. More intriguingly, however, light is being shone on the activities of the Northern Revival from other directions. In 2002 Jeffrey Dudgeon's *Roger Casement: The Black Diaries*[15] was published, a work which transformed understanding of the Northern Revival as much as it sent reverberations through the world of Casement studies. While previous books such as B. L. Reid's *The Lives of Roger Casement*[16] and Austen Morgan's *Labour and Partition: The Belfast Working Class 1905–23*[17] had suggested the double occlusion of nationalist life and dissident sexuality, it was not until the publication of Dudgeon's book that the complexities of Casement's, Bigger's and (to a lesser extent) O'Byrne's private and public lives were significantly revealed. In the case of Casement, this was a comparatively straightforward task – his Black Diaries describe a gay lifestyle that was perhaps unusual for the period only in the extent of its geographical spread. What is more remarkable about O'Byrne and Bigger, however, is the extent to which they were able to obscure their tracks so effectively. Although in many of the interviews and discussions I undertook with those who remembered O'Byrne in Belfast the matter of his homosexuality tended to be asserted without any great controversy, there is simply no corroboration of this in any of the textual evidence that remains. Indeed, judged purely by such sources – and in a manner similar to that of his friend Bigger – O'Byrne appears to have been a man of no sex life whatsoever. Is this a realistic possibility? The fact that O'Byrne's piety was so intense (and certainly of a different order to that experienced by Bigger or Casement) might suggest the possibility of lifelong sexual abstinence, but Dudgeon's comment on this issue remains persuasive:

> here is no evidence to suggest [O'Byrne] was gay but none to suggest he was not. It just seems unlikely, again, that a man who could be so emotional and passionate, was unable to arrange any sexual life for himself.[18]

Just as rumours have long gathered around O'Byrne, so have those who seek to protect his reputation. Most notable in this regard was Seamus

O'Neill, who, in an article for the Catholic journal *Studies*,[19] mounted a defence of O'Byrne's sexual reputation following a few mild speculations about his private life and relationship with Casement contained in Reid's *The Lives of Roger Casement*. O'Neill's refutation is remarkable and speaks, in turn, of its own confusions:

> Was Cathal a homosexual as Professor Reid believes him to have been? It is, I suppose, impossible to give a positive answer to such a question. It may be significant, however, that Professor Reid, who did not know Cathal, believes he was, whilst I and others who knew him do not believe it. At any rate, if he was, I must have been exceedingly unattractive to him, for I sat alone with him in the small parlour of the house in which he lived with his sister in Cavendish Street in Belfast and he certainly made no advances towards me. Nor, at the time did I ever think of such a thing....
>
> If Cathal had been a homosexual, I should not have been visiting him because in a close community like that of the Cavendish Street area his repute would have been known to everyone, and ill-repute it would have been, and Cathal a man to avoid, for at that time homosexuality was not looked upon as something bright and gay. It is said that no one is a prophet in his own country, but I am aware that Cathal was held in the highest esteem by his neighbours. He had some of the airs and graces that come naturally to a man who spends his life on the stage, but in everything else he was one of them, and he had served them well.

As O'Neill observes, it is indeed impossible to give a definite answer as to the question of O'Byrne's sexuality, but the bizarre – not to say downright menacing – terms of this defence certainly indicate why O'Byrne might have taken steps to conceal any such desires. Unlike Bigger and Casement, O'Byrne lacked the financial resources to lead a dual life. Moreover, in the atmosphere of Catholic working-class Belfast as described by O'Neill, the consequences of an indiscretion becoming known would have been unbearable for O'Byrne to contemplate. If he was, indeed, a man of no sex life, then in O'Neill's description we can glimpse a plausible reason why.

But the issue cannot quite be left at that. Rereading O'Byrne's collection of poems *The Grey Feet of the Wind* from 1917 in light of these speculations, it is impossible not to notice how frequently the many poems of desire and longing refuse any gender specificity. Indeed, there is no first-person statement of desire for a woman in the collection at all. In place of this, however, are many dramatisations of female longing for a male lover, and it is in these poems that O'Byrne's descriptions of male physical beauty are at their most intense. Such poetic encryption was hardly unusual in this period, but even in that context the emotional intensity of some of O'Byrne's poems is striking. Of these, 'A silent mouth', the lament of a woman for an unknowing lover, is perhaps the most tortured:

> I have made my heart as the stones in the street for his tread,
> I have made my love as the shadow that falls from his dear gold head.
> But the stones with his footsteps ring,
> And the shadow keeps following,
> And just as the quiet shadow goes ever beside or before
> So must I go silent and lonely and loveless for ever and evermore.[20]

The unhappy prophecy of the final line was one that would have spoken eloquently to many gay men in this period, and it was a fate that I fear O'Byrne, too, was to suffer.

It is frustrating to conclude this study with so many speculations, but is also appropriate. Much of O'Byrne's life will remain unknown to us, and in many ways it is this unknowability that renders him typical. His motivations are often elusive, his perceptions shrouded and his contradictions glaring. Biographical practice, or its more respectable cousin, life writing, remains an activity often dependent on the idea of a materially privileged individual – the figure whose activities can be recorded, archived and reconstituted through institutions. Indeed, it is this material base which allows for the idea of the individual in the first instance. Wealth might have enabled Casement and Bigger to conceal aspects of their private lives, but in death it was this very material security that would lead to their revelation. As this suggests, it is ultimately not O'Byrne's putative sexual dissidence nor his republican activities that has obscured his face from our view, but rather his class position, that fundamental social element which the Northern Revival instinctively sought to suppress and which frequently remains shadowed in Irish political and cultural discourse even today. Understood in these terms, then, the course of O'Byrne's life was a struggle between voicelessness and articulation and, as such, it is fitting that the blue plaque on his house remembers him as 'singer, poet, writer' – three modes of speech, three refusals of silence. The nobility in O'Byrne's legacy lies with this refusal. Silence is the perennial condition of the oppressed. In giving voice to the people and places that he loved, O'Byrne's life contested that oppression.

NOTES

1 Quoted by Seán Lysaght, *Robert Lloyd Praeger: The Life of a Naturalist* (Dublin: Four Courts Press, 1998), p. 42.

2 I. T. Galwey, *Hybrasil and Other Verses* (Dublin: George Herbert, 1872), p. 9.

3 Dora Sigerson Shorter, 'I have been to Hy-Brasail', in *Ballads and Poems* (London: James Bowden, 1899), pp. 62–3.
4 Dora Sigerson Shorter, *The Tricolour* (Cork: CFN, 1976), back cover.
5 Shorter, *The Tricolour*, p. 6.
6 Ethna Carbery, *The Four Winds of Eirinn: Twenty-Fifth Anniversary Edition* (Dublin: Gill and Son, 1927), p. 54.
7 *John Mitchell's Jail Journal* (London: Sphere Books, 1983, first published 1854), p. 61.
8 Shane Leslie, *Doomsland* (London: Chatto and Windus, 1923), p. 40.
9 Interview article by Sean O'Hagan, 'A family touched with madness', *Observer*, 28 August 2005, p. 7.
10 Austen Morgan, *Labour and Partition: The Belfast Working Class 1905–23* (London: Pluto, 1991), p. 198.
11 Brian Moore, *The Lonely Passion of Judith Hearne* (London: Penguin, 1959, first published 1955).
12 John Boyd, *The Middle of My Journey* (Belfast: Blackstaff Press, 1990).
13 It is worth noting, for instance, how three (though in other ways laudable) recent general studies of this period have practically nothing to say about the North at all: Chris Morash, *A History of Irish Theatre 1601–2000* (Cambridge: Cambridge University Press, 2002); Shaun Richards, *The Cambridge Companion to Twentieth-Century Irish Drama* (Cambridge: Cambridge University Press, 2004); and Gregory Castle, *Modernism and the Celtic Revival* (Cambridge: Cambridge University Press, 2001).
14 'Gaelic Revivalist at last honoured in his native city', *Irish News*, 18 October 2004, p. 4.
15 Jeffrey Dudgeon, *Roger Casement: The Black Diaries* (Belfast: Belfast Press, 2002).
16 B. L. Reid, *The Lives of Roger Casement* (New Haven: Yale University Press, 1976).
17 Morgan, *Labour and Partition.*
18 Dudgeon, *Roger Casement*, pp. 589–90.
19 Seamus O'Neill, 'Note: Roger Casement, Cathal O'Byrne and Professor Reid', *Studies*, 68 (spring/summer 1979), pp. 117–21.
20 Cathal O'Byrne, 'A silent mouth', in *The Grey Feet of the Wind* (Dublin: Talbot Press, 1917), p. 9.

Bibliography

BOOKS AND SELECTED ARTICLES BY CATHAL O'BYRNE

A Jug of Punch, Belfast: details lost, 1900.
The Lane of the Thrushes: Some Ulster Love Songs, with C. Healy, Dublin: Sealy, Bryers and Walker, 1905.
Six Songs of Ireland: The Poems by Moira O'Neill, Lizzie Twigg, Cahir Healy and Cahal O'Byrne, the Music by Hamilton Harty, London: Boosey, 1908.
The Grey Feet of the Wind, Dublin: Talbot Press, 1917.
The Grey Feet of the Wind, Chicago: Ard-Ree Press, 1928.
Pilgrim in Italy, Dublin: At the Sign of the Three Candles, 1930.
The Gaelic Source of the Brontë Genius, Edinburgh: Sands, 1933.
'The red cock's cry', 'To one who is monsignor' and 'The one thing needful', in *Capuchin Annual*, Dublin: Capuchin Franciscan Fathers, 1933, pp. 73, 147, 273.
'Shakespeare's debt to Ireland', *Irish News*, 2 May 1934, p. 8.
Catholic Truth Society of Ireland pamphlets, *Mrs Farrell's Fancies* (no. 879), *The Green Willow: An Irish Tale Told in the Gaelic Fashion* (no. 1225), *Our Lady's Brooch* (no. 1444), *The Legend of the Cave of Lough Derg* (no. 1638), Dublin: Veritas, 1934–42.
From Far Green Hills, Dublin: Browne and Nolan, 1935.
'Roger Casement's last will', *Irish Monthly*, 65, October 1937, pp. 668–72.
Christmas Wayfarers, Dublin: At the Sign of the Three Candles, undated.
'The humour of Ulster', *Irish Monthly*, 66, December 1938, pp. 842–5.
'An appreciation of Carl Gilbert Hardebeck', in *Capuchin Annual*, Dublin: Capuchin Franciscan Fathers, 1943, pp. 235–6.
As I Roved Out, Belfast: Irish News Ltd, 1946.
'Roger Casement's ceilidhe', in *Capuchin Annual*, Dublin: Capuchin Franciscan Fathers, 1946–47, pp. 312–14.
'Sunny days in Hollywood California', in *Capuchin Annual*, Dublin: Capuchin Franciscan Fathers, 1948, pp. 268–71.
The Burthen: A One-Act Comedy, Dublin: James Duffy, 1948.
The Ashes on the Hearth, Dublin: At the Sign of the Three Candles, 1948.

As I Roved Out, Dublin: At the Sign of the Three Candles, 1957.
As I Roved Out, Foreword by J. J. Campbell, Wakefield: SR Publishers, 1970.
As I Roved Out, Foreword by John Hewitt, Belfast: Blackstaff, 1982.

NEWSPAPERS AND MAGAZINES

Belfast Evening Telegraph (Belfast)
Belfast Morning News (Belfast)
Belfast News-Letter (Belfast)
Causeway: Cultural Traditions Journal (Belfast)
Chicago Tribune (Chicago)
Guardian (Manchester, London)
Hansard (London)
Ireland's Saturday Night (Belfast)
Irish Book Lover (Dublin)
Irish News (Belfast)
Irish Press (Dublin)
Irish Times (Dublin)
New York Evening Post (New York)
New York Times (New York)
Northern Patriot (Belfast)
Northern Whig (Belfast)
Observer (London)
Rushlight (Belfast)
Shan Van Vocht (Belfast)
The Times (London)
Uladh (Belfast)
Ulster Guardian (Belfast)
Ulster Journal of Archaeology (Belfast)
Workers' Republic (Dublin)

GENERAL BIBLIOGRAPHY

Adams, G., *Falls Memories*, Dingle: Brandon Books, 1983.
Aldrich, R., *The Seduction of the Mediterranean: Writing, Art and Homosexual Fantasy*, London: Routledge, 1993.
Alexander, E., *Lady Anne's Walk*, London: Edward Arnold, 1903.
Allen, N., A. Kelly, eds, *The Cities of Belfast*, Dublin: Four Courts Press, 2003.
Anonymous, *The Heckled Unionist: Hints to Irish Unionists on English Platforms*, Dublin: E. Ponsonby, 1906.
—, *The Irish Unionist Pocket-Book for the Use of Unionist Workers in Great Britain*, Dublin: Unionist Associations of Ireland, 1911.
—, *Fashionable Thoroughfares of Great Britain and Ireland*, London: Advertising Concessions, 1911.
—, 'Sir Roger Casement's last speech from the dock done into verse: the ideal recitation for volunteers' (handbill), Dublin: Independent Newspapers, 1916.

—, Review of *The Grey Feet of the Wind* by C. O'Byrne, *Studies*, 6.23, September 1917, pp. 512–13.
—, Review of *The Grey Feet of the Wind* by C. O'Byrne, *Irish Book Lover*, 11.3, October/November 1917, p. 34.
—, 'Bookman's gossip', *Irish Bookman*, 1.2, September 1946, p. 73.
—, *The City of Belfast Tourist Handbook*, Belfast: Belfast City Council, 1958.
Bannister, G., 'Events in Easter 1916', National Library of Ireland, MS 7946.
Bardon, J., *A History of Ulster*, Belfast: Blackstaff Press, 1992.
Beckett, J. C., *et al.*, eds, *Belfast: The Making of the City*, Belfast: Appletree Press, 1988.
Bell, S. H., *The Theatre in Ulster*, Dublin: Gill and Macmillan, 1972.
—, N. A. Robb and J. Hewitt, eds, *The Arts in Ulster: A Symposium*, London: George G. Harrap, 1951.
Benjamin, W., *Illuminations*, ed. H. Arendt, trans. H. Zohn, London: Fontana, 1973.
Bigger, F. J., *Remember Orr*, Dublin: Maunsel, 1906.
Birmingham, G., *The Northern Iron*, Dublin: Maunsel, 1907.
—, *Pleasant Places*, London: Heinemann, 1934.
Blakeston, O., *Thank You Now: An Exploration of Ulster*, London: Anthony Bond, 1960.
Blaney, R., *Presbyterians and the Irish Language*, Belfast: Ulster Historical Foundation, 1996.
Boyce, G., *Nationalism in Ireland*, London: Routledge, 1991.
Boyd, E., *Ireland's Literary Renaissance*, London: Grant Richards, 1923.
Boyd, J., 'Ulster prose', in *The Arts in Ulster: A Symposium*, eds S. H. Bell, N. A. Robb and J. Hewitt, London: George G. Harrap, 1951.
—, *The Middle of My Journey*, Belfast: Blackstaff Press, 1990.
Bradley, A., and M. Gialanella Valiulis, eds, *Gender and Sexuality in Modern Ireland*, Amherst: University of Massachusetts Press, 1997.
Brearton, F., *The Great War in Irish Poetry: W. B. Yeats to Michael Longley*, Oxford: Oxford University Press, 2000.
Brown, M., *The Politics of Irish Literature: From Thomas Davis to W. B. Yeats*, London: Allen and Unwin, 1972.
Brown, S. J., and D. Clarke, eds, *Ireland in Fiction: A Guide to Irish Novels, Tales, Romances and Folklore, Vol.* 2, Cork: Royal Carbery Books, 1985.
Brown, T., *Ireland: A Social and Cultural History 1922–85*, London: Fontana, 1990.
—, 'Cultural nationalism, 1880–1930', in *The Field Day Anthology of Irish Writing, Vol.* 2, eds Seamus Deane *et al.*, Derry: Field Day, 1991, p. 516.
Browne, J. N., 'Poetry in Ulster', in *The Arts in Ulster: A Symposium*, eds S. H. Bell, N. A. Robb and J. Hewitt, London: George G. Harrap, 1951, pp. 131–52.
Byrne, O., *The Stage in Ulster from the Eighteenth Century*, Belfast: Linen Hall Library, 1997.
Campbell, F., *The Dissenting Voice: Protestant Democracy in Ulster from Plantation to Partition*, Belfast: Blackstaff Press, 1991.
Campbell, J., *The Garden of Bees*, Belfast: Erskine Mayne, 1905.
—, *The Mountainy Singer*, Dublin: Maunsel, 1909.

—, *Irishry*, Dublin: Maunsel, 1913.
—, and H. Hughes, *Songs of Uladh*, Belfast: W. J. Baird, 1904.
Campbell, J. H., 'A visit to Ardglass', *Irish News*, 26 June 1913, p. 7.
Campbell, T. J., *Fifty Years of Ulster: 1890–1940*, Belfast: Irish News Ltd, 1941.
Carbery, E., *The Four Winds of Eirinn*, Dublin: M. H. Gill, 1902.
—, *The Four Winds of Eirinn: Poems by Ethna Carbery*, Dublin: M. H. Gill, 1918.
—, *In the Celtic Past*, Cork: Mercier Press, 1978 edition (first published 1904).
—, S. MacManus and A. Milligan, *We Sang for Ireland: Poems of Ethna Carbery, Seumas MacManus, Alice Milligan*, Dundalk: Dundalgan Press, 1950.
Carroll, F. M., 'The American Committee for Relief in Ireland, 1920–2', *Irish Historical Studies*, 23.89, May 1982, pp. 30–49.
Carson, C., 'Interesting times', *Honest Ulsterman*, 74, winter 1983, pp. 36–40.
—, *The Irish for No*, Dublin: Gallery Press, 1987.
—, *Belfast Confetti*, Dublin: Gallery Press, 1989.
—, *The Star Factory*, London: Granta, 1997.
Carson, M., *The Knight of the Flaming Heart*, London: Doubleday, 1995.
—, 'A homosexual hero for our times', *Guardian*, 3 March 1998, p. 15.
Castle, G., *Modernism and the Celtic Revival*, Cambridge: Cambridge University Press, 2001.
Clyde, T., '*Uladh*, *Lagan* and *Rann*: the "little magazine" comes to Ulster', in *Returning to Ourselves: Second Volume of Papers from the John Hewitt Summer School*, ed. E. Patten, Belfast: Lagan Press, 1995, pp. 145–53.
—, *Irish Literary Magazines: An Outline History and Descriptive Bibliography*, Dublin: Irish Academic Press, 2003.
Coates, T., ed., *The Irish Uprising 1914–21: Papers from the British Parliamentary Archive*, London: The Stationery Office, 2000.
Connolly, J., *Labour in Irish History*, Dublin: New Books, 1973 edition (first published 1910).
—, 'Press poisoners in Ireland', *Forward*, 30 August 1913.
—, 'Wee Joe Devlin', *Workers' Republic*, 28 August 1915, p. 2.
—, *Ireland Upon the Dissecting Table*, Cork: Cork Workers' Club, 1975.
Conrad, J., *Heart of Darkness*, London: Penguin, 1987 edition (first published 1902).
Conrad, K., 'Queer treasons: homosexuality and Irish national identity', *Cultural Studies*, 15.1, January 2001, pp. 124–37.
Conway, J. J., *Bolshevism: Considered in its Economics, Civics and Religious Attitude*, Catholic Truth Society of Ireland pamphlet, Dublin: Veritas, 1934.
Coogan, T. P., *De Valera: Long Fellow, Tall Shadow*, London: Arrow Books, 1995.
Cooke, J., ed., *Dublin Book of Irish Verse 1728–1909*, Dublin: Hodges, Figgis, 1924.
Craig, P., *The Rattle of the North*, Belfast: Blackstaff Press, 1992.
—, 'The liberal imagination in Northern Irish prose', in E. Patten, ed., *Returning to Ourselves: Second Volume of Papers from the John Hewitt Summer School*, Belfast: Lagan Press, 1995, pp. 130–44.
Cranmer, P., 'Vocal music', in *Hamilton Harty: His Life and Music*, ed. D. Greer, Belfast: Blackstaff Press, 1978.

Crone, J. S., 'Necrology: Francis Joseph Bigger', *Journal of the Cork Historical and Archaeological Society*, 32, 1927, pp. 113–17.
—, and F. C. Bigger, eds, *In Remembrance: Articles and Sketches by Francis Joseph Bigger*, Dublin: Talbot Press, 1927.
Danaher, K., 'The plays of Gerald MacNamara', *Journal of Irish Literature*, 18.2–3, 1988, pp. 24–55.
Darby, J., *Conflict in Northern Ireland*, Dublin: Gill and Macmillan, 1976.
Dawe, G., and J. W. Foster, eds, *The Poet's Place: Ulster Literature and Society. Essays in Honour of John Hewitt, 1907–1987*, Belfast: Institute of Irish Studies, 1991.
Deane, S., 'Wherever green is read', in *Revising the Rising*, eds M. Ní Dhonnchadha and T. Dorgan, Derry: Field Day, 1991, pp. 91–105.
—, *et al.*, eds, *The Field Day Anthology of Irish Writing*, Derry: Field Day, 1991.
De Blácam, A., *The Black North. An Account of the Six Counties of Unrecovered Ireland: Their People, Their Treasures, and Their History*, Dublin: M. H. Gill, 1938.
Devlin, P., *Straight Left: An Autobiography*, Belfast: Blackstaff Press, 1993.
Dixon, R., 'F. J. Bigger: romantic, enthusiast and antiquary', *Causeway: Cultural Traditions Journal*, 1.2, spring 1994, pp. 5–7.
—, 'Heroes for a new Ireland: Francis Joseph Bigger and the leaders of the '98', in *From Corrib to Cultra: Folklife Essays in Honour of Alan Gailey*, ed. T. M. Owen, Belfast: Institute of Irish Studies, 2000, pp. 29–38.
Douglas, J., *The Unpardonable Sin*, London: Grant Richards, 1907.
Doyle, L., *An Ulster Childhood*, Dublin: Maunsel, 1921.
Dudgeon, J., *Roger Casement: The Black Diaries*, Belfast: Belfast Press, 2002.
Duffy, C. G., *The Revival of Irish Literature*, London: T. Fisher Unwin, 1893.
Eagleton, T., *Heathcliff and the Great Hunger: Studies in Irish Culture*, London: Verso, 1995.
Elliott, M., *The Catholics of Ulster: A History*, London: Penguin, 2000.
Ellmann, R., *Oscar Wilde*, London: Penguin, 1997 edition (first published 1988).
Ervine, S. J., 'The return to Belfast', *New Age*, 14.4, 27 November 1913, pp. 102–4.
Fallon, P., and D. Mahon, eds, *The Penguin Book of Contemporary Irish Poetry*, London: Penguin, 1990.
Farrell, M., *Northern Ireland: The Orange State*, London: Pluto Press, 1976.
Fitzhenry, E. C., *Henry Joy McCracken*, Dublin: Talbot Press, 1936.
Forster, E. M., *Abinger Harvest*, London: Arnold, 1936.
Foster, J. W., *Fictions of the Irish Literary Revival: A Changeling Art*, Syracuse: Gill and Macmillan, 1987.
—, 'Natural history, science and Irish culture', in *The Poet's Place: Ulster Literature and Society. Essays in Honour of John Hewitt, 1907–1987*, eds G. Dawe and J. W. Foster, Belfast: Institute of Irish Studies, 1991, pp. 119–29.
Foster, R. F., *Modern Ireland: 1600–1972*, London: Penguin, 1989.
—, *Paddy and Mr Punch: Connections in Irish and English History*, London: Penguin, 1993.
Fox, T., Review of *As I Roved Out*, *Irish Bookman*, 1.5, December 1946, pp. 84–7.

Gailey, A., ed., *The Use of Tradition: Essays Presented to GB Thompson*, Cultra: Ulster Folk and Transport Museum, 1988.
Galwey, I. T., *Hybrasil and Other Verses*, Dublin: George Herbert, 1872.
Gardiner, D., 'The other Irish renaissance: the Maunsel poets', *New Hibernia Review/Iris Éireannach Nua*, 8.1, spring 2004, pp. 54–79.
Gaughan, J. A., ed., *Memoirs of Senator Joseph Connolly (1885–1961): A Founder of Modern Ireland*, Dublin: Irish Academic Press, 1996.
Graves, A. P., ed., *The Book of Irish Poetry*, Dublin: Talbot Press, 1915.
Greacen, R., ed., *Northern Harvest: An Anthology of Ulster Writing*, Belfast: Derek MacCord, 1944.
Green, A. S., *The Making of Ireland and its Undoing 1200–1600*, London: Macmillan, 1908.
—, *The Old Irish World*, Dublin: M. H. Gill, 1912.
—, *Ourselves Alone in Ulster*, Dublin: Maunsel, 1918.
Greer, D., ed., *Hamilton Harty: His Life and Music*, Belfast: Blackstaff Press, 1978.
—, 'The collaboration of Cathal O'Byrne and Cahir Healy in *The Lane of the Thrushes*', *Irish Booklore*, 4, 1978–80, pp. 109–12.
Gregory, A., *Lady Gregory's Journals: 1916–1930*, London: Putnam, 1946.
Gregory, P., ed., *Modern Anglo-Irish Verse*, London: David Nutt, 1914.
Gwynn, D., 'Roger Casement's last weeks', *Studies*, 54, spring 1965, p. 71.
Hardebeck, C. G., *Gems of Melody*, Dublin: Pohlmann, 1908.
Harvey, D., *The Condition of Postmodernity*, London: Blackwell, 1990.
Hay, M., 'Explaining *Uladh*: cultural nationalism in Ulster', in *The Irish Revival Reappraised*, eds B. Taylor FitzSimon and J. H. Murphy, Dublin: Four Courts Press, 2004, pp. 119–31.
Hayes, M., *Black Puddings with Slim: A Downpatrick Boyhood*, Belfast: Blackstaff, 1996.
Hayward, R., *In Praise of Ulster*, London: Arthur Baker, 1938.
—, *Belfast Through the Ages*, Dundalk: Dundalgan Press, 1952.
Headlam, M., *Irish Reminiscences*, London: Robert Hale, 1947.
Heatley, F., *Henry Joy McCracken and His Times*, Belfast: Belfast Wolfe Tone Society, 1967.
Hennessey, T., *A History of Northern Ireland*, Dublin: Gill and Macmillan, 1997.
Henry, P., *An Irish Portrait*, London: Batsford, 1988 edition (first published 1951).
Hewitt, J., Foreword, in Cathal O'Byrne, *As I Roved Out*, Belfast: Blackstaff Press, 1982.
—, '"The Northern Athens" and after', in *Belfast: The Making of the City*, eds J. C. Beckett, *et al.*, Belfast: Appletree Press, 1988, pp. 71–82.
Hobson, B., *Ireland Yesterday and Tomorrow*, Tralee: Anvil Books, 1968.
Hutchinson, J., *The Dynamics of Cultural Nationalism: The Gaelic Revival and the Creation of the Irish Nation State*, London: Allen and Unwin, 1987.
Hyland, P., *The Black Heart: A Voyage to Central Africa*, London: Gollancz, 1988.
Inglis, B., *Roger Casement*, London: Hodder and Stoughton, 1973.
Ireland, D., *From the Irish Shore*, London: Rich and Cowan, 1936.

—, 'Prince of storytellers: Cathal O'Byrne', *Belfast Telegraph*, 26 May 1956, p. 5.
—, *From the Jungle of Belfast: Footnotes to History 1904–1972*, Belfast: Blackstaff Press, 1973.
'J.J.H.', 'Review of two one-act comedies by Cathal O'Byrne', *Irish Book Lover*, 21.1, January/February 1933, p. 23.
Jackson, T. A., *Ireland Her Own: An Outline History of the Irish Struggle for National Freedom and Independence*, London: Cobbett Press, 1946.
Joyce, J., *Dubliners*, London: Penguin, 2000 edition (first published 1914).
—, *Ulysses*, London: Penguin, 2000 edition (first published 1922).
Kane, W., *Are We All Met?*, London: Elkin Mathews and Marrot, 1931.
Kelly, A., and A. A. Gillis, eds, *Critical Ireland: New Essays in Literature and Culture*, Dublin: Four Courts Press, 2001.
Kelly, B. M., *The Valley of Vision*, New York: Encyclopaedia Press, 1916.
Kelly, J., *Bonfires on the Hillside: An Eyewitness Account of Political Upheaval in Northern Ireland*, Belfast: Fountain Publishing, 1995.
Kenna, G. B., *Facts and Figures: The Belfast Pogroms 1920–2*, Belfast: Donaldson Archives, 1997 edition (first published 1922).
Keogh, D., *Twentieth-Century Ireland: Nation and State*, Dublin: Gill and Macmillan, 1994.
Kiberd, D., *Inventing Ireland: The Literature of the Modern Nation*, London: Jonathan Cape, 1995.
Kirkland, R., '"The *shanachie* of Belfast and its red-brick Gaeltacht": Cathal O'Byrne', *Bullán: An Irish Studies Journal*, 4.2, winter 1999/spring 2000, pp. 67–82.
Krause, D., ed., *The Letters of Sean O'Casey. Vol. 1: 1910–41*, London: Cassell, 1975.
—, *The Letters of Sean O'Casey. Vol. 2: 1942–54*, New York: Macmillan, 1980.
Lawlor, H. C., *Ulster: Its Archaeology and Antiquities*, Belfast: Carswell, 1928.
—, 'Bun-na-Mairghie Friary: Ballycastle's great Franciscan link', *Glensman*, 1.3, 1931, pp. 26–32.
Leslie, S., *The End of a Chapter*, London: Constable, 1916.
—, *Doomsland*, London: Chatto and Windus, 1923.
—, *The Film of Memory*, London: Michael Joseph, 1938.
—, *The Irish Tangle for English Readers*, London: MacDonald, 1946.
—, *Long Shadows*, London: John Murray, 1966.
Levenson, S., *Maud Gonne*, London: Cassell, 1977.
Longley, E., 'The rising, the Somme and Irish memory', in *Revising the Rising*, eds M. Ní Dhonnchadha and T. Dorgan, Derry: Field Day, 1991, p. 39.
Lysaght, S., *Robert Lloyd Praeger: The Life of a Naturalist*, Dublin: Four Courts Press, 1998.
MacBride White, A., and A. Norman Jeffares, eds, *The Gonne–Yeats Letters 1893–1938*, London: Pimlico, 1993.
MacCartan, H. A.,*The Little White Roads and Other Poems*, London: Heath Cranton, 1917.
—, *Silhouettes: Some Character Studies from North and South*, Dublin: Talbot Press, 1921.

—, *The Glamour of Belfast*, Dublin: Talbot Press, 1921.

—, 'Belfast: some backward glances', in *Capuchin Annual*, Dublin: Capuchin Franciscan Fathers, 1943, pp. 171–8.

MacColl, R., *Roger Casement: A New Judgement*, London: Hamish Hamilton, 1956.

MacGreevy, T., 'Cathal O'Byrne, Dublinman', *Father Mathew Record*, May 1948, p. 11.

Mackey, H. O. ed., *The Crime Against Europe: Writings and Poems of Roger Casement*, Dublin: C. J. Fallon, 1958.

MacManus, L., *White Light and Flame: Memories of the Irish Literary Revival and the Anglo-Irish War*, Dublin: Talbot Press, 1929.

MacManus, S., 'A memoir of Ethna Carbery', in *The Four Winds of Eirinn: Poems by Ethna Carbery*, Dublin: M. H. Gill, 1918. See http://digital.library.upenn.edu/women/carbery/carbery.html.

MacNamara, G., *Thompson in Tir-na-n-Óg*, Dublin: Talbot Press, 1912.

MacNeice, L., *Selected Poems*, ed. M. Longley, London: Faber, 1988.

Maguire, W. A., *Caught in Time: The Photographs of Alexander Hogg of Belfast, 1870–1939*, Belfast: Friar's Bush, 1986.

Maloney, W. J., *The Forged Casement Diaries*, Dublin: Talbot Press, 1936.

Martindale, C. C., *Pope Pius XI*, unnumbered Catholic Truth Society of Ireland pamphlet, Dublin: Veritas, 1937.

Maume, P., *The Long Gestation: Irish Nationalist Life, 1891–1918*, Dublin: Gill and Macmillan, 1999.

McCarroll, J., *Passages Taken from the Manuscript Written by Roger Casement in the Condemned Cell at Pentonville Prison* (private circulation). A short memoir by Father James McCarroll. Preface by Herbert O. Mackey, 18 January 1950.

McCormack, W. J., *Roger Casement in Death or Haunting the Free State*, Dublin: University College Dublin Press, 2002.

McDiarmid, L., 'The posthumous life of Roger Casement', in *Gender and Sexuality in Modern Ireland*, eds A. Bradley and M. Gialanella Valiulis, Amherst: University of Massachusetts Press, 1997, pp. 127–58.

McDowell, R. B., *Alice Stopford Green: A Passionate Historian*, Dublin: Allen Figgis, 1967.

McGuinne, D., 'Colm O Lochlainn and the Sign of the Three Candles: the early decades', *Long Room*, 41, 1996, pp. 43–51.

McHugh, R., ed., *Ireland's Field Day,* London: Hutchinson, 1985.

McMinn, J. R. B., 'Liberalism in North Antrim 1900–14', *Irish Historical Studies*, 23.89, May 1982, pp. 17–29.

—, *Against the Tide: A Calendar of the Papers of Rev. J. B. Armour, Irish Presbyterian Minister and Home Ruler 1869–1914*, Belfast: Public Record Office of Northern Ireland, 1985.

McPhillips, K., *The Falls: A History*, Belfast: private publication, undated.

Mengel, H., *Sam Thompson and Modern Drama in Ulster*, Frankfurt am Main: Lang, 1986.

Meredith, R., '*The Shan Van Vocht*: notes from the North', in *Critical Ireland: New Essays in Literature and Culture*, eds Aaron Kelly and Alan A. Gillis, Dublin: Four Courts Press, 2001, pp. 173–80.

Mhic Sheáin, B., *Glimpses of Erin. Alice Milligan: Poet, Protestant, Patriot*, Belfast: Fortnight Educational Trust Supplement, undated.
Milligan, A., 'The boys who are true to Erin oh!', *Northern Patriot*, 3, 1895, p. 33.
—, *Hero Lays*, Dublin: Maunsel, 1908.
—, *Poems*, ed. H. Mangan, Dublin: Gill, 1954.
Mitchell, A., ed., *The Amazon Journal of Roger Casement*, London: Anaconda, 1997.
Mitchell, J., *John Mitchell's Jail Journal*, London: Sphere Books, 1983 edition (first published 1854).
Moberly, C., and E. Jourdain, *An Adventure*, London: Macmillan, 1911.
Monteith, R., *Casement's Last Adventure*, Dublin: Michael Moynihan, 1953.
Moore, B., *The Lonely Passion of Judith Hearne*, London: Penguin, 1959 edition (first published 1955).
—, *The Emperor of Ice-Cream*, London: Paladin, 1987 edition (first published 1965).
Morash, C., *A History of Irish Theatre 1601–2000*, Cambridge: Cambridge University Press, 2002.
Morgan, A., *Labour and Partition. The Belfast Working Class 1905–23*, London: Pluto, 1991.
Morris, C., 'Becoming Irish? Alice Milligan and the Revival', *Irish University Review*, 33.1, spring/summer 2003, pp. 79–98.
Muldoon, P., *Kerry Slides*, Oldcastle: Gallery Press, 1988.
Najder, Z., 'Conrad's Casement letters', *Polish Perspectives*, 17.12, 1974, pp. 25–30.
Newmann, K., *Dictionary of Ulster Biography*, Belfast: Institute of Irish Studies, 1993.
Ní Chuilleanáin, E., ed., *As I Was Among the Captives: Joseph Campbell's Prison Diaries 1922–1923*, Cork: Cork University Press, 2001.
Ní Dhonnchadha, M., and T. Dorgan, eds, *Revising the Rising*, Derry: Field Day, 1991.
Noyes, A., *The Accusing Ghost or Justice for Casement*, London: Gollancz, 1957.
O'Brien, C. C., 'A slow north-east wind', review of *North* by S. Heaney, *Listener*, 25 September 1975, pp. 23–4.
O'Brien, F., *The Poor Mouth*, trans. P. C. Power, London: Grafton, 1986 edition (first published 1941).
—, *The Dalkey Archive*, London: Grafton, 1986 edition (first published 1964).
Ó Broin, L., *Revolutionary Underground: The Story of the Irish Republican Brotherhood 1858–1924*, London: Gill and Macmillan, 1976.
—, *Protestant Nationalists in Revolutionary Ireland: The Stopford Connection*, Dublin: Gill and Macmillan, 1985.
Ó Buachalla, S., ed., *The Letters of P. H. Pearse*, Gerrards Cross: Colin Smythe, 1980.
O'Connor, F., *In Search of a State: Catholics in Northern Ireland*, Belfast: Blackstaff Press, 1993.
O Lochlainn, C., *Anglo-Irish Song-Writers Since Moore*, Dublin: At the Sign of the Three Candles, 1950.

O'Malley, C., *A Poet's Theatre*, Dublin: Elo Press, 1988.
O'Neill, G., Review of *The Grey Feet of the Wind* by C. O'Byrne, *Studies*, 6.23, September 1917, pp. 512–13.
O'Neill, S., 'Note: Roger Casement, Cathal O'Byrne and Professor Reid', *Studies*, 68, spring/summer 1979, pp. 117–21.
Ó Snodaigh, P., *Hidden Ulster: Protestants and the Irish Language*, Belfast: Lagan Press, 1995.
O'Sullivan, S., *The Rose and the Bottle*, Dublin: Talbot Press, 1946.
Owen, T. M., ed., *From Corrib to Cultra: Folklife Essays in Honour of Alan Gailey*, Belfast: Institute of Irish Studies, 2000.
Patten, E., ed., *Returning to Ourselves: Second Volume of Papers from the John Hewitt Summer School*, Belfast: Lagan Press, 1995.
Patterson, G., *Fat Lad*, London: Chatto and Windus, 1992.
Paulin, T., *Liberty Tree*, London: Faber and Faber, 1983.
Phoenix, E., *Northern Nationalism: Nationalist Politics, Partition and the Catholic Minority in Northern Ireland 1890–1940*, Belfast: Ulster Historical Foundation, 1994.
—, ed., *A Century of Northern Life: The Irish News and 100 Years of Ulster History 1890s–1990s*, Belfast: Ulster Historical Foundation, 1995.
—, 'The history of a newspaper: the *Irish News* 1855–1995', in E. Phoenix, ed., *A Century of Northern Life: The Irish News and 100 Years of Ulster History 1890s–1990s*, Belfast: Ulster Historical Foundation, 1995.
Rafferty, O. P., *Catholicism in Ulster 1603–1983*, London: Hurst, 1994.
—, 'Catholicism in the North of Ireland since 1891', in *A Century of Northern Life: The Irish News and 100 Years of Ulster History 1890s–1990s*, ed. E. Phoenix, Belfast: Ulster Historical Foundation, 1995.
Reid, B. L., *Lives of Roger Casement*, New Haven: Yale University Press, 1976.
Reid, F., *Apostate*, London: Constable, 1926.
—, *Private Road*, London: Faber and Faber, 1940.
Richards, S., *The Cambridge Companion to Twentieth-Century Irish Drama*, Cambridge: Cambridge University Press, 2004.
Ruane, M., 'Who owns Casement?', *Irish Times*, 14 October 1997, p. 17.
Rudkin, D., 'The chameleon and the kilt: the complexities of Roger Casement', *Encounter*, 41, August 1973, pp. 70–7.
—, *Cries from Casement as His Bones Are Brought to Dublin*, London: British Broadcasting Corporation, 1974.
Russell, G. (AE), ed., *New Songs, Selected by AE from the Poems of Padraic Colum, Eva Gore Booth, Thomas Keohler, Alice Milligan, Susan Mitchell, Seumas O'Sullivan, George Roberts, and Ella Young*, Dublin: O'Donoghue, 1904.
Ryan, W. P., *The Irish Literary Revival: Its History, Pioneers and Possibilities*, London: privately published, 1894.
Saunders, N., and A. A. Kelly, *Joseph Campbell: Poet and Nationalist 1879–1944. A Critical Biography*, Dublin: Wolfhound Press, 1988.
Sawyer, R., *Casement: The Flawed Hero*, London: Routledge and Kegan Paul, 1984.
—, *Roger Casement's Diaries, 1910: The Black and the White*, London: Pimlico, 1997.

Shea, P., *A History of the Ulster Arts Club*, Belfast: Mayne, Boyd, 1971.
Shorter, C., *In Memoriam Dora Sigerson 1918–1923*, London: privately published, 1923.
Sigerson Shorter, D., *Ballads and Poems*, London: James Bowden, 1899.
—, *Sixteen Dead Men and Other Poems of Easter Week*, New York: M. Kennerley, 1919.
—, *The Tricolour*, Cork: CFN, 1976.
Singleton-Gates, P., and M. Girodias, *The Black Diaries: An Account of Roger Casement's Life and Times with a Collection of his Diaries and Public Writings*, London: Sidgwick and Jackson, 1959.
Smith, F. E., *Famous Trials of History*, London: Hutchinson, 1920.
Squire, J. C., *Tricks of the Trade*, London: Martin Secker, 1917.
Swanton, M. R., *Feeding Your Family*, Catholic Truth Society of Ireland pamphlet, Dublin: Veritas, 1936.
Taylor FitzSimon, B., and J. H. Murphy, eds, *The Irish Revival Reappraised*, Dublin: Four Courts Press, 2004.
Tomelty, J., Review, *Irish Bookman*, 1.10, June 1947, pp. 90–4.
Trench, C., 'The Three Candles Press in the "thirties"', *Long Room*, 41, 1996, pp. 35–42.
Ulster Society for the Prevention of Cruelty to Animals, *The Tree*, Belfast: USPCA, 1936.
Vandevelde, K., 'An open national identity: Rutherford Mayne, Gerald MacNamara, and the plays of the Ulster Literary Theatre', *Eire–Ireland: Journal of Irish Studies*, 39, spring/summer 2004, pp. 36–58.
Walshe, É., ed., *Sex, Nation and Dissent in Irish Writing*, Cork: Cork University Press, 1997.
Yeats, W. B., *Autobiographies*, London: Macmillan, 1992 edition (first published 1955).
—, *Collected Plays of W. B. Yeats*, Dublin: Gill and Macmillan, 1982.
—, *Collected Poems of W. B. Yeats*, London: Macmillan, 1982.
—, *The Collected Letters of W. B. Yeats. Vol. 1: 1865–1895*, ed. J. Kelly, Oxford: Clarendon Press, 1986.
—, *The Collected Letters of W. B. Yeats. Vol. 3: 1901–1904*, eds J. Kelly and R. Schuchard, Oxford: Clarendon Press, 1994.

Index